The End of Policing

The End of Policing

Alex S. Vitale

London • New York

This paperback edition first published by Verso 2018

7 9 10 8

Verso
UK: 6 Meard Street, London W1F 0EG
US: 20 Jay Street, Suite 1010, Brooklyn, NY 11201
versobooks.com

Verso is the imprint of New Left Books

ISBN-13: 978-1-78478-292-4
ISBN-13: 978-1-78478-291-7 (US EBK)
ISBN-13: 978-1-78478-290-0 (UK EBK)

British Library Cataloguing in Publication Data
A catalogue record for this book is available from the British Library

The Library of Congress Has Cataloged the Hardback Edition as Follows:

Names: Vitale, Alex S., author.
Title: The end of policing / Alex Vitale.
Description: Brooklyn : Verso, 2017.
Identifiers: LCCN 2017020713| ISBN 9781784782894 (hardback) | ISBN 9781784782917 (US ebk) | ISBN 9781784782900 (UK ebk)
Subjects: LCSH: Police—United States. | Police misconduct—United States. | BISAC: POLITICAL SCIENCE / Political Freedom & Security / Law Enforcement. | SOCIAL SCIENCE / Discrimination & Race Relations. | POLITICAL SCIENCE / Public Policy / General.
Classification: LCC HV8139 .V58 2017 | DDC 363.20973—dc23
LC record available at https://lccn.loc.gov/2017020713

Typeset in Sabon by MJ & N Gavan, Truro, Cornwall
Printed and bound by CPI Group (UK) Ltd, Croydon, CR0 4YY

Contents

1

The Limits of Police Reform

Tamir Rice and John Crawford were both shot to death in Ohio because an officer's first instinct was to shoot. Anthony Hill outside Atlanta, Antonio Zambrano-Montes in Pasco, California, and Jason Harris in Dallas were all shot to death by police who misunderstood their mental illnesses. Oscar Grant in Oakland, Akai Gurley in Brooklyn, and Eric Harris in Tulsa were all shot "by mistake" because officers didn't use enough care in handling their weapons. North Charleston, South Carolina, police officer Michael Slager shot Walter Scott in the back for fleeing a traffic stop and potential arrest for missed child support—then planted evidence on him as part of a cover-up, which was backed up by other officers. On Staten Island, Eric Garner was killed in part because of an overly aggressive police response to his allegedly selling loose cigarettes. The recent killings of so many unarmed black men by police, in so many different circumstances, have pushed the issue of police reform onto the national agenda in a way not seen in over a generation.[1]

Is there an explosive increase in police violence? There is no question that American police use their weapons more than police in any other developed democracy. Unfortunately, we don't have fully accurate information about the number or nature of homicides at the hands of police. Despite a 2006 law requiring the reporting of this information (reauthorized in 2014), many police departments do not comply. Researchers have had to rely on independent information such as local news stories to cobble together numbers. One effort by the *Guardian* and *Washington Post* documented 1,100 deaths in 2014, 991 in 2015, and 1,080 in 2016—fewer than in the 1960s and 1970s, but still far too many.[2]

African Americans are disproportionately victims of police shootings; black teens are up to twenty-one times more likely than white teens to be killed by police,[3] though these rates are often proportional to the race of gun offenders and shooting victims more broadly.[4] Racial profiling remains widespread, and many communities of color experience invasive and disrespectful policing. The recent cases of Ferguson and North Charleston are hardly outliers; blacks and Latinos are overwhelmingly the targets of low-level police interactions, from traffic tickets to searches to arrests for minor infractions, and frequently report being treated in a hostile and degrading manner despite having done nothing wrong.[5] In New York City 80 to 90 percent of those targeted for such interactions are people of color.[6]

This form of policing is based on a mindset that people of color commit more crime and therefore must be subjected to harsher police tactics. Police argue that residents in high-crime communities often demand police action. What is left out is that these communities also ask for better schools, parks, libraries, and jobs, but these services are rarely provided. They lack the political power to obtain real services and support to make their communities safer and healthier. The reality is that middle-class and wealthy white communities would put a stop to the constant harassment and humiliation meted out by police in communities of color, no matter the crime rate.

Those who question the police or their authority are frequently subjected to verbal threats and physical attacks. In 2012, young Harlem resident Alvin Cruz, who had been repeatedly stopped and searched by police without justification, taped an encounter with police in which he questioned the reason for the stop. In response, the police officer cursed at him, twisted his arm behind his back, and said, "Dude, I'm gonna break your fuckin' arm, then I'm gonna punch you in the fuckin' face."[7]

Even wealthy and more powerful people of color are not immune: in 2009, Harvard professor and PBS personality Henry Louis Gates Jr. was arrested by Cambridge police in his own home; he had lost his keys, and a neighbor had called the police to report a break-in. The incident prompted President Obama to state:

> I think it's fair to say, number one, any of us would be pretty angry; number two, that the Cambridge police acted stupidly in arresting somebody when there was already proof that they were in their own home, and, number three, what I think we know separate and apart from this incident is that there's a long history in this country of African Americans and Latinos being stopped by law enforcement disproportionately.[8]

Part of the problem stems from a "warrior mentality."[9] Police often think of themselves as soldiers in a battle with the public rather than guardians of public safety. That they are provided with tanks and other military-grade weapons, that many are military veterans,[10] and that militarized units like Special Weapons and Tactics (SWAT) proliferated during the 1980s War on Drugs and post-9/11 War on Terror[11] only fuels this perception, as well as a belief that entire communities are disorderly, dangerous, suspicious, and ultimately criminal. When this happens, police are too quick to use force.

Excessive use of force, however, is just the tip of the iceberg of over-policing. There are currently more than 2 million Americans in prison or jail and another 4 million on probation or parole. Many have lost the right to vote; most will have severe difficulties in finding work upon release and will never recover from the lost earnings and work experience. Many have had their ties to their families irrevocably damaged and have been driven into more serious and violent criminality. Despite numerous well-documented cases of false arrests and convictions, the vast majority of these arrests and convictions have been conducted lawfully and according to proper procedure—but their effects on individuals and communities are incredibly destructive.

Reforms

Any effort to make policing more just must address the problems of excessive force, overpolicing, and disrespect for the public. Much of the public debate has focused on new and enhanced training, diversifying the police, and embracing community policing as strategies for reform, along with enhanced accountability measures. However, most of these reforms fail to deal with the fundamental problems inherent to policing.

Training

The videotaped death of Eric Garner for allegedly selling loose cigarettes immediately spurred calls for additional training of officers in how to use force in making arrests. Officers were accused of using a prohibited chokehold and of failing to respond to his pleas that he couldn't breathe. In response, Mayor Bill de Blasio and Police Commissioner William Bratton announced that all New York Police Department (NYPD) officers would undergo additional use-of-force training so that they could make arrests in the future in ways that were less likely to result in serious injury, as well as training in methods to de-escalate conflicts and more effectively communicate with the public.

Such training ignores two important factors in Garner's death. The first is the officers' casual disregard for his well-being, ignoring his cries of "I can't breathe," and their seeming indifferent reaction to his near lifelessness while awaiting an ambulance. This is a problem of values and seems to go to the heart of the claim that, for too many police, black lives *don't* matter. The second is "broken windows"-style policing, which targets low-level infractions for intensive, invasive, and aggressive enforcement. This theory was first laid out in 1982 by criminologists James Q. Wilson and George Kelling.[12] They presented existing behavioral research that showed that when a car is left unattended on a street it is usually left alone, but if just one window of the car is broken, the car is quickly vandalized. The lesson: failure to indicate care and maintenance will unleash people's latent destructive tendencies. Therefore, if cities want to establish or maintain crime-free neighborhoods they must take action to ensure that residents feel the pressure to conform to civilized norms of public behavior. The best way to accomplish this is to use police to remind people in subtle and not-so-subtle ways that disorderly, unruly, and antisocial behavior are unacceptable. When this doesn't happen, people's baser instincts will take hold and predatory behavior will reign, in a return to a Hobbesian "war of all against all."

The emergence of this theory in 1982 is tied to a larger arc of urban neoconservative thinking going back to the 1960s. Wilson's former mentor and collaborator, Edward Banfield, a close associate of neoliberal economist Milton Friedman at the University of Chicago, parented many of the ideas that came to make up the new conservative consensus on cities. In his seminal 1970 work *The Unheavenly City,* Banfield argues that the poor are trapped in a culture of poverty that makes them largely immune to government assistance:

> Although he has more "leisure" than almost anyone, the indifference ("apathy" if one prefers) of the lower-class person is such that he seldom makes even the simplest repairs to the place that he lives in. He is not troubled by dirt or dilapidation and he does not mind the inadequacy of public facilities such as schools, parks, hospitals, and libraries; indeed, where such

> things exist he may destroy them by carelessness or even by vandalism.[13]

Unlike Banfield, who in many ways championed the abandonment of cities, Wilson decried the decline of urban areas. Along with writers like Fred Siegel,[14] Wilson pointed at the twin threats of failed liberal leadership and the supposed moral failings of African Americans. All three of them argued that liberals had unwittingly unleashed urban chaos by undermining the formal social control mechanisms that made city living possible. By supporting the more radical demands of the later urban expressions of the civil rights movement, they had so weakened the police, teachers, and other government forces of behavioral regulation that chaos came to reign.

Wilson, following Banfield, believed strongly that there were profound limits on what government could do to help the poor. Financial investment in them would be squandered; new services would go unused or be destroyed; they would continue in their slothful and destructive ways. Since the root of the problem was either an essentially moral and cultural failure or a lack of external controls to regulate inherently destructive human urges, the solution had to take the form of punitive social control mechanisms to restore order and neighborhood stability.[15]

Wilson's views were informed by a borderline racism that emerged as a mix of biological and cultural explanations for the "inferiority" of poor blacks. Wilson co-authored the book *Crime and Human Nature* with Richard Herrnstein, which argued that there were important biological determinants of criminality.[16] While race was not one of the core determinants, language about IQ and body type opened the door to a kind of sociobiology that led Herrnstein to coauthor the openly racist *The Bell Curve* with Charles Murray, who was also a close associate of Wilson.[17]

What was needed to stem this tide of declining civility, they argued, was to empower the police to not just fight crime but to become agents of moral authority on the streets. The new role for the police was to intervene in the quotidian disorders of urban life that contributed to the sense that "anything goes." The broken-windows theory magically reverses the well-understood causal relationship between crime and poverty, arguing that poverty and social disorganization are the result, not the cause, of crime and that the disorderly behavior of the growing "underclass" threatens to destroy the very fabric of cities.

Broken-windows policing is at root a deeply conservative attempt to shift the burden of responsibility for declining living conditions onto the poor themselves and to argue that the solution to all social ills is increasingly aggressive, invasive, and restrictive forms of policing that involve more arrests, more harassment, and ultimately more violence. As inequality continues to increase, so will homelessness and public disorder, and as long as people continue to embrace the use of police to manage disorder, we will see a continual increase in the scope of police power and authority at the expense of human and civil rights.

The order to arrest Eric Garner came from the very top echelons of the department, in response to complaints from local merchants about illegal cigarette sales. Treating this as a crime requiring the deployment of a special plainclothes unit, two sergeants, and uniformed backup seems excessive and pointless. Garner had experienced over a dozen previous police contacts in similar circumstances, including stints in jail; this had done nothing to change his behavior or improve his or the community's circumstances. No amount of procedural training will solve this fundamental flaw in public policy.

Many advocates also call for cultural sensitivity trainings designed to reduce racial and ethnic bias. A lot of this training is based on the idea that most people have at least some unexamined stereotypes and biases that they are not consciously aware of but that influence their behavior. Controlled experiments consistently show that people are quicker and more likely to shoot at a black target than a white one in simulations. Trainings such as "Fair and Impartial Policing" use role-playing and simulations to help officers see and consciously adjust for these biases.[18] Diversity and multicultural training is not a new idea, nor is it terribly effective. Most officers have already been through some form of diversity training and tend to describe it as politically motived, feel-good programming divorced from the realities of street policing. Researchers have found no impact on problems like racial disparities in traffic stops or marijuana arrests; both implicit and explicit bias remain, even after targeted and intensive training. This is not necessarily because officers remain committed to their racial biases, though this can be true,[19] but because institutional pressures remain intact.

American police receive a great deal of training. Almost all officers attend an organized police academy and many have prior college and or military experience. There is also ongoing training; large departments have their own large training staff, while smaller departments rely on state and regional training centers. Many states have unified Police Officer Standards and Training (POST) agencies that set minimum standards, develop training plans, and advise on best practices. While police training standards are still more decentralized in the United States than in many countries that have national police forces and academies, the new POST system has gone a long way in raising standards and creating greater uniformity of procedures.

However, even after training officers often have inadequate knowledge of the laws they are tasked to enforce. Police regularly disperse young people from street corners without a legal basis, conduct searches without probable cause, and in some cases take enforcement action based on inaccurate knowledge of the law. In Victoria, Texas, an officer assaulted an elderly man he had pulled over for not having a registration sticker on his license plate. The man tried to explain that the vehicle had a dealers' plate, which in Texas is exempt from the sticker requirement. When the officer refused to listen, the man attempted to summon his boss at the car dealership where the confrontation was occurring. Rather than working to resolve the mistake, the officer attempted to arrest the man and in the process injured him with a Taser so badly that he was hospitalized.[20] In the subsequent inquiry, the officer insisted that the man's passive resistance was a threat that had to be neutralized. Since the incident was recorded on the dashboard camera of the police cruiser, the officer was fired.

The training police receive at the academy is often quite different from what they learn from training officers and peers. The emphasis is on strict discipline and rote learning of laws and rules, and emphasizes proper appearance over substance. Cadets are given little in the way of substantial advice about how to make decisions in a complex environment, according to two veteran officers' memoirs.[21] Even sympathetic portrayals, such as the reality television show *The Academy*, provide stark evidence of a militarized training environment run by drill sergeants who attempt to "break down" recruits through punitive drilling and humiliating personal attacks. When officers start working, the first thing their peers often tell them is to forget everything they learned in the academy.

In some ways, training is actually part of the problem. In recent decades, the emphasis has shifted heavily toward officer safety training. Seth Stoughton, a former police officer turned law professor, shows how officers are repeatedly exposed to scenarios in which seemingly innocuous interactions with the public, such as traffic stops, turn deadly.[22] The endlessly repeated point is that any encounter can turn deadly in a split second if officers don't remain ready to use lethal force at any moment. When police come into every situation imagining it may be their last, they treat those they encounter with fear and hostility and attempt to control them rather than communicate with them—and are much quicker to use force at the slightest provocation or even uncertainty.

Take the case of John Crawford, an African American man shot to death by an officer in a Walmart in Ohio. Crawford had picked up an air gun off a shelf and was carrying it around the store while shopping. Another shopper called 911 to report a man with a gun in the store. The store's video camera shows that one of the responding officers shot without warning while Crawford was talking on the phone.[23] In Ohio it is legal to carry a gun openly, but the officer had been trained to use deadly force upon seeing a gun. The officer involved was not charged, and Crawford's girlfriend was intimidated and threatened while being questioned after the incident.[24]

Similarly, in South Carolina, a state trooper drove up to a young man in his car at a gas station and asked him for his driver's license. He leaned into the car to comply and the officer shot him without warning: see unexpected movement, shoot.[25]

Part of this emphasis on the use of deadly force comes from the rise of independent training companies that specialize in inservice training, staffed by former police and military personnel. Some of these groups serve both military and police clients and emphasize military-style approaches and the "warrior mentality." The company CQB (Close Quarters Battle) boasts of training thousands of local, state, and federal police as well as American and foreign military units such as the US Marines, Navy Seals, and Danish, Canadian, and Peruvian special forces. Its emphasis is on "battle-proven tactics."[26] Trojan Securities trains both military and police units and offers police training in a variety of weapons in numerous settings, including a five-day "Police Covert Surveillance and Intelligence Operations" course.[27]

This problem is especially acute when it comes to SWAT teams. Initially created in the early 1970s to deal with rare acts of extremist violence, barricaded suspects, or armed confrontations with police, these units now deal almost exclusively with serving drug warrants and even engage in regular patrol functions armed with automatic weapons and body armor. These units regularly violate people's constitutional rights, kill and maim innocent people—often as a result of being in the wrong location—and kill people's pets.[28] These paramilitary units are increasingly being used to respond to protest activity. The militarized response to the Ferguson protests may have served to escalate the conflict there; it's probably no accident that the Saint Louis County police chief's prior position had been as head of the SWAT team. These units undergo a huge amount of inservice training, funded in part by seizing alleged drug money.

The federal government also began to fund training and equipment for SWAT teams in the 1970s as part of the last round of major national policing reforms, which were intended to improve police-community relations and reducing police brutality through enhanced training. These reforms instead poured millions into training programs that resulted in the rise of SWAT teams, drug enforcement, and militarized crowd control tactics.

Diversity

There is no question that the racial difference between the mostly white police and the mostly African American policed in Ferguson, Missouri, contributed to the intensity of protests over the killing of Mike Brown. Reformers often call for recruiting more officers of color in the hopes that they will treat communities with greater dignity, respect, and fairness. Unfortunately, there is little evidence to back up this hope. Even the most diverse forces have major problems with racial profiling and bias, and individual black and Latino officers appear to perform very much like their white counterparts.

Nationally, the racial makeup of the police hews closely to national population figures. The US population is 72 percent white; 75 percent of police nationally are white. Blacks make up 13 percent of the population and 12 percent of police. Asians and Latinos are somewhat less well represented relative to their numbers but not dramatically so.[29] In the largest departments, only 56 percent of officers are white. The disparities seem greater in communities of color because of the deep segregation there. In these cases, there are invariably large numbers of white officers patrolling primarily nonwhite areas. This contrast stands out more than its converse, because whites are rarely concerned about being policed by nonwhite officers and because white communities tend to have fewer negative interactions with the police.

There is now a large body of evidence measuring whether the race of individual officers affects their use of force. Most studies show no effect.[30] More distressingly, a few indicate that black officers are *more* likely to use force or make arrests, especially of black civilians.[31] One new study suggests that small increases in diversity produce worse outcomes, while large increases begin to show some improvements; but only a handful of departments met this criterion. In the end, the authors conclude, "There's no evidence to suggest that increasing the proportion of officers that are black is going to offer a direct solution."[32] Use of force is highly concentrated in a small group of officers who tend to be male, young, and working in high-crime areas.[33] This high concentration of use of force may be exacerbated by weak accountability mechanisms and a culture of machismo that rewards aggressive policing, formally and informally. These same cultural and institutional forces militate against differential behavior by nonwhite officers.

At the department level, more diverse police forces fare no better in measures of community satisfaction, especially among nonwhite residents. These departments are also often just as likely to have systematic problems with excessive use of force, as seen in federal interventions in Detroit, Miami, and Cleveland in recent years. Both New York and Philadelphia have highly diverse forces (though not as diverse as their populations), yet both have come under intense scrutiny for excessive use of force and discriminatory practices such as "stop and frisk." This is in large part because departmental priorities are set by local political leaders, who have driven the adoption of a wide variety of intensive, invasive, and aggressive crime-control policies that by their nature disproportionately target communities of color. These include broken-windows policing, with its emphasis on public disorder, and the War on Drugs, which is waged almost exclusively in nonwhite neighborhoods. Having more black and brown police officers may sound like an appealing reform, but as long as larger systems of policing are left in place, there is no evidence that would give cause to expect a significant reduction in brutality or overpolicing.

Procedural Justice

Procedural justice deals with *how* the law is enforced, as opposed to substantive justice, which involves the actual outcomes of the functioning of the system. President Obama's Task Force on 21st Century Policing report focuses on procedural reforms such as training and encourages officers to work harder to explain why they are stopping, questioning, or arresting people.[34] Departments are advised to create consistent use-of-force policies and mechanisms for civilian oversight and transparency. The report implies that more training, diversity, and communication will lead to enhanced police-community relations, more effective crime control, and greater police legitimacy.

Similar goals were set in the late 1960s. The Katzenbach report of 1967 argued that the roots of crime lie in poverty and racial exclusion, but also argued that a central part of the solution was the development of a more robust and procedurally fair criminal justice system that would uphold the rights of all people to be free of crime. In keeping with this, it called for a major expansion of federal spending on criminal justice. Just as local housing and social services programs needed federal support, so too did prisons, courts, and police. "Every part of the system is undernourished. There is too little manpower and what there is is not well enough trained or well enough paid."[35] The Commission called for improved training, racial diversity in hiring, programmatic innovations, and research. The Kerner Commission on Civil Disorders reached similar conclusion calling for "training, planning, adequate intelligence systems, and knowledge of the ghetto community."[36]

Similarly, Johnson's initial draft of the 1968 Safe Streets bill called for resources to recruit and train police, modernize equipment, better coordinate between criminal justice agencies, and begin innovative prevention and rehabilitation efforts; it had the support of the American Civil Liberties Union (ACLU) and other liberal reform groups.[37] After Congress finished with it, the bill primarily granted funds in large blocs to states to use as they saw fit. Johnson signed the bill anyway, claiming that the core goals of professionalizing the police would be achieved. Over the next decade, the result was a massive expansion in police hardware, SWAT teams, and drug enforcement teams—and almost no money toward prevention and rehabilitation.

By conceptualizing the problem of policing as one of inadequate training and professionalization, reformers fail to directly address how the very nature of policing and the legal system served to maintain and exacerbate racial inequality. By calling for colorblind "law and order" they strengthen a system that puts people of color at a structural disadvantage and contributes to their deep social and legal estrangement.[38]

At root, they fail to appreciate that the basic nature of the law and the police, since its earliest origins, is to be a tool for managing inequality and maintaining the status quo. Police reforms that fail to directly address this reality are doomed to reproduce it.

The Justice Department makes the same mistake in its report on the Ferguson Police Department.[39] It relies heavily on improving training and expanding community policing initiatives to address racial bias and excessive use of force. It also calls for police to acknowledge their historical role in racial oppression, as was recently done by FBI director James Comey and, to a lesser extent, Commissioner William Bratton in New York.[40] Otherwise, the document largely lays out procedural reforms designed to make the policing process more democratic through internal consultation with officers and their unions and external consultation with the public. Departments are urged to think of how the community will perceive their actions and to pursue nonpunitive interactions with people to build trust. These reforms may improve the efficiency of police bureaucracies and improve relations with those active in police-community dialogues between communities and the police but will do little to address the racially disparate outcomes of policing. That is because even racially neutral enforcement of traffic laws will invariably punish poorer residents who are least able to maintain their vehicles and pay fines. Well-trained police following proper procedure are still going to be arresting people for mostly low-level offenses, and the burden will continue to fall primarily on communities of color because *that is how the system is designed to operate*—not because of the biases or misunderstandings of officers.

Community Policing

Everyone likes the idea of a neighborhood police officer who knows and respects the community. Unfortunately, this is a mythic understanding of the history and nature of urban policing, as we will see in chapter 2. What distinguishes the police from other city agencies is that they can legally use force.

While we need police to follow the law and be restrained in their use of force, we cannot expect them to be significantly more friendly than they are, given their current role in society. When their job is to criminalize all disorderly behavior and fund local government through massive ticketing-writing campaigns, their interactions with the public in high-crime areas will be at best gruff and distant and at worst hostile and abusive. The public will resist them and view their efforts as intrusive and illegitimate; the police will react to this resistance with defensiveness and increased assertiveness. Community policing is not possible under these conditions.

Another part of the problem lies in the nature of community. Steve Herbert shows that community meetings tend to be populated by long-time residents, those who own rather than rent their homes, business owners, and landlords.[41] The views of renters, youth, homeless people, immigrants, and the most socially marginalized are rarely represented. As a result, they tend to focus on "quality of life" concerns involving low-level disorderly behavior rather than serious crime.

Across the country, community police programs have been based on the idea that the "community" should bring concerns of all kinds about neighborhood conditions to the police, who will work with them on developing solutions. The tools that police have for solving these problems, however, are generally limited to punitive enforcement actions such as arrests and ticketing. Community policing programs regularly call for increasing reliance on Police Athletic Leagues, positive nonenforcement activities with youth, and more focus on getting to know community members. There is little research, however, to suggest that these endeavors reduce crime or help to overcome overpolicing.

Low-level drug dealing and use generates a tremendous number of calls for police service. Criminalizing these activities has done nothing to reduce the availability and negative effects of drugs on individuals or communities. It has produced substantial negative consequences for those arrested, however, and has been a major drain on local and state resources.

The research shows that community policing does not empower communities in meaningful ways. It expands police power, but does nothing to reduce the burden of overpolicing on people of color and the poor. It is time to invest in communities instead. Participatory budgeting and enhanced local political accountability will do more to improve the well-being of communities than enhancing the power and scope of policing.

Enhanced Accountability

Holding police accountable is another focus of reformers. Activists have called for police to be prosecuted criminally in most cases, though this is rarely successful, leading some to call for new forms of police prosecution. Many reformers frustrated with local inaction have looked to the federal government to intervene, though with little past success to point to. Finally, police body cameras have emerged as a possible technological fix, but raise serious privacy concerns.

Independent Prosecutors

There are major legal, institutional, and social impediments to prosecuting police. While hard numbers are difficult to come by, a successful prosecution of a police officer for killing someone in the line of duty, where no corruption is alleged, is extremely rare. A recent report found only fifty-four officers charged for fatal on-duty shootings in the last ten years; of those, only eleven were convicted.[42] Their average sentence is only four years, with some receiving only a few weeks. The few convictions that have occurred have resulted primarily from clear video evidence or the testimony of fellow officers.

From the moment an investigation into a police shooting begins, there are structural barriers to indictment and prosecution. When there is reason to believe that the shooting might not be justified, prosecutors tend to take a greater role. However, they must rely on the cooperation of the police to gather necessary evidence, including witness statements. Police officers at the scene are sometimes the only witnesses to the event. The close working relationship between police and prosecutors, normally an asset in homicide investigations, becomes a fundamental conflict of interest in all but the most straightforward cases. As a result, prosecutors are often reluctant to pursue such cases aggressively.

Furthermore, because DAs are usually elected, they are often reluctant to be seen as inhibiting the police, since the public sees district attorneys as defenders of law and order. Even in periods of heightened concern about police misconduct, most citizens retain a strong bias in favor of police. We can see the effects of this in the case of Darren Wilson, the officer who shot Michael Brown in Ferguson. Prosecutors spent months collecting and presenting evidence. While this made them appear thorough, it also created a public "cooling off" period, allowing the possibility that demands for prosecution would die down.

Also, the Saint Louis County DA decided to use a radically different approach in this case. Usually, prosecutors make a short presentation of the evidence to the grand jury in which they call for specific charges to be considered. Given the low threshold of probable cause and the one-sided nature of the proceedings, successful indictments are the norm. In this case, the DA decided to provide the grand jury with a wide variety of conflicting evidence and little framework to evaluate it, and allow them to decide, without any prompting, whether an indictment was justified and for what offense. This allowed the DA to absolve himself from any responsibility for the outcome and served to confuse and undermine the confidence of the grand jury, gambling that it would be likely to err on the side of caution and hold back on an indictment. Normally, this body is given clear guidance and only overrules prosecutors in extreme cases.

One alternative being pursued in several states is the creation of an independent police prosecutor's office that is more removed from local politics. The hope is that such independent prosecutions would be viewed as more legitimate, regardless of the outcome. In addition, such so-called "blue desks" could become repositories of expertise on police prosecutions. While still tied to politics at the state level, these bureaus, because of their singular focus, might be better able to insulate themselves from accusations of overly aggressive prosecutions, as well as charges of not supporting the police—since this is their primary purpose.

However, even when a prosecutor is motivated, there are huge legal hurdles. State laws authorizing police use of force, backed up by Supreme Court decisions, give police significant latitude in using deadly force. In the 1989 case *Graham v. Connor*, the Supreme Court ruled that officers may use force to make a lawful arrest or if they reasonably believe the person represents a serious physical threat to the officer or others.[43] This means that police can initiate the use of force over any resistance to arrest. In Missouri and many other places, any perceived effort to take an officer's gun justifies the use of deadly force. The court also said that the totality of circumstances must be judged with an understanding of the split-second nature of police decision-making.

Therefore, considerations like the size and previous actions of the alleged perpetrator, as well as the training and guidance of the officer, are factors a jury may consider. In some cases, state laws don't even reflect the new federal standards. Recent police prosecutions in Missouri and South Carolina were clouded by state laws that allow police to shoot fleeing suspects.

Another challenge that won't be fixed by independent prosecutors is the mindset of juries. Popular culture and political discourse are suffused with commentaries about the central importance of police in maintaining the basic structural integrity of society as well as the dangerous nature of their work—as misguided as both may be. The legal standard for judging police intensifies this tendency to identify with them.

Finally, despite the "post-racial society" rhetoric, racism and bias remain omnipresent in American society—nowhere more than in the realm of criminal justice. There is abundant evidence that jury bias exacerbates racial disparities in criminal justice outcomes, including false convictions, application of the death penalty, and drug convictions. Recent research shows that the closer whites live to blacks, the more positive their views of the police are—which did not augur well for an indictment in a place like Saint Louis County. White jurors are much more likely to side with police, regardless of the race of the officer and the person killed.

Federal Intervention

Many advocates have called on the federal government to be more involved in holding local police accountable and in investigating systematic policies and practices, citing the conflicts we have noted about local police and district attorneys.[44] Since the civil rights era, when the government acknowledged that local legal systems were refusing to prosecute perpetrators of racist violence, the Justice Department (DOJ) has been authorized to bring criminal cases against individual officers through civil rights prosecutions.

Local activists have also turned to the DOJ when they feel local police and political officials are unresponsive to their demands for systemic reforms. Since 1994, in the wake of the Rodney King incident, the DOJ has been allowed to undertake investigations, reports, and even litigation in cases where there is an indication of a pattern of constitutional violations.[45] Its ability to expose problems and pressure local officials is seen as an important check on local political and police power. In addition, many activists hope that federal intervention will give them more power in their ongoing dealings with local police.

In practice, such prosecutions and investigations are rare. Local police are often reluctant to cooperate, with some outright refusing to comply, forcing additional litigation, which raises costs and delays reforms. The DOJ's Civil Rights Division has only fifty lawyers, some of whom are assigned to other tasks.[46] In individual actions, the standard of proof requires that there be evidence of intent to deprive someone of their rights. Actions undertaken in the heat of the moment combined with any indication of a possible threat to the officer generally undermine such prosecutions. In addition, concerns about major federal intrusions into local justice systems mean that only the most clear-cut cases are brought—only around a hundred a year. The country's approximately 17,000 independent police departments all have their own ways of doing things, with remarkable autonomy. A political or legal victory imposing changes on one local police department may have no bearing on the one next door.

Even when cases end in voluntary agreements or court-imposed consent decrees, the results are rarely significant or long-lasting. In 1999, the DOJ entered into a consent decree with the New Jersey state police to address "driving while black" cases by making a number of changes in how they trained officers, assigned them to duty, conducted stops and searches, and maintained paperwork. In the end, however, a study of their practices five years later showed that 75 percent of all stops were still directed at black and Latino motorists.[47] In Cleveland, the DOJ got the local police to agree to prohibit shooting at fleeing vehicles unless there was an immediate threat to life. That agreement seemed to have little effect when officers killed an unarmed driver and passenger after firing 137 shots at them, because they mistook an engine backfire for a gunshot.[48] The DOJ has the power to withhold federal grants from departments that don't make changes, but this is never done in practice. Instead of taking often cosmetic steps to enhance police legitimacy, the DOJ should be demanding a long-term reexamination of the expanding role of the police in racial and class inequality.

Part of the weakness of this process is that the changes imposed tend to mirror the failed reforms outlined in this chapter: improved training, installing dashboard and body cameras, and improving record keeping. The DOJ's report on police practices in Ferguson did help expose inadequate federal and state funding for municipal operations and racially biased, poor-quality police and court services. It even recommended restricting the use of highly discretionary summonses and low-level arrests, as well as reducing police enforcement in schools. Unfortunately, its main recommendation was to implement a system of "community policing," without addressing all the problems that entails. It did not discuss dialing back the War on Drugs, police militarization, or broken-windows policing.

Under the Trump administration, there is even less reason to rely on this strategy to rein in local police. Attorney General Jeff Sessions has made it clear he will be giving local police a free hand and that federal investigations and prosecutions will be few and far between, as they were under George W. Bush. Instead, we must hold local officials directly accountable for the behavior and mission of local police.

Body Cameras

Reformers have pointed to body cameras as a way to deter and hold officers accountable for improper behavior. The Obama administration embraced this reform and put tens of millions of dollars into police budgets for it. Dash cameras, which have been around for longer, are becoming widespread; police departments like to keep an eye on officers, and the cameras seem to have reduced the number of civilian complaints and lawsuits against officers. In some cases they have also aided in prosecutions.

There is a problem of officer compliance. In numerous shooting cases, officers have failed to turn on their cameras. For example: One of the officers present at the shooting of Walter Scott in Charleston did not have his camera turned on. Not a single one of the officers present at a shooting in Washington, D.C., in 2016 had their camera on. Eighteen-year-old Paul O'Neil was killed by police in Chicago who did not have their cameras on.[49] One study actually found that departments using cameras had *higher* rates of shootings.[50]

Ultimately, body cameras are only as effective as the accountability mechanisms in place. If local DAs and grand juries are unwilling to act on the evidence cameras provide, then the courts won't be an effective accountability tool. Giving local complaint review boards access to the tapes could aid some investigations, but often these boards have only limited authority.

Body cameras also raise important privacy and civil liberties concerns. What will happen to the videos? In the past, police have used the information they gather to establish gang databases, "red files" of political activists, and huge databases on individuals who are not accused of engaging in criminal behavior. Who will have access to these images? In some cases the public may have access to this material. In Seattle, where Washington State has strong sunshine laws, police have started posting videos on YouTube with the images of individuals blurred. While this provides some sense of anonymity, people familiar with the circumstances involved may find it quite possible to identify individuals. If the primary reason for public support of body cameras is to enhance accountability, then perhaps the footage should be under the control of an independent body and not the police.[51]

Alternatives

Any hope we have of holding police more accountable must be based on greater openness and transparency. Police departments are notoriously defensive and insular. Their special status as the sole legitimate users of force has contributed to a mindset of "them against us," which has engendered a culture of secrecy. For too long police have walled themselves off from public inspection, open academic research, and media investigations. Entrenched practices that serve no legitimate purpose, failed policies, implicit and explicit racism among the rank and file, and a culture of hostility toward the public must be rooted out.

Police should stop fighting requests for information from the public, researchers, and the media. They should encourage more public oversight by including civilians on major decision-making bodies. Just as many hospitals, universities, and corporations have outside directors drawn from the communities they serve, the police should be bringing people in, not shutting them out. This is being done in places like Seattle and Oakland, which have created civilian police commissions with encouraging results. Ideally, these people should be chosen by communities, rather than the police or even political leaders. This is a basic requirement of democratic policing. As NYU law professor Barry Friedman notes, our failure to adequately oversee the actions of police puts our society at peril, especially as new technologies give police the ability to see into ever more aspects of our private lives.[52]

We can't rely on a few well-intentioned individuals to rein in excessive police power. Countervailing institutional bases of power must be positioned to monitor the police actively and thoroughly.

Disarm the Police

Since 2000, the police in Great Britain have killed a total of forty-two people. In March 2016 alone, US police killed one hundred people.[53] Yes, there are more people and more guns in the United States, but the scale of police killings goes far beyond these differences. US police are armed with an amazing array of weapons from semiautomatic handguns and fully automatic AR-15 rifles to grenade launchers and .50-caliber machine guns. Much of the militarized weaponry comes directly from the Pentagon through the 1033 Program, a weapons transfer program that began in 1997. This program has resulted in the distribution of $4 billion worth of equipment. Local police departments can get surplus armaments at no cost—with no questions asked about how they will be used. Small communities now have access to armored personnel carriers, assault rifles, grenade launchers, and a variety of "less lethal" weaponry, such as rubber bullets and pepper-spray rounds. The Department of Homeland Security (DHS) has also given out $34 billion in "terrorism grants," a tremendous boon for military contractors trying to expand their reach into civilian policing markets.[54]

SWAT teams have become the primary consumers of militarized weaponry and tactics.[55] These heavily armed teams are almost never used for their original purpose of dealing with hostage situations or barricaded suspects. Instead, their function is now to serve warrants, back up low-level buy-and-bust drug operations, and patrol high-crime areas. Much of this expansion was driven by federal policies that funded the equipment for such teams either directly or through asset forfeiture laws.

The increased use of paramilitary units has resulted in dozens of incidents in which police have wrongfully killed or injured people—including throwing a flashbang grenade into a toddler's crib during a Georgia drug raid in May 2014.[56] The child was severely burned and entered a coma. No drugs were found and no arrests made. One officer was charged with perjury but found not guilty at trial. In fact, the local prosecutor threatened to charge family members for the child's injuries. This near total lack of accountability for botched raids, excessive use of force, and the dehumanization of suspects must be corrected. Getting rid of this military hardware would be a start, but even handguns pose a major problem. Are armed police really the most appropriate tool in most cases?

Even when officers are injured or killed, the officer's possession of a weapon sometimes contributes to their victimization. Offenders who are committed to evading police are more likely to use deadly force precisely because they know the officer is armed. This means they are prone to escalate dramatically. An armed suspect is much less likely to shoot an unarmed officer. Does that mean that some people may evade capture? Yes. But it also means that many lives are saved, including the lives of officers, and police legitimacy is broadly enhanced. Traffic stops would be less deadly for officers and the public if police carried no weapons.[57]

While police insist on the need for firearms, the vast majority of officers never fire their weapons and some brag of long careers without even drawing one on duty. Some will say it acts as a deterrent and bolsters police authority so that other force isn't necessary. This may be true at the margins, but to rely on the threat of lethal force to obtain compliance flies in the face of "policing by consent." The fact that police feel the need to constantly bolster their authority with the threat of lethal violence indicates a fundamental crisis in police legitimacy.

Police Role

More than anything, however, what we really need is to rethink the role of police in society. The origins and function of the police are intimately tied to the management of inequalities of race and class. The suppression of workers and the tight surveillance and micromanagement of black and brown lives have always been at the center of policing. Any police reform strategy that does not address this reality is doomed to fail. We must stop looking to procedural reforms and critically evaluate the substantive outcomes of policing. We must constantly reevaluate what the police are asked to do and what impact policing has on the lives of the policed. A kinder, gentler, and more diverse war on the poor is still a war on the poor. As Chris Hayes points out, organizing policing around the collection of fees and fines to fund local government undermines the basic ideals of democracy.[58] And as long as the police are tasked with waging simultaneous wars on drugs, crime, disorder, and terrorism, we will have aggressive and invasive policing that disproportionately criminalizes the young, poor, male, and nonwhite. We need to push back on this dramatic expansion of police power and its role in the mass incarceration at the heart of the "New Jim Crow."

What we are witnessing is a political crisis. At all levels and in both parties, our political leaders have embraced a neoconservative politics that sees all social problems as police problems. They have given up on using government to improve racial and economic inequality and seem hellbent on worsening these inequalities and using the police to manage the consequences. For decades, they have pitted police against the public while also telling them to be friendlier and improve community relations. They can't do both.

A growing number of police leaders are speaking out about the failures of this approach. In the wake of the tragic deaths of five police officers in Dallas, Chief David Brown said:

> We're asking cops to do too much in this country. We are. Every societal failure, we put it off on the cops to solve. Not enough mental health funding, let the cops handle it … Here in Dallas we got a loose dog problem; let's have the cops chase loose dogs. Schools fail, let's give it to the cops … That's too much to ask. Policing was never meant to solve all those problems.[59]

We are told that the police are the bringers of justice. They are here to help maintain social order so that no one should be subjected to abuse. The neutral enforcement of the law sets us all free. This understanding of policing, however, is largely mythical. American police function, despite whatever good intentions they have, as a tool for managing deeply entrenched inequalities in a way that systematically produces injustices for the poor, socially marginal, and nonwhite.

Part of the problem is that our politicians, media, and criminal justice institutions too often equate justice with revenge. Popular culture is suffused with revenge fantasies in which the aggrieved bring horrible retribution down on those who have hurt them. Often this involves a fantasy of those who have been placed on the margins taking aim at the powerful; it's a fantasy of empowerment through violence. Police and prisons have come to be our preferred tools for inflicting punishment. Our entire criminal justice system has become a gigantic revenge factory. Three-strikes laws, sex-offender registries, the death penalty, and abolishing parole are about retribution, not safety. Whole segments of our society have been deemed always-already guilty. This is not justice; it is oppression. Real justice would look to restore people and communities, to rebuild trust and social cohesion, to offer people a way forward, to reduce the social forces that drive crime, and to treat both victims and perpetrators as full human beings. Our police and larger criminal justice system not only fail at this but rarely see it as even related to their mission.

There are police and other criminal justice agents who want to use their power to improve communities and individuals and protect the "good" people from the "bad" ones. But this relies on the same degraded notion of punishment as justice and runs counter to the political imperatives of the institutions in which they operate. There are growing numbers of disgruntled police officers across the country who are deeply frustrated about the mission they've been given and the tools they've been told to use. They are sick and tired of being part of a system of mass criminalization and punishment. This is especially acute among African American officers, who see the terrible consequences of so much that police do in their communities. Some are beginning to speak out, such as the NYPD Twelve, who filed suit against their department for its use of illegal quotas.[60] Many more, however, fear speaking out.

But not all police mean well. Too many engage in abuse based on race, gender, religion, or economic condition. Explicit and intentional racism is alive and well in American policing. We are asked to believe that these incidents are the misdeeds of "a few bad apples." But why does the institution of policing so consistently shield these misdeeds? Too often, when biased policing is pointed out, the response is to circle the wagons, deny any intent to do harm, and block any discipline against the officers involved. This sends an unambiguous message that officers are above the law and free to act on their biases without consequence. It also says that the institution is more concerned about defending itself than rooting out these problems.

Is our society really made safer and more just by incarcerating millions of people? Is asking the police to be the lead agency in dealing with homelessness, mental illness, school discipline, youth unemployment, immigration, youth violence, sex work, and drugs really a way to achieve a better society?

Can police really be trained to perform all these tasks in a professional and uncoercive manner? In the pages that follow I lay out the case for why the answer to these questions is no, and sketch out a plan for constructing an alternative.

Any real agenda for police reform must replace police with empowered communities working to solve their own problems. Poor communities of color have suffered the consequences of high crime and disorder. It is their children who are shot and robbed. They have also had to bear the brunt of aggressive, invasive, and humiliating policing. Policing will never be a just or effective tool for community empowerment, much less racial justice. Communities must directly confront the political, economic, and social arrangements that produce the vast gulfs between the races and the growing gaps between the haves and the have-nots. We don't need empty police reforms; we need a robust democracy that gives people the capacity to demand of their government and themselves real, nonpunitive solutions to their problems.

2

The Police Are Not Here to Protect You

The police exist to keep us safe, or so we are told by mainstream media and popular culture. TV shows exaggerate the amount of serious crime and the nature of what most police officers actually do all day. Crime control is a small part of policing, and it always has been.

Felony arrests of any kind are a rarity for uniformed officers, with most making no more than one a year. When a patrol officer actually apprehends a violent criminal in the act, it is a major moment in their career. The bulk of police officers work in patrol. They take reports, engage in random patrol, address parking and driving violations and noise complaints, issue tickets, and make misdemeanor arrests for drinking in public, possession of small amounts of drugs, or the vague "disorderly conduct." Officers I've shadowed on patrol describe their days as "99 percent boredom and 1 percent sheer terror"—and even that 1 percent is a bit of an exaggeration for most officers.

Even detectives (who make up only about 15 percent of police forces) spend most of their time taking reports of crimes that they will never solve—and in many cases will never even investigate. There is no possible way for police to investigate every reported crime. Even homicide investigations can be brought to a quick conclusion if no clear suspect is identified within two days, as the television reality show *The First 48* emphasizes. Burglaries and larcenies are even less likely to be investigated thoroughly, or at all. Most crimes that are investigated are not solved.

The Liberal View of Policing

I grew up on shows like *Adam-12*, which portrayed police as dispassionate enforcers of the law. Hollywood, in the sixties and seventies, was helping the Los Angeles Police Department (LAPD) manufacture a professional image for itself in the wake of the 1965 Watts riots. Today, we are awash in police dramas and reality TV shows with a similar ethos and purpose. Some are more nuanced than others, but by and large these shows portray the police as struggling to fight crime in a complex and at times morally contradictory environment. Even when police are portrayed as engaging in corrupt or brutal behavior, as in *Dirty Harry* or *The Shield*, it is understood that their primary motivation is to get the bad guys.

It is largely a liberal fantasy that the police exist to protect us from the bad guys. As the veteran police scholar David Bayley argues,

> The police do not prevent crime. This is one of the best kept secrets of modern life. Experts know it, the police know it, but the public does not know it. Yet the police pretend that they are society's best defense against crime and continually argue that if they are given more resources, especially personnel, they will be able to protect communities against crime. This is a myth.[1]

Bayley goes on to point out that there is no correlation between the number of police and crime rates.

Liberals think of the police as the legitimate mechanism for using force in the interests of the whole society. For them, the state, through elections and other democratic processes, represents the general will of society as well as any system could; those who act against those interests, therefore, should face the police. The police must maintain their public legitimacy by acting in a way that the public respects and is in keeping with the rule of law. For liberals, police reform is always a question of taking steps to restore that legitimacy. That is what separates the police of a liberal democracy from those of a dictatorship.

This is not to say that liberals believe that US policing is without problems. They acknowledge that police sometimes violate their principles, but see this as an individual failing to be dealt with through disciplinary procedures or improvements to training and oversight. If entire police departments are discriminatory, abusive, or unprofessional, then they advocate efforts to stamp out bias and bad practices through training, changes in leadership, and a variety of oversight mechanisms until legitimacy is reestablished. They argue that racist and brutal cops can be purged from the profession and an unbiased system of law enforcement reestablished in the interest of the whole society. They want the police to be better trained, more accountable, and less brutal and racist—laudable goals, but they leave intact the basic institutional functions of the police, which have never really been about public safety or crime control.

Political scientist Naomi Murakawa points out that this liberal misconception led to the inadequate police and criminal justice reforms of the past.[2] Liberals, according to Murakawa, want to ignore the profound legacy of racism. Rather than admit the central role of slavery and Jim Crow in both producing wealth for whites and denying basic life opportunities for blacks, they prefer to focus on using a few remedial programs—backed up by a robust criminal justice system to transform black people's attitudes so that they will be better able to perform competitively in the labor market. The result, however, is that black Americans start from a diminished position that makes them more likely to come into contact with the criminal justice system and to be treated more harshly by it. What is missing from this liberal approach is any critical assessment of what problems the state is asking the police to solve and whether the police are really the best suited to solve them.

The reality is that the police exist primarily as a system for managing and even producing inequality by suppressing social movements and tightly managing the behaviors of poor and nonwhite people: those on the losing end of economic and political arrangements. Bayley argues that policing emerged as new political and economic formations developed, producing social upheavals that could no longer be managed by existing private, communal, and informal processes.[3] This can be seen in the earliest origins of policing, which were tied to three basic social arrangements of inequality in the eighteenth century: slavery, colonialism, and the control of a new industrial working class. This created what Allan Silver calls a "policed society," in which state power was significantly expanded in the face of social upheavals and demands for justice.[4] As Kristian Williams points out, "The police represent the point of contact between the coercive apparatus of the state and the lives of its citizens."[5] In the words of Mark Neocleous, police exist to "fabricate social order," but that order rests on systems of exploitation—and when elites feel that this system is at risk, whether from slave revolts, general strikes, or crime and rioting in the streets, they rely on the police to control those activities.[6] When possible, the police aggressively and proactively prevent the formation of movements and public expressions of rage, but when necessary they will fall back on brute force. Therefore, while the specific forms that policing takes have changed as the nature of inequality and the forms of resistance to it have shifted over time, the basic function of managing the poor, foreign, and nonwhite on behalf of a system of economic and political inequality remains.

The Original Police Force

Most liberal and conservative academics attempt to counter this argument by pointing to the London Metropolitan Police, held up as the "original" police force. Created in 1829 by Sir Robert Peel, from whom the "Bobbies" get their name, this new force was more effective than the informal and unprofessional "watch" or the excessively violent and often hated militia and army. But even this noble endeavor had at its core not fighting crime, but managing disorder and protecting the propertied classes from the rabble. Peel developed his ideas while managing the British colonial occupation of Ireland and seeking new forms of social control that would allow for continued political and economic domination in the face of growing insurrections, riots, and political uprisings.[7] For years, such "outrages" had been managed by the local militia and, if necessary, the British Army. However, colonial expansion and the Napoleonic Wars dramatically reduced the availability of these forces just as resistance to British occupation increased. Furthermore, armed troops had limited tools for dealing with riots and others forms of mass disorder. Too often they were called upon to open fire on crowds, creating martyrs and further inflaming Irish resistance. Peel was forced to develop a lower-cost and more legitimate form of policing: a "Peace Preservation Force," made up of professional police who attempted to manage crowds by embedding themselves more fully in rebellious localities, then identifying and neutralizing troublemakers and ringleaders through threats and arrests. This led eventually to the creation of the Royal Irish Constabulary, which for about a century was the main rural police force in Ireland. It played a central role in maintaining British rule and an oppressive agricultural system dominated by British loyalists, a system that produced widespread poverty, famine, and displacement.

The signal event that showed the need for a professional police force was the Peterloo Massacre of 1819. In the face of widespread poverty combined with the displacement of skilled work by industrialization, movements emerged across the country to call for political reforms. In August 1819, tens of thousands of people gathered in central Manchester, only to have the rally declared illegal. A cavalry charge with sabers killed a dozen protestors and injured several hundred more. In response, the British state developed a series of vagrancy laws designed to force people into "productive" work. What was needed was a force that could both maintain political control and help produce a new economic order of industrial capitalism.[8] As home secretary, Peel created the London Metropolitan Police to do this. The main functions of the new police, despite their claims of political neutrality, were to protect property, quell riots, put down strikes and other industrial actions, and produce a disciplined industrial work force. This system was expanded throughout England, which was awash in movements against industrialization. Luddites resisted exploitation through workplace sabotage. Jacobins, inspired by the French Revolution, were a constant source of concern. The most threatening, however, were the Chartists, who called for fundamental democratic reforms on behalf of impoverished English workers. Local, nonprofessional constables and militias were unable to deal with these movements effectively or enforce the new vagrancy laws.[9] At first they requested the services of the new London Police, who had proven quite capable of putting down disturbances and strikes with minimal force. That force, however, always had the patina of central government intervention, which often further inflamed movements, so eventually towns created their own full-time professional police departments, based on the London model.

The London model was imported into Boston in 1838 and spread through Northern cities over the next few decades. That model had to adapt to the United States, where massive immigration and rapid industrialization created an even more socially and politically chaotic environment. Boston's economic and political leaders needed a new police force to manage riots and the widespread social disorder associated with the working classes.[10] In 1837, the Broad Street riots involved a mob of 15,000 attacking Irish immigrants. This was quelled only after a regiment of militia, including 800 cavalry, was called onto the streets. Following this, Mayor Samuel Elliot moved to create a professional civilian police force.

New York leapfrogged over Boston, creating an even larger and more formal police force in 1844. New York was exploding with new immigrants who were being chewed up by rapid and often cruel industrialization, producing social upheaval and immiseration that was expressed as crime, racial and ethnic strife, and labor unrest. White and black dockworkers went on strike and undertook destructive sabotage actions in 1802, 1825, and 1828. There were larger waves of strikes by skilled workers being displaced by mass production in 1809, 1822, and 1829. These culminated in the formation of the Workingmen's Party in 1829, which demanded a ten-hour day, and led to the founding of the General Trade Union in 1833. Rioting that was less obviously political was widespread during this period, sometimes occurring monthly. During the 1828 Christmas riot, four thousand workers marched on the wealthy districts, beating up blacks and looting stores along the way. The night watch assembled to block them, but gave way—to the horror of the city's elite, who watched events unfold from their mansions and a party at the City Hotel. In response, newspapers began calling for a major expansion and professionalization of the watch, which ended with the formation of the police.[11]

Wealthy Protestant nativists feared and resented the new immigrants, who were often Catholic, uneducated, disorderly, politically militant, and prone to voting Democratic. They attempted to discipline and control this population by restricting drinking, gambling, and prostitution, as well as much more mundane behaviors like how women wore their hair, the lengths of bathing suits, and public kissing.[12] The formation of the Chicago police was directly tied to such efforts. Law and Order Party mayor Levi Boone established the first "special police" force following his election in 1855 with the express intent of enforcing a variety of nativist morality laws, including restrictions on drinking. In response to the arrest of several dozen saloonkeepers, a group comprised mostly of German workers attempted to free them, leading to the Lager Beer Riots. According to historian Sam Mitrani, local elites responded by holding a "Law and Order" meeting to demand an even larger and more professional police body. The next week the City Council responded by creating Chicago's first official police force.[13]

It was the creation of police that made widespread enforcement of vice laws and even the criminal code possible for the first time.[14] These morality laws both gave the state greater power to intervene in the social lives of the new immigrants and opened the door to widespread corruption. Vice corruption was endemic in police departments across the country. While station house basements often housed the homeless, and officers managed a large population of orphaned youth, as Eric Monkkonen points out, these efforts were primarily designed to surveil and control this population rather than provide meaningful assistance.[15]

America's early urban police were both corrupt and incompetent. Officers were usually chosen based on political connections and bribery. There were no civil service exams or even formal training in most places. They were also used as a tool of political parties to suppress opposition voting and spy on and suppress workers' organizations, meetings, and strikes. If a local businessman had close ties to a local politician, he needed only to go to the station and a squad of police would be sent to threaten, beat, and arrest workers as needed. Payments from gamblers and, later, bootleggers were a major source of income for officers, with payments increasing up the chain of command. This system of being "on the take" remained standard procedure in many major departments until the 1970s, when resistance emerged in the form of whistleblowers like Frank Serpico. Corruption remains an issue, especially in relation to drugs and sex work, but tends to be more isolated, less systemic, and subject to some internal disciplinary controls, as liberal reformers have worked to shore up police legitimacy.

The primary jobs of early detectives were to spy on political radicals and other troublemakers and to replace private thief catchers, who recovered stolen goods for a reward. Interestingly, very few thieves ended up getting caught by the new police. In many instances they worked closely with thieves and pickpockets, taking a cut of their earnings and acting as fences by exchanging stolen merchandise for a reward rather than having to sell the goods on the black market at a heavy discount. Early detectives like Alexander "Clubber" Williams amassed significant fortunes in this trade.[16]

The extent of police corruption was so great that business leaders, journalists, and religious leaders banded together to expose corruption and inefficiency and demand that police both become more professional and more effectively crack down on crime, vice, and radical politics.[17] In response to this and similar efforts in the late nineteenth and early twentieth century, policing was professionalized through the use of civil service exams and centralized hiring processes, training, and new technology. Overt corruption and brutality were reined in and management sciences were introduced. Reformers like August Vollmer developed police science courses and textbooks, utilized new transportation and communication technologies, and introduced fingerprinting and police labs. As we will see later, many of these ideas emerged from his experiences as part of the US occupation forces in the Philippines.

From the Philippines to Pennsylvania

In some cases, early police forces were created specifically for purposes of suppressing workers' movements. Pennsylvania was home to some of the most militant unionism of the late nineteenth and early twentieth century. Local police were too few in number and were sometimes sympathetic to the workers, so mine and factory owners turned to the state to provide them with armed forces to control strikes and intimidate organizers. The state's initial response was to authorize a completely privatized police force called the Coal and Iron Police.[18] Local employers had only to pay a commission fee of one dollar per person to deputize anyone of their choosing as an official officer of the law. These forces worked directly for the employer, often under the supervision of Pinkertons or other private security forces, and were typically used as strike breakers and were often implicated as agents provocateurs, fomenting violence as a way of breaking up workers' movements and justifying their continued paychecks. The Coal and Iron Police committed numerous atrocities, including the Latimer Massacre of 1897, in which they killed nineteen unarmed miners and wounded thirty-two others. The final straw was the Anthracite Coal Strike of 1902, a pitched battle that lasted five months and created national coal shortages.

In the aftermath, political leaders and employers decided that a new system of labor management paid for out of the public coffers would be cheaper for them and have greater public legitimacy and effectiveness. The result was the creation of the Pennsylvania State Police in 1905, the first state police force in the country. It was modeled after the Philippine Constabulary, used to maintain the US occupation there, which became a testing ground for new police techniques and technologies.[19] The local population resented US occupation and developed anticolonial organizations and struggles. The national police force attempted to develop close ties to local communities to allow it to monitor subversive activities. The United States also moved quickly to erect telephone and telegraph wires, to allow quick communication of emerging intelligence. When demonstrations emerged, the police, through a huge network of informants, could anticipate them and place spies and agents provocateurs among them to sow dissent and allow leaders and other agitators to be quickly arrested and neutralized.

In Pennsylvania, this new paramilitary force represented an important shift of power away from local communities. This shift unambiguously favored the interests of large employers, who had significantly more influence over state level politicians. While putatively under civilian political control, the reality was that the state police remained a major force in putting down strikes, though often with less violence and greater legal and political authority. The consequences, however, were largely the same, as they participated in strikebreaking and the killing of miners, such as in the Westmoreland County Coal Strike of 1910 and 1911. Their frequent attacks led Slovak miners to give them the nickname "Pennsylvania Cossacks" and prompted Socialist state legislator James H. Maurer to solicit, compile, and publish a huge amount of correspondence describing their heavy-handed tactics under the title *The American Cossack*.[20] Interestingly, many of the letters point out that the new state police routinely showed no interest in crime control, serving strictly as publicly financed strikebreakers. In 1915, the State Commission on Industrial Relations described them as

> an extremely efficient force for crushing strikes, but ... not successful in preventing violence in connection with strikes, in maintaining legal and civil rights of the parties to the dispute, nor in protecting of the public. On the contrary, violence seems to increase rather than diminish when the constabulary is

> brought into an industrial dispute, the legal and civil rights of the workers have on numerous occasions been violated.[21]

Jesse Garwood, a major figure in the US occupation forces in the Philippines, brought the methods of militarized espionage and political suppression to bear on Pennsylvania miners and factory workers.

These practices then fed back into domestic American policing. The most important police leader of the twentieth century, August Vollmer, after serving in the Philippines, became chief of police in Berkeley, California, and wrote the most influential textbook of modern policing. Vollmer went on to pioneer the use of radio patrol cars, fingerprinting, and other techniques now considered standard practice. Marine General Smedley Butler, who created the Haitian police and played a major role in the US occupation of Nicaragua, served as police chief of Philadelphia in 1924, ushering in a wave of technological modernization and militarized police tactics. He was removed from office after a public outcry over his repressive methods.[22]

The US went on to set up additional colonial police forces in Central America and the Caribbean in the early twentieth century. Jeremy Kuzmarov documents US involvement in creating repressive police forces in Haiti, the Dominican Republic, and Nicaragua.[23] These forces were designed to be part of a Progressive Era program of modernization and nation-building, but were quickly turned into forces of brutal repression in the service of US-backed regimes. These US-trained security forces went on to commit horrific human rights abuses, including torture, extortion, kidnapping, and mass murder.

The US continued to set up police forces as part of its foreign policy objectives throughout the postwar period. Japan, South Korea, and South Vietnam all had US-created police forces whose primary purposes were intelligence and counterinsurgency. Postwar police reformer O.W. Wilson, a colonel in the military police during World War II, was involved in the denazification of Germany following the war. Afterwards he went on to teach police science at Berkeley and was appointed Commissioner of Police in Chicago in 1960 and influenced a generation of police executives with his ideas of preventative policing.

The Texas Rangers

The US also had its own domestic version of colonial policing: the Texas Rangers. Initially a loose band of irregulars, the Rangers were hired to protect the interests of newly arriving white colonists, first under the Mexican government, later under an independent Republic of Texas, and finally as part of the state of Texas. Their main work was to hunt down native populations accused of attacking white settlers, as well as investigating crimes like cattle rustling.

The Rangers also frequently acted as vigilantes on behalf of whites in disputes with the Spanish and Mexican populations. For more than a century they were a major force for white colonial expansion pushing out Mexicans through violence, intimidation, and political interference. In some cases, whites would raid cattle from Mexican ranches and then, when Mexican *vaqueros* tried to take them back, call in the Rangers to retrieve their "stolen property." Mexicans and Native Americans who resisted Ranger authority could be killed, beaten, arrested, or intimidated. Mike Cox describes this as nothing short of an extermination campaign in which almost the entire indigenous population was killed or driven out of the territory.[24]

Carrigan and Webb's *Forgotten Dead: Mob Violence against Mexicans in the United States, 1848–1928*,[25] is part of an effort involving families, academics, and the larger Tejano community to uncover this hidden history that culminated in an exhibit at the Bullock State History Museum, entitled "Life and Death on the Border," which chronicled the many abuses of Texans of Mexican heritage, who were pushed out by white settlers with the help of the Texas Rangers.[26] This includes the horrific 1918 massacre at Porvenir, in which Rangers killed fifteen unarmed locals and drove the remaining community into Mexico for fear of further violence. This led to a series of state legislative hearings in 1919 about extrajudicial killings and racially motivated brutality on behalf of white ranchers. Those hearings resulted in no formal changes; the graphic records of abuse were sealed for the next fifty years to avoid any stain on the Rangers' "heroic" record.

This intense violence was in part driven by separatists among the Mexican population of Texas who were tired of the constant usurpation of their lands, segregationist policies, and exclusion from the political process, all of which was enforced by the Rangers and local police. This movement of *sediciosos* engendered a horrific backlash that was celebrated by local newspapers: "The known bandits and outlaws are being hunted like coyotes and one by one are being killed ... The war of extermination will be carried on until every man known to have been involved with the uprising will have been wiped out."[27]

In the sixties and seventies, local and state elites used Rangers to suppress the political and economic rights of Mexican Americans and played a central role in subverting farmworker movements by shutting down meetings, intimidating supporters, and arresting and brutalizing picketers and union leaders.[28] They were also frequently called in to intimidate Mexican Americans out of voting in local elections. Most Latinos were subjected to a kind of "Juan Crow" in which they were denied the right to vote and barred from private and public accommodations such as hotels, restaurants, bus station waiting rooms, public pools, and bathrooms. The first direct assault on this system occurred in 1963 in the small farming town of Crystal City, in which Tejanos made up a majority of the population but had no political representation. The white political establishment enforced segregation, charged Latinos higher taxes, and provided them with substandard services. In 1962, local Mexican Americans began attempting to register to vote, only to be faced with harassment and intimidation from local police and employers. After an extended effort involving outside monitors, press attention, and lawsuits, they registerered and, in 1963, ran a slate of candidates for the local city council. In response, the Texas Rangers undertook a program of intimidation. They tried to prevent voter rallies, threatened candidates and their supporters, and even engaged in physical attacks and arrests. In the end, because of extensive outside press attention, the Rangers had to back down and the slate swept the election, ushering in a period of greater civil rights for Mexican Americans.

In 1935 Walter Webb wrote a massive history of the Rangers called *The Texas Rangers: A Century of Frontier Defense* that unambiguously sang their praises and held them up as a model for American policing.[29] President Lyndon B. Johnson even wrote the foreword to a later edition.[30] Webb's book inspired a generation of films and novels lionizing the Rangers, culminating in the 1990s television series, *Walker, Texas Ranger*, starring right-wing martial-arts expert Chuck Norris.

The Role of Slavery

Slavery was another major force that shaped early US policing. Well before the London Metropolitan Police were formed, Southern cities like New Orleans, Savannah, and Charleston had paid full-time police who wore uniforms, were accountable to local civilian officials, and were connected to a broader criminal justice system. These early police forces were derived not from the informal watch system as happened in the Northeast, but instead from slave patrols, and developed to prevent revolts.[31] They had the power to ride onto private property to ensure that slaves were not harboring weapons or fugitives, conducting meetings, or learning to read or write. They also played a major role in preventing slaves from escaping to the North, through regular patrols on rural roads.

While most slave patrols were rural and nonprofessional, urban patrols like the Charleston City Guard and Watch became professionalized as early as 1783. By 1831, the Charleston police had a hundred paid City Guards and sixty State Guards on duty twenty-four hours a day, including foot and mounted patrols. Enslaved people often worked away from their owners' property in warehouses, workshops, and other workplaces, as part of industrialization. This meant that large numbers of unaccompanied enslaved people could move about the city on their own as long as they had a proper pass. They could congregate with others, frequent illicit underground taverns, and even establish religious and benevolent associations, often in conjunction with free blacks, which produced tremendous social anxiety among whites. Professional police were thus deemed essential. Richard Wade quotes a Charlestonian in 1845:

> Over the sparsely populated country, where gangs of negros are restricted within settled plantations under immediate control and discipline of their respective owners, slaves were not permitted to idle and roam about in pursuit of mischief. ... The mere occasional riding about and general supervision of a patrol may be sufficient. But, some more energetic and scrutinizing system is absolutely necessary in cities, where from the very denseness of population and closely contiguous settlements there must be need of closer and more careful circumspection.[32]

The result, according to Wade, was "a persistent struggle to minimize Negro fraternizing and, more especially, to prevent the growth of an organized colored community."[33] This was done through constant monitoring and inspection of the black population. The heavily armed police regularly inspected the passes of employed slaves and the papers of free blacks. Police waged a constant battle to close down underground bars, study groups, and religious gatherings. The only limit on police power was that enslaved people were someone else's property; killing one could result in civil liability to the owner. In rural areas the transition from slave patrols to police was slower, but the basic functional connection was just as strong.[34]

When slavery was abolished, the slave patrol system was too; small towns and rural areas developed new and more professional forms of policing to deal with the newly freed black population. The main concern of this period was not so much preventing rebellion as forcing newly freed blacks into subservient economic and political roles. New laws outlawing vagrancy were used extensively to force blacks to accept employment, mostly in the sharecropping system. Local police enforced poll taxes and other voter suppression efforts to ensure white control of the political system.

Anyone on the roads without proof of employment was quickly subjected to police action. Local police were the essential front door of the twin evils of convict leasing and prison farms. Local sheriffs would arrest free blacks on flimsy to nonexistent evidence, then drive them into a cruel and inhuman criminal justice system whose punishments often resulted in death. These same sheriffs and judges also received kickbacks and in some cases generated lists of fit and hardworking blacks to be incarcerated on behalf of employers, who would then lease them out to perform forced labor for profit. Douglas Blackmon chronicles the appalling conditions of mines and lumber camps where thousands perished.[35] By the Jim Crow era, policing had become a central tool of maintaining racial inequality throughout the South, supplemented by ad hoc vigilantes such as the Ku Klux Klan, which often worked closely with—and was populated by—local police.[36]

Northern policing was also deeply affected by emancipation. Northern political leaders deeply feared the northern migration of newly freed rural blacks, whom they often viewed as socially, if not racially, inferior, uneducated, and criminal. Ghettos were established in Northern cities to control this growing population, with police playing the role of both containment and pacification. Up until the 1960s, this was largely accomplished through the racially discriminatory enforcement of the law and widespread use of excessive force. Blacks knew very well what the behavioral and geographic limits were and the role that police played in maintaining them in both the Jim Crow South and the ghettoized North.

Political Policing in the Postwar Era

With the rise of the civil rights movement came more repressive policing. In the South police became the front line for suppressing the movement. They denied protest permits, threated and beat demonstrators, made discriminatory arrests, and failed to protect demonstrators from angry mobs and vigilante actions, including beatings, disappearances, bombings, and assassinations. All of this occurred to preserve a system of formal racial discrimination and economic exploitation.

In Northern and Western cities the suppression of the movement sometimes took a more nuanced approach at first, but when that failed, overt violence soon followed. Many cities allowed a wide variety of protest actions to occur with only minor restrictions. Boycotts and pickets in support of Southern organizing were largely tolerated, as was protest aimed at local governments calling for jobs, education, and social services. As these movements grew and became more militant, however, they were subjected to ever more repressive tactics. New "Red Squads" were developed that gathered intelligence through informants, infiltrators, and even agents provocateurs, who actively worked to undermine groups like the Black Panthers and the Congress of Racial Equality (CORE). Eventually local police, often working in cooperation with the FBI, undertook the overt suppression of these movements through targeted arrests on trumped-up charges and ultimately even assassinations of prominent leaders such as Fred Hampton, the Black Panther leader killed in a hail of gunfire in the middle of the night during a police raid of his Chicago apartment. The American Indian Movement and the Latino-based Brown Berets and Young Lords faced similar forms of repression.

These movements were suppressed in part based on counterinsurgency strategies that emerged out of the foreign policy of that era. From 1962 to 1974, the US government operated a major international police training initiative, staffed by experienced American police executives, called the Office of Public Safety (OPS). This agency worked closely with the CIA to train police in areas of Cold War conflict, including South Vietnam, Iran, Uruguay, Argentina, and Brazil. According to internal documents, the training emphasized counterinsurgency, including espionage, bomb making, and interrogation techniques. In many parts of the world these officers were involved in human-rights abuses including torture, disappearance, and extrajudicial killings. Over $200 million in firearms and equipment was distributed to foreign police departments and 1,500 US personnel were involved in training a million officers overseas. Even more troubling is that many of the trainers moved in large numbers into law enforcement, including the Drug Enforcement Agency (DEA), FBI, and numerous local and state police forces, bringing with them a more militarized vision of policing steeped in Cold War imperatives of suppressing social movements through counterintelligence, militarized riot-suppression techniques, and heavy-handed crime control.[37] They applied this counterinsurgency mindset to the political uprisings occurring at home.

OPS director Byron Engle testified before the Kerner Commission on Civil Disorders that "in working with the police in various countries we have acquired a great deal of experience in dealing with violence ranging from demonstrations and riots to guerrilla warfare. Much of this experience may be useful in the US."[38] The result was a massive expansion of federal funding for the police under the Johnson administration. Under the guise of professionalizing the police, the federal government began spending hundreds of millions of dollars to provide police with more training and equipment with few strings attached. Unfortunately, and unsurprisingly, rather than reducing the burden of racialized policing, this new professionalization movement merely enhanced police power and led directly to the development of SWAT teams and mass incarceration.

Policing Today

The past few decades have seen a dramatic expansion in the scope and intensity of police activity. More police than ever before are engaged in more enforcement of more laws, resulting in astronomical levels of incarceration, economic exploitation, and abuse. This expansion mirrors the rise of mass incarceration. It began with the War on Crime rhetoric of the 1960s and continued to develop and intensify until today, with support from both political parties.

This increase in the power of police is tied to a set of economic and political crises. At the political level, politicians were anxious to find new ways to harness the support of white voters in the wake of the civil rights movement. As Michelle Alexander and others have pointed out, Nixon mobilized racial fears through the lens of "law and order" to convince Southern whites to vote Republican for the first time since Reconstruction. Following the disastrous defeat of Michael Dukakis in 1988 for being "soft on crime," Democrats came to fully embrace this strategy as well, leading to disasters like Bill Clinton's 1994 Crime Bill, which added tens of thousands of additional police and expanded the drug and crime wars.

America's changing economic realities have played a central role in this process as well. Christian Parenti has shown how the federal government crashed the economy in the 1970s to stem the rise of workers' power, leaving millions out of work and creating a new, mostly African American permanent underclass largely excluded from the formal economy.[39] In response, government mobilized at all levels to manage this new "surplus population" through intensive policing and mass incarceration. The policing of poor and nonwhite communities became much more intense. As unemployment, poverty, and homelessness increased, government, police, and prosecutors worked together to criminalize huge swaths of the population aided by ideologies like the broken-windows theory and the superpredator myth.

We cannot reduce all policing to the active suppression of social movements and the control of racial minorities. Today's police are clearly concerned with matters of public safety and crime control, however misguided their methods are. The advent of Compstat and other management techniques are in fact designed to address serious crime problems, and significant resources go into these efforts. But this crime-fighting orientation is itself a form of social control. From Jonathan Simon's *Governing Through Crime*[40] to Michelle Alexander's *The New Jim Crow*,[41] there is extensive research to show that what counts as crime and what gets targeted for control is shaped by concerns about race and class inequality and the potential for social and political upheaval. As Jeffrey Reiman points out in the *Rich Get Richer and the Poor Get Prison*, the criminal justice system excuses and ignores crimes of the rich that produce profound social harms while intensely criminalizing the behaviors of the poor and nonwhite, including those behaviors that produce few social harms.[42] When the crimes of the rich *are* dealt with, it's generally through administrative controls and civil enforcement rather than aggressive policing, criminal prosecution, and incarceration, which are reserved largely for the poor and nonwhite. No bankers have been jailed for the 2008 financial crisis despite widespread fraud and the looting of the American economy, which resulted in mass unemployment, homelessness, and economic dislocation.

American crime control policy is structured around the use of punishment to manage the "dangerous classes," masquerading as a system of justice. The police's concern with crime makes their social control functions more palatable. The transition from the use of militias and military troops to civilian police was a process of engineering greater public acceptance of the social-control functions of the state, whether abroad or at home.

Today's modern police are not that far removed from their colonialist forebears. They too enforce a system of laws designed to reproduce and maintain economic inequality, usually along racialized lines. As Michelle Alexander has put it,

> We *need* an effective system of crime prevention and control in our communities, but that is not what the current system is. This system is better designed to create crime, and a perpetual class of people labeled criminals ... Saying mass incarceration is an abysmal failure makes sense, though only if one assumes that the criminal justice system is designed to prevent and control crime. But if mass incarceration is understood as a system of social control—specifically, racial control—then the system is a fantastic success.[43]

The most damning example of this is the War on Drugs, in which millions of mostly black and brown people have been ground through the criminal justice system, their lives destroyed and their communities destabilized, without reduction in the use or availability of drugs.

Everyone wants to live in safe communities but when individuals and communities look to the police to solve their problems they are in essence mobilizing the machinery of their own oppression. While the police will often go through the motions of crime control—though not always—it is through a lens of class and race skepticism if not outright animus. While individual officers may not harbor deep biases—though many do—the institution's ultimate purpose has always been one of managing the poor and non-white, rather than producing anything resembling true justice. It is understandable that people have come to look to the police to provide them with safety and security. Poor people in particular bear the brunt of street crime. After decades of neoliberal austerity, local governments have no will or ability to pursue the kinds of ameliorative social policies that might address crime and disorder without the use of armed police; as Simon points out, government has basically abandoned poor neighborhoods to market forces, backed up by a repressive criminal justice system. That system stays in power by creating a culture of fear that it claims to be uniquely suited to address.[44] As poverty deepens and housing prices rise, government support for affordable housing has evaporated, leaving in its wake a combination of homeless shelters and aggressive broken-windows-oriented policing. As mental health facilities close, police become the first responders to calls for assistance with mental health crisies. As youth are left without adequate schools, jobs, or recreational facilities, they form gangs for mutual protection or participate in the black markets of stolen goods, drugs, and sex to survive and are ruthlessly criminalized. Modern policing is largely a war on the poor that does little to make people safer or communities stronger, and even when it does, this is accomplished through the most coercive forms of state power that destroy the lives of millions. Instead of asking the police to solve our problems we must organize for real justice. We need to produce a society designed to meet people's human needs, rather than wallow in the pursuit of wealth at the expense of all else.

3

The School-to-Prison Pipeline

In 2005, three police officers in Florida forcibly arrested a five-year-old African American girl for misbehaving in school. It was captured on video. The singer and civil rights activist Harry Belafonte, like most others, was appalled by what he saw and initiated a campaign to train the next generation of civil rights activists: the Gathering for Justice, which in turn created the Justice League, an important force in the Black Lives Matter movement. At the core of the group's demands is a call to end the criminalization of young people in schools.[1]

"School Resource Officers"

Over the last twenty years there has been an explosion in the number of police officers stationed in schools—one of the most dramatic and clearly counterproductive expansions of police scope and power. In the 2013–14 academic year, there were more than forty-three thousand school-based police officers in the United States.[2] Over 40 percent of all schools now have police officers assigned to them, 69 percent of whom engage in school discipline enforcement rather than just maintaining security and enforcing the law.

While the origins of "school resource officers" (SROs) can be traced back to the 1950s, there was a dramatic change in their number and focus in the 1990s, thanks in large part to the Justice Department's "Cops in Schools" program, which gave out $750 million to hire 6,500 new school-based police.[3] While many of these officers work hard to maintain a safe environment for students and to act as mentors and advisors, the overall approach of relying on armed police to deal with safety issues has led to a massive increase in arrests of students that fundamentally undermines the educational mission of schools, turning them into an extension of the larger carceral state and feeding what has come to be called the school-to-prison pipeline.

This increase in the number of school-based police is tied to a variety of social and political factors that converged in the 1990s and continues today. First, conservative criminologist John Dilulio, along with broken-windows theory author James Q. Wilson, argued in 1995 that the United States would soon experience a wave of youth crime driven by the crack trade, high rates of single-parent families, and a series of racially coded concerns about declining values and public morality.[4] He predicted that by 2010 there would be an additional 270,000 of these youthful predators on the streets, leading to a massive increase in violent crime. He described these young people as hardened criminals: "radically impulsive, brutally remorseless ... elementary school youngsters who pack guns instead of lunches" and "have absolutely no respect for human life."[5] Dilulio and his colleagues argued that there was nothing to be done but to exclude such children from settings where they could harm others and, ultimately, to incarcerate them for as long as possible. Dilulio's ideas were based on spurious evidence and ideologically motivated assumptions that turned out to be totally inaccurate. Every year since, juvenile crime in and out of schools in the US has declined.[6]

However, the "superpredator" myth was extremely influential. It generated a huge amount of press coverage, editorials, and legislative action. One of the immediate consequences was a rash of new laws lowering the age of adult criminal responsibility, making it easier to incarcerate young people in adult jails, in keeping with the broader politics of incapacitation and mass incarceration. It was also at the center of efforts to tighten school discipline policies and increase police presence in schools.

The second major factor was the Columbine school massacre of 1999, in which two Colorado high school students murdered twelve classmates and a teacher, despite the presence of armed police on campus. This tragic incident received incredible attention due to its extreme nature and the fact that it occurred in a normally low-crime white suburban area. It was easy enough for middle-class families to ignore the more frequent outbursts of violence in nonwhite urban schools, but this incident drove them to want action taken to make schools safer for young people.

In keeping with the broader ethos of get-tough criminal-justice measures, the response was to increase the presence of armed police in schools rather than dealing with the underlying social issues of bullying, mental illness, and the availability of guns. While there was some focus on bullying, much of it took a punitive form, driving additional "zero tolerance" disciplinary procedures and further contributing to suspensions, expulsions, and arrests on flimsy evidence and for minor infractions.

The third major factor was the rise of neoliberal school reorganization, with its emphasis on high-stakes testing, reduced budgets, and punitive disciplinary systems. Increasingly, schools are being judged almost exclusively based on student performance on standardized tests. Teacher pay, discretionary spending, and even the survival of the school are tied to these tests. This creates a pressure-cooker atmosphere in schools in which improving test scores becomes the primary focus, pitting teachers' and administrators' interests against those of students.[7] A teacher or administrator who wants to keep their job or earn a bonus has an incentive to get rid of students who are dragging down test scores through low performance or behaviors that disrupt the performances of other students. This gives those schools a strong incentive to drive those students out, either temporarily through suspensions or permanently through expulsions or dropping out.

High-Stakes Testing and Social Control

States that rely heavily on high-stakes tests tend to shift teaching toward test prep and rote learning; this drives out creativity and individualized learning, which contributes to discipline problems as students grow uninterested or resentful. Schools too often respond to this dynamic by adopting ever more restrictive and punitive disciplinary systems. As a result, suspension, arrests, and expulsions increase, driving students out of school and into the criminal justice system. In this environment, teacher morale declines and dropout rates increase.

North Carolina became one of the first states to fully embrace these measures in 1996. Teachers there report spending more and more time on test preparation, while subjects not covered by the tests, such as social studies, science, and physical education, have been dramatically scaled back. New punitive disciplinary systems, created in the wake of the passage of No Child Left Behind, led to increased suspensions and arrests. Suspensions of less than ten days increased 41 percent, long-term suspensions increased 135 percent, and by 2008, the number of SROs had doubled, leading to 16,499 students being arrested. Racial disparities in suspensions became worse as well, with black students three and a half times more likely to be suspended.[8]

Florida adopted a high-stakes testing regime in 1998. By 2003, out-of-school suspensions had increased by almost 20 percent. In 2004, 28,000 students were arrested at school, almost two-thirds for minor offenses that previously were dealt with in school. In addition, more students have been classified as disabled, taking them out of the test pool. Teacher morale plummeted; more than half of all teachers in a 2006 survey reported that they were thinking of giving up teaching. By that same year Florida's graduation rate had fallen to 57 percent, the fourth-lowest in the country. Because of high expulsion and dropout rates, GED test taking increased by 25 percent from 2003 to 2007.[9]

At the epicenter of this transformation is Texas, where privatization and drastic cuts to the public sector meet the expansion of punitive mechanisms of social control. Texas was an early adopter of high-stakes testing in the 1990s. As governor, George W. Bush expanded its role and implemented a series of punitive measures, mostly focused on zero-tolerance approaches. Since, as we've seen, testing motivates teachers to remove low-performing and disruptive students from class, suspension rates went through the roof—95 percent of them for minor infractions.[10] By 2009–10 there were 2 million suspensions in Texas, 1.9 million of which were for "violating local code of conduct" rather than a more serious offense. To deal with this onslaught of suspensions, for-profit companies with close ties to state Republican leaders developed what Annette Fuentes calls "supermax schools."[11] These schools use fingerprint scanners, metal detectors, frequent searches, heavy video surveillance, and intense disciplinary systems to manage kids kicked out of regular schools. In many cases there is no talking allowed in hallways or lunchrooms. Teachers have little specialized training, and the low pay means fewer certified teachers than in regular schools. The emphasis is on computer-based learning and frequent testing. Outside evaluations have been tightly controlled; the few external reviews have found terrible performance and prison-like conditions.

Overall, the claimed "Texas Miracle" of improved test scores was based on faked test results, astronomical suspension and dropout rates, and the shunting of problem students to prison-like schools outside the state testing regime. Bush rode this chicanery all the way to the White House, where he instituted it nationally in the form of the No Child Left Behind Act.

The ultimate expression of this transformation in education is the charter-school movement, which fully embraces high-stakes testing and punitive disciplinary systems. Proponents have called for widespread adoption of broken-windows-based policies in charter schools as a way to instill greater classroom discipline.[12] Eventually the discourse around such methods was transformed into "sweating the small stuff" and "no excuses"–based discipline. These methods are also heavily emphasized by Teach for America and the Center for Transformative Teaching, both of which have a significant influence on teacher training for traditional public schools as well. While these phrases evoke dedicated teaching professionals working hard to overcome any impediment, what it really meant is creating ever more restrictive rules and increasing the frequency and severity of punishments, weeding out students who may be a drag on those test scores. Black boys in particular are being driven out of these schools, not for educational failure but for failure to sit still in class and wear the right color shoes. One student at a New York charter school was suspended nineteen times in first grade. The school said he was "intellectually gifted, but struggled with his behavior."[13] *PBS NewsHour* found charter schools suspending kids as young as kindergarten for behavioral infractions.[14] These children disproportionately leave the charter schools, in part because parents can't manage the constant disciplinary conferences and suspensions. The *New York Times* found that the large Success Academy charter-school network in New York had a suspension rate of 10 percent, with some schools as high as 23 percent, while city public schools had a rate of only 3 percent.[15] One mother was told that if her six-year-old daughter's misbehavior in class didn't stop, the teacher would be forced to call 911. One school even had a "got to go" list, with students they deemed inappropriate matches for the school's rigid behavioral rules.

As a result, many charter schools end up graduating a skewed population of mostly girls. The schools then claim very high graduation rates, because the students who leave do so voluntarily, for reasons other than educational failure.

The School-to-Prison Pipeline

Finally, these forces have meshed with the overall trend toward harsher punishments driving the rise of mass incarceration more generally. Politicians in the 1990s had already embraced the idea that criminality was a deeply embedded moral failing that was largely impervious to reform. The only appropriate response, they argued, was long-term incarceration, as seen in the rise of "three strikes" laws and other mandatory minimum sentencing schemes. In this political environment, every public safety threat was immediately turned into another opportunity to roll out more punishment and control.

President Bill Clinton was more than happy to oblige. In 1994 he introduced the Gun-Free Schools Act, which ushered in "zero tolerance" school discipline policies. Following that lead, legislators and school administrators embraced a raft of harsh disciplinary codes, placing surveillance systems, metal detectors, and huge numbers of police in schools.

These policies have led to the growing criminalization of young people, despite falling crime rates. According to the Department of Education, 92,000 arrests were made in the 2011–2012 school year.[16] One study shows that schools with SROs had nearly five times the arrest rate of non-SRO schools even after controlling for student demographics like race and income.[17] The impact of these policies has been especially harsh for students of color and those with disabilities. Schools with high percentages of students of color are more likely to have zero tolerance policies and generate more suspensions, expulsions, and arrests.[18]

The US Department of Education found in a 2011–2012 survey of 72,000 schools that black, Latino, and special-needs students were all disproportionately subjected to criminal justice actions.[19] While black students represent 16 percent of student enrollment, they represent 27 percent of students referred to law enforcement and 31 percent of students subjected to a school-related arrest. In comparison, white students represent 51 percent of enrollment, 41 percent of students referred to law enforcement, and 39 percent of those arrested. Some individual districts have even starker numbers. In Chicago, in 2013–2014 black students were twenty-seven times more likely to be arrested than white students leading to 8,000 arrests in a two-year period.[20] Over 50 percent of those arrested were under fifteen.

Students are frequently arrested for minor acts of disobedience and disruption such as using cell phones, disrespecting teachers, and getting into loud arguments. Schools with SROs increasingly turn over more and more school discipline to those officers, finding it easier just to have a police officer come in and remove and arrest a student than to put in the hard work of establishing a reasonable classroom environment through enlightened disciplinary systems. Even well-intentioned teachers have limited options. Healthy and effective disciplinary systems take work and resources, though they are usually a lot cheaper than paying for extra armed police.

Suspensions, which are a huge predictor of future arrest, are also highly racially disproportionate. A 2010 national study by the Southern Poverty Law Center found that in 9,000 middle schools, 28 percent of black male students were suspended three times as often as white males. Black female students were suspended more than four times as often as white females.[21] The Children's Defense Fund of Ohio found that black students were four times more likely to be suspended than their white counterparts. These results have been duplicated by studies all over the country.[22]

Special-needs children make up over a quarter of those referred to police (even though they represent just 14 percent of students), sometimes leading to horrific results.[23] In spring of 2015 Public Radio International profiled the case of an eleven-year-old boy with autism from Lynchburg, Virginia, who was repeatedly charged with criminal offenses by the school's SRO.[24] In one incident, the youth kicked a garbage can after being scolded for misbehavior, prompting the officer to file disorderly conduct charges against him in juvenile court. In another incident, the boy was slammed to the ground and handcuffed by the same SRO after resisting being dragged out of the classroom. This resulted in a misdemeanor charge of disorderly conduct and a felony charge of assault on a police officer. Shockingly, a family court judge found the youth guilty of all charges. As it turns out, Virginia leads the nation in the rate of children being charged with school-related crimes.[25] LGBTQ students are also at higher risk of punitive discipline and arrest; they are frequently ostracized by students and even teachers, leading to behaviors that are deemed "anti-social."

In August of 2015 the ACLU filed a federal lawsuit against a Kentucky sheriff's deputy for handcuffing two disabled students, an eight-year-old boy and a nine-year-old girl, for minor disorderly behavior related to their disabilities. The children were so small that the officer handcuffed their biceps, further traumatizing them. The handcuffing of the boy was caught on tape. The officers told him, "You can do what we ask you to, or you can suffer the consequences."[26] Obviously the officer had received no special training in dealing with special-needs children; the school's decision to rely on untrained armed police to manage the behavior of special-needs students is deeply problematic and, as the ACLU claims, a fundamental violation of the Americans with Disabilities Act (ADA) and civil and human rights.

The Militarization of Schools

Another area of concern is the growing militarization of schools. Nationally, police have been taking on tremendous amounts of surplus military hardware from the Pentagon. School police agencies have joined in as well. Such agencies have purchased mine-resistant ambush protection (MRAP) vehicles, AR-15 assault rifles, shotguns, and grenade launchers. According to the *Washington Post*, at least 120 school-affiliated police forces in thirty states have utilized the 1033 weapons transfer program (discussed in chapter 1).[27] In 2003, administrators at Goose Creek High School in South Carolina coordinated a massive SWAT team raid of their school in an effort to ferret out drugs and guns. Armored police, with guns drawn, ordered hundreds of mostly black students onto the ground without any specific probable cause as administrators went around identifying students to be searched and arrested. A video of the incident shows students freezing or fleeing in terror as black-clad officers burst out of closets and stairwells screaming commands and pointing guns.[28] Police dogs were brought in to find the drugs that supposedly necessitated the raid. None were found. The administrator who had organized the raid apologized to parents but pointed out that "once police are on campus, they are in control"—which is exactly the problem.[29]

The use of guns and militarized equipment undermines the basic ethos of school as a supportive learning environment and replaces it with fear and control.[30] The National Association of School Resource Officers has become a bastion of this process. Its annual convention is a panoply of military contractors trying to sell schools new security systems, train officers in paramilitary techniques, and make the case that students are at constant risk from themselves and outsiders. Annette Fuentes attended one such convention and was appalled at the keynote speaker, an "anti-terrorism expert" with no domestic law enforcement or pedagogical training who warned the hundreds of officers present,

> You've got people in your schools right now planning a Columbine. Every town, every university now has a Cho [the Virginia Tech shooter] and in every state, we have Al-Qaeda cells thinking of it. Every school is a possible target of attack ... You've got to be a one-man fighting force ... You've got to have enough guns and ammunition and body armor to stay alive ... You should be walking around in school every day in complete tactical equipment, with semi-automatic weapons and five rounds of ammo ... You can no longer afford to think of yourselves as peace officers ... You must think of yourself as soldiers at war, because we're going to ask you to act like soldiers.[31]

This mindset is permeating school policing. In 2010 the Southern Poverty Law Center filed a class-action lawsuit against the Birmingham, Alabama schools claiming that they were systematically using excessive force.[32] They allege that from 2006 to 2014, 199 students have been sprayed with a combination pepper spray and tear gas agent called Freeze + P, which causes extreme pain and skin irritation and can impede breathing and vision. All of the students sprayed were African American. One student was pregnant, many were innocent bystanders, and some were completely nonviolent when sprayed. In most cases, officers made no effort to treat those sprayed and some were held in police custody to await arraignment wearing chemically coated clothing. In 2015, a federal court found the school district guilty of civil rights violations and banned the use of the spray.[33] A seventeen-year-old high school student in Texas was tasered by an SRO while trying to break up a school fight. The student was critically injured by the resulting fall and blow to the head and spent fifty-two days in a medically induced coma.[34] Surveillance video showed that the young man was actually stepping away from the officers when he was tasered.

More mundane violence by SROs is also widespread. In October 2015 a student recorded a South Carolina sheriff's deputy assigned to the school violently arresting a teenage girl for having a phone in class. The officer flipped the young woman and her desk over, then dragged, threw, and tackled her.[35] A fellow student who videotaped the incident was physically threatened and arrested when she vocally protested what was happening. In 2010 a fifteen-year-old student with a past traumatic brain injury was beaten by a Dalton, Illinois police officer at a special-needs school for having his shirt untucked. The incident was captured on surveillance video and no action was taken against the officer, who didn't even report the incident.[36] Such complaints are pervasive in schools across the country.

According to a report by *Mother Jones* magazine, between 2010 and 2015, twenty-eight US students were severely injured by SROs and one was killed.[37] In 2010, fourteen-year-old Derek Lopez was shot to death by an SRO in suburban San Antonio. Lopez punched a student on school grounds. Officer Daniel Alvarado witnessed it and ordered Lopez to freeze, then chased him to a nearby backyard shed, where he shot Lopez. Alvarado claimed that Lopez had "bull-rushed" him as he opened the shed door. In August 2012, a grand jury declined to indict Alvarado.[38]

Lower levels of force are much more prevalent. While no national data is available, in part because there is no federal or state reporting requirements, local studies show heavy use of force. The *Houston Chronicle* found that, from 2010 to 2014, police in ten suburban Houston school districts reported 1,300 use-of-force incidents.[39] Many large districts had no data or refused to cooperate; neither education nor police oversight bodies require such reporting.

The massive expansion of school police is predicated on the idea that it makes schools safer, but this just isn't true. Schools with heavy police presence consistently report feeling less safe than similar schools with no police. There is no evidence that SROs reduce crime, and there have been only a few instances where officers played a role in averting a potential gun crime (these mostly involved threats). In one 2013 case an officer in Atlanta stopped a school shooting in progress; the intended target had already been shot, along with a school employee, and the perpetrator was no longer shooting when apprehended.[40] Research generally shows that reported crimes actually increase with the presence of SROs.[41] This is in part because they uncover more contraband and treat more things as criminal matters than would have been the case previously. There is no solid evidence that they reduce thefts or violence.[42]

Reforms

The role of SROs has continually expanded as officers are given more responsibilities and find more to do with their time in the absence of actual security threats. Armed police officers are now acting either formally or informally as guidance counselors in many schools. They conduct Drug Abuse Resistance Education (DARE) and other drug-prevention programs. Unfortunately, there is little oversight or training for these roles. SROs typically receive little or no instruction in counseling, mentoring, or pedagogy. While some of their efforts are laudable, others are laughable. Decades of research have shown the consistent ineffectiveness of programs like DARE. Furthermore, there is a fundamental conflict in asking kids to treat police as mentors and counselors. While officers want young people to confide in them, they are also law enforcement agents, meaning that these communications can be used as evidence and can lead very quickly to police enforcement action, possibly even against the youth being mentored. In an age of zero tolerance, this could have devastating consequences.

The DOE, in its 2014 *Guiding Principles* report on best practices in discipline, calls for school-based police officers to be trained in adolescent development, de-escalation, implicit bias, and how best to deal with students with disabilities and a history of trauma.[43] Others continue to point to the value of police as role models and mentors, but only if they understand their role as providing security for the students and the school, not as agents of school discipline.[44] This approach, however, assumes an inherent value in having uniformed police officers play this role rather than, say, a coach, teacher, counselor, or administrator. The implicit goal is to establish the importance and legitimacy of the police in the eyes of students; by virtue of being a formal authority figure, police in schools are valuable. This view argues that young people can benefit from the appreciation of authority well instituted. This is an inherent aspect of the liberal adherence to procedural justice discussed in chapter 1: the problem is not that there are agents of formal state control in schools, it's that they sometimes act improperly and abuse that all-important authority.

In fact, the earliest origins of police in school are suffused with this mindset. In the 1950s, police were placed in schools in Flint, Michigan, with the intent of reestablishing the legitimacy and value of the police in the eyes of young people at a time of high youth violence and social disaffection. The 1960s saw another period of expansion, again with the same intent.[45] This was not about the safety and security of schools or youth. In fact, most of these early programs were established in elementary and middle schools, where crime and violence are much lower than in high schools. In many ways this is an extension of the community policing mindset, in which police become embedded in the community to collect information and generate goodwill that then feeds into more intensive and invasive forms of policing. According to Kevin Quinn, president of the National Association of School Resource Officers, developing rapport to facilitate intelligence gathering is a central component of their work: "Once school resource officers establish themselves in a community, kids are willing to come forward and report things, send an e-mail, leave a voicemail, come by the office."[46] Couldn't that rapport be generated just as well by counselors with more appropriate training and more of an allegiance to the well-being of students than the enforcement of the law?

Some have suggested there need to be national standards for training and best practices.[47] The Obama Task Force on Twenty-First Century Policing has some mixed recommendations about this issue. It recommends that police agencies reform the policies and procedures that end up pushing children into the criminal justice system, but says nothing about removing police from schools. In fact, it expands the role of police by calling on them to "develop and monitor" discipline policies and work with school administrators to "create a continuum of developmentally appropriate and proportionate consequences." But, as Lisa Thurau and Johanna Wald ask, "Why should police without any training or background help schools devise educational policy and practices?"[48]

Recently some school districts have begun to search for alternatives to police-enforced zero tolerance approaches, but have been reluctant to totally abandon a punitive orientation. In 2007 the Los Angeles Unified School District embraced a new approach called Positive Behavioral Intervention and Supports, in which schools integrate social skill-building and behavioral management into their lesson plans.[49] Students who are not doing well in school are targeted for additional interventions such as tutoring and counseling on self-management skills. Teachers work on labeling "good" and "bad" behaviors, closely monitor student behavior, and apply graduated sanctions to ensure compliance. While this has reduced suspensions and police enforcement, it still relies on a top-down form of discipline similar to classic control theory, in which parents and others are encourage to socialize their children through the identification and control of improper behavior. School discipline specialist Alfi Kohn has come to refer to this as TKLP (Treating Kids Like Pets), because it is a control-based approach that uses bribes rather than threats.

Alternatives

A task force in New York found that schools with less punitive disciplinary systems were able to achieve a greater sense of safety for students, lower arrest and suspension rates, and fewer crimes, even in poor and high-crime neighborhoods.[50] What is needed, but often not supplied by school officials, is a set of nonpunitive disciplinary measures designed to keep kids in school while getting to the root of disruptive behavior. Schools cannot solve all the problems students bring in, but they can be part of the solution rather than part of the criminal justice system. To do that, they need more resources to deal with the whole student. You can't just teach to the test or focus on fundamental knowledge and skills at the expense of the bodies and emotions of young people. Abundant research shows that learning can't happen effectively when young people are emotionally or physically distracted. Relying on school police, however, removes the bodily, emotional, and behavioral aspects of the student from the responsibility of teachers and outsources it to police. This is a huge mistake.

What teachers need is training, counselors, and support staff with access to meaningful services for students and their families. There are currently more NYPD personnel in New York City schools than there are counselors of all types at an estimated cost of $750 million a year.[51] We need to invest in both school and after-school services that address problems at home and in the community. On their own, especially with diminishing budgets and high-stakes testing regimes, teachers can't deal with these problems. Instead they find themselves pressured to push kids out of their classrooms and ultimately out of school and into the criminal justice system.

To respond to these needs, the American Federation of Teachers (AFT) has recently been supporting the creation of "community schools."[52] These schools provide a range of wraparound services, such as medical and mental health care, personal counseling, tutoring, community service, and social-justice programming, as well as adult education and counseling for parents. Services are often provided by community organizations working in partnership with the schools, allowing services to be tailored to the particular needs of that community. In Salt Lake City, Utah, the United Way has partnered with eleven community schools that serve more than ten thousand students, over half of whom are very low income and over a quarter of whom are English language learners. The program has increased academic achievement and reduced chronic absenteeism, a strong indicator of future problems. Baltimore has forty-five community schools serving an overwhelmingly poor and minority student body. These schools have improved attendance rates and, with restorative justice programs, have reduced suspensions. In many, graduation rates and test scores have improved significantly as well. There are some uniformed police in Baltimore schools, but state law requires that they be unarmed and there is public pressure to further reduce their presence.[53]

In addition to better funding for high-needs schools more generally, officials should adopt a variety of evidence-based reforms that are cheaper and more effective than police. Social and emotional learning, behavioral monitoring and reinforcement, peaceable-schools programs, and restorative justice systems have all been shown to reduce discipline problems in schools without relying on the logic of control and punishment.

Restorative justice programs are the most established of these alternatives. They were originally conceived to deal with crime in communities but have taken off in schools. Across the country, schools are implementing programs that turn away from punitive approaches to managing student behavior, embracing mechanisms for addressing the underlying causes of student misbehavior and working to integrate students into the community as a responsible community members rather than pushing them out, as current disciplinary systems tend to do.

Restorative justice practices are based on a variety of indigenous practices from around the world that predominate in traditional, close-knit communities, in which problems need to be resolved in ways that encourage community stability, cohesion, and self-sustainability. These practices are being implemented in many forms, including peer juries, problem-solving circles, community service, and conflict mediation. To be truly effective, these programs need buy-in from teachers and administrators over time in order to build student trust. At the core of all these mechanisms is the desire to make schools a welcoming place for young people regardless of the problems they bring to school and to try to work out those problems cooperatively in a way that is in the best interest of the student and the larger school community.

The National Education Association, the American Federation of Teachers, and the Advancement Project have teamed up to promote these efforts by producing a guide for teachers.[54] *Restorative Practices: Fostering Healthy Relationships and Promoting Positive Discipline in Schools* lays out basic principles, such as resolving conflicts in ways that demand that people take meaningful responsibility for their actions and work to change them, build healthy relationships throughout the school, reduce harmful behaviors, repair harms, and restore positive relationships.

These programs take resources. Teachers need to be trained and class time needs to be set aside. Further, schools that are undergoing stress from budget cuts and chasing after test scores to stay open will find it difficult to cultivate a supportive and caring atmosphere and will be reluctant to take the time away from instruction necessary to implement these programs in an effective way. Replacing suspensions with forced community service, like cleaning hallways, won't turn things around.

In Social and Emotional Learning, students and teachers work together to develop a variety of life skills to help them deal with conflict and be more effective at school.[55] The program is guided by five principles that are instilled through the process: self-awareness, self-management, social awareness, relationship skills, and responsible decision making. The best known implementation of this approach is the Resolving Conflict Creatively Program (RCCP), begun in 1995. The program, which has been active in New York City schools and dozens of others, uses interactive methods to teach children skills in anger management, negotiation, mediation, cooperation, and intercultural understanding. Extensive research shows that these programs consistently improve both school discipline and educational outcomes. This is true for in-school and after-school programs and for students with or without disabilities, regardless of race.[56] A Columbia University study found that children receiving RCCP instruction from their teachers developed more positively than their peers: they saw their social world in a less hostile way, saw violence as an unacceptable option, and chose nonviolent ways to resolve conflict. They also scored higher on standardized tests in reading and math.[57]

Behavioral Monitoring and Reinforcement is a primarily middle school program designed to help students who are at high risk of coming into contact with the criminal justice system, using drugs, or dropping out. This program relies on positive reinforcement and empowerment strategies. Students in the program had higher grades and better attendance compared to students in a control group. A one-year follow-up study showed that students in the program had less self-reported delinquency, drug abuse, suspension, absenteeism, tardiness, academic failure, and unemployment compared to control students. A five-year follow-up study found that these students had fewer county court records than students in the control group.[58]

These programs are incompatible with the current emphasis on high-stakes testing that measures school success almost entirely on student performance on these tests. Programs that deal with students' overall wellbeing are too often viewed as a distraction from teaching to the all-important test. Any effort, then, to make school safer and less punitive has to break away from that approach to education and address student needs more holistically in a way that takes in their specific needs and the larger context in which learning is occurring. The research shows that when students feel safe and supported their learning improves. Armed police enforcing zero-tolerance discipline systems undermine that, even when they are well trained and well intentioned. The nature of police is to be a force for order and control. Even when they attempt to be positive mentors, it is always backed up by the punitive and coercive capacities that distinguish them from teachers and counselors.

Metal detectors, police on campus, and zero-tolerance disciplinary codes drive a wedge between students and teachers and create a climate of distrust that can actually increase disruptive and criminal behavior, as education professors Matthew Mayer and Peter Leone found in their groundbreaking 1999 study of school crime.[59] It also reduces the chances that students will alert teachers and administrators to real threats. In most of the mass school shootings committed by students, there were other students who were aware that plans and threats were in place. Too often, they did not report those concerns. According to Mayer and Leone, "creating an unwelcoming, almost jail-like, heavily scrutinized environment may foster the violence and disorder school administrators hope to avoid."[60] Schools, they argue, should "focus their effort;

effective communication rather than control is the best way to establish the legitimacy of the school's system of law in the minds of students."[61]

We must break completely with the idea of using police in schools. They have no positive role to play that couldn't be better handled by nonpolice personnel. There may be a need to protect schools from intruders, but so far, having armed police in schools does not appear to be the solution. Even if armed police are needed, they have no business operating on school grounds. If necessary, they can be stationed at the school's perimeter or dispatched as needed. Will there be tragic events on school campuses? Yes, and having more armed police on campus has not proven effective in reducing them. Instead, they have been incredibly effective at driving young people out of school and into the criminal justice system by the hundreds of thousands. Even if armed police on campus were an effective tool for reducing a few violent incidents, the social costs of that approach are not acceptable. We must find better ways to keep kids safe than turning their schools into armed fortresses and prisons. It's time to take police out of the schools and reject the harsh punitive focus of school management. Our young people need compassion and care, not coercion and control.

4

"We Called for Help, and They Killed My Son"

One of the most tragic developments in policing in the last forty years has been the massive expansion of their role in managing people with mental illness and other psychiatric disabilities.[1] The police have always had to deal with mentally ill individuals whose behaviors are criminal or create a substantial public nuisance. With the massive deterioration in mental health services, the scope and number of these interactions have changed. The police are often the main agency engaged in both emergency and ongoing management of segments of this population. While most such interactions are handled reasonably well, too many result in arrest, incarceration, injury, and even death. The police are particularly ill-suited for this role, given their other functions; relying on police, jails, and emergency rooms to "manage" people suffering from mental health problems is expensive and inefficient, and does little to improve their quality of life.

The United States suffers from particularly inadequate mental health care services. While psychoactive drugs have brought increased independence for many in recent decades, many are unable or unwilling to maintain pharmacological treatment, many do not have access to basic mental health services, and ongoing community-based services are few and far between. As a result, in a crisis, patients and families have little choice but to call 911—and it's typically the police who respond.

Egon Bittner, in his classic 1967 study, identified the difficult choices officers face when they arrive at a scene.[2] Ideally, an officer assesses the situation and decides whether the person should be taken to a psychiatric emergency room for temporary voluntary or possibly involuntary committal, arrests the individual, or attempts to resolve the issue informally. Police typically prefer the latter option, but often feel compelled to take one of the others because the behavior is serious or seems likely to continue unabated if not addressed. In these former cases, the officer must take the person into custody, sometimes against their will. This means using verbal coaxing if possible but, if necessary, force.

US police officers kill hundreds of people with mental illness (PMI) every year, according to a count by the *Guardian*.[3] The Treatment Advocacy Center reviewed the literature on fatal police encounters and estimates that one in every four police killings is of a person with a mental illness, meaning they are sixteen times more likely to be killed by police than other people.[4] The killings of PMI take a few general forms. In some cases, police arrive on the scene and encounter someone with something they perceive to be a weapon, such as a screwdriver or kitchen implement. That person refuses to drop the object and sometimes threatens the officer or others, prompting police to open fire. This can be seen in three recent videotaped incidents:

- In August 2014, Kajieme Powell was clearly mentally distraught and had a knife. Officers arrived on the scene and yelled commands at him from dozens of feet away. When Powell took a few steps toward them, they shot him to death.[5]
- In May 2015, the mother of Jason Harrison called 911 requesting help for her son, who was refusing to take his medication. When police arrived, she casually walked outside, followed by her son, who was carrying a screwdriver. When the officer saw him, he began yelling commands to drop it and within seconds opened fire, killing Harrison.[6]

- In December 2014, New York police killed a man with a knife who had stabbed someone in a Jewish religious school and was shouting about killing Jews. The video shows local congregants trying to calm him and pleading with police not to shoot, but police destabilized the situation by yelling commands and pointing weapons.[7]

In each of these cases, officers relied on standard procedure for an armed suspect, which is to yell commands and prepare to use deadly force—even though most of them had received training in how to deescalate confrontations with PMI.

In the United Kingdom and other places where police are less likely to be armed, this dynamic is less common. Police use less lethal means to manage them. Three recent cases reflect this.

- In September 2014, Nicholas Salvador, who had paranoid schizophrenia, beheaded a neighbor and went on a rampage in his London neighborhood. Local unarmed police encountered the suspect and rescued nearby children while engaging him verbally. Eventually, armed police arrived and used Taser shocks to subdue him.[8]
- In August 2014, a knife-wielding man outside Buckingham Palace was Tasered by police rather than shot.[9]
- In 2011, a man with a machete was captured after a seven-minute confrontation with up to thirty police officers in South London. Officers used trash cans, batons, and eventually riot shields to contain him and finally overwhelm and tackle him.[10]

In each of these cases, police put themselves at risk to try to resolve the situation without deadly force, even though they might have been legally justified in using it. In the United States, it seems likely that any if not all of these incidents would have resulted in the person's death.

Another form of this dynamic is "suicide by cop," in which someone who is suicidal counts on the willingness of an armed police officer to respond to a threat with deadly force. In these tragic cases, the suicidal individuals arm themselves with toy guns or other harmless devices in hopes that they will be sufficient to provoke a deadly response by police, who too often quickly oblige them. In some ways this seems like an unavoidable problem. There are, however, some important caveats. This whole scenario rests on the suicidal person's assumption that they will be confronted by an armed police officer. The dynamic might be very different if the responder instead was an experienced civilian mental health worker, or even an unarmed police officer. Suicide by cop is extremely rare in the United Kingdom, where police are unlikely to be armed.[11]

This is not to say that mental health policing in Britain is without problems. The National Health Service offers substantial options for people in crisis or with chronic mental health needs. Police are instructed to take someone with a mental health crisis to a "place of safety," which could be a hospital, community-based care provider, or, as a last resort, a police station. The UK police rely on a Mental Health Liaison Officer (MHLO) system, in which a few officers receive extensive training and are supposed to respond to difficult calls and smooth bureaucratic processes between service providers and police. In addition, mental health nurse practitioners are stationed in police dispatch rooms to give responding officers patient histories and real-time advice. They are also expanding the number of street triage teams in which a nurse rides along with the responding officer. The overall attitude is one of care rather than threat neutralization. In practice, however, problems remain. After several high-profile deaths and other mishandled incidents, a national commission found in 2013 that training was inadequate, MHLOs were not well supported by the police services, health services in police stations were inadequate, too much force was used to restrain

PMI, and there was not always a good working relationship between police, hospitals, and community mental health workers.[12]

Studies suggest that anywhere from 5 to 20 percent of all US police incidents involve a PMI, and that these incidents take longer to resolve and are more likely to result in arrest.[13] In addition, the number of incarcerated PMI has grown dramatically. The National Alliance on Mental Illness (NAMI) found that 11 million people a year are admitted to US jails; of them, 15 percent of men and 30 percent of women have a serious mental illness.[14] The largest inpatient psychiatric facilities in the United States are the LA County Jail, New York's Rikers Island Jail, and Chicago's Cook County Jail; the PMI in jails and prisons outnumber those in state hospitals ten to one.[15] The number-two cause of death in jails and prisons is suicide; jails, which generally receive people straight from police custody, provide only limited screening and inconsistent mental health care.[16] NAMI estimates that 83 percent of PMI in jail don't have access to the treatments they need.[17] People are often given medication while in jail and, at best, a bottle of pills and a referral when they are released, leading to a revolving door of arrests and short-term incarceration with no real improvement in the person's underlying mental health, which is often at the root of the behaviors that get them arrested in the first place.

What we are witnessing is, in essence, the criminalization of mental illness, with police on the front lines of this process. This is especially true for those who are homeless and/or lack access to quality mental health services. Both groups of people have grown significantly in recent decades. While the Affordable Care Act holds the promise of some improvement, as recently as 2011, over 60 percent of people experiencing a mental health problem reported that they had no access to mental health services.[18] Even when mental health services are available, they are often inadequate. A lack of stable housing and income exacerbates mental health problems, makes treatment more difficult, and contributes to the public display of disability-related behaviors, all of which make it more likely that the police will be called.

Reducing social services and replacing them with punitive social control mechanisms works less well and is more expensive. The cost of housing people and providing then with mental health services is actually lower than cycling them through emergency rooms, homeless shelters, and jails, as numerous studies have shown.[19] The drive to criminalize has more to do with ideology than effectiveness: the mentally ill are seen not as victims of the neoliberal restructuring of public health services but as a dangerous source of disorder to be controlled through intensive and aggressive policing. Any attempt to reduce the negative effects of policing on this population must directly challenge this ideological approach to policing.

Reforms

Training

Efforts to increase and improve officer training attempt several things. First, training details the signs of serious suicidal thinking and actions and offers strategies for stabilizing people so that they can be taken into custody. Second, it provides information about available services such as community-based or outpatient clinics and ways of accessing emergency acute care, including temporary commitment at an emergency room. Officers are also taught about the nature of different mental illnesses and strategies for dealing with a crisis without traditional use of force.

There are severe drawbacks to this approach. First, it is not reasonable to expect a patrol officer to make a meaningful clinical assessment of patients in the field. While experience may help some officers identify certain more common behaviors, a nuanced assessment just isn't likely, and this could have significant consequences for how the officer approaches the interaction. While some people might respond well to limit-setting language, others might find this threatening and become aggressive, especially when it is attempted by an inexperienced practitioner.

Second, there are few services available in most places, especially for people who are not in severe crisis. A huge amount of police interactions are with PMI they encounter somewhat regularly, often in public places, who are more a nuisance than an actual threat to public safety. Emergency rooms are not appropriate and will generally not accept people in this condition. Telling them about available services—or lack thereof—often just communicates that officers are on their own and must instead rely on either informal resolutions or arrests.

Finally, as mentioned in chapter 1, standard police training instills a warrior mentality. Police are trained to see the potential threat in any encounter and to use their presence, body language, and verbal commands to take charge and to react quickly and aggressively to any threat of violence or the presence of a weapon. This goes directly against best practices for dealing with most PMI. Studies show that standard police approaches actually tend to escalate and destabilize encounters. Yelling commands and displaying weapons may cause a mentally ill person to flee or become more aggressive. Just as problematic, someone having delusions or a psychotic episode may be unable to hear, understand, or comply with police orders. This can have tragic consequences.

More recently, some departments have adopted training that emphasizes communication, containment, and coordination with appropriate service providers as an alternative to the command-and-control approach. While this new training has some advantages for de-escalation, it can still lead to tragic results. Officers in New York were using this exact policy when they confronted an Orthodox Jewish man in his apartment after receiving a call. The man had a small decorative hammer used in religious ceremonies. When the man tried to leave his basement apartment with the hammer, officers tried to surround him, in keeping with their training on containment. However, when the man tried to evade containment, they shot and killed him.[20] More recently, police in San Francisco used similar tactics in trying to apprehend a man with a knife who had stabbed someone nearby. Officers cornered and surrounded the assailant, demanding that he drop the knife, and fired two beanbag rounds at him, but he continued to hold onto the knife and attempt to leave. Officers then fired fifteen rounds at him, killing him.[21] Containment and less lethal weaponry can still lead to deadly encounters.

It is not reasonable to expect that officers who spend the bulk of their time using aggressive methods to establish their authority can just turn that off in a situation where someone might be mentally ill and appears to be a threat to the officer or others. This is why so many encounters with PMI holding weapons end up escalating, even when the officers involved have received mental health training.

Crisis Intervention Teams

The "Memphis Model" relies on a small number of specialized officers who can be routed to calls to deal with a person experiencing a mental health crisis.[22] These officers become more knowledgeable and experienced and are better able to assess the situation accurately and take clinically appropriate steps to reduce the chance of escalation. This model has shown signs of success in cities that have embraced it, but only when there are meaningful mental health care services available for police to rely on. The problem is that these services often don't exist; in addition, it is still a police-centered model with a strong tendency to resolve situations through arrest and other uses of force.

Some places have tried to mitigate this tendency by creating crisis response teams that include trained mental health workers. This approach is common in places like Canada, Britain, Europe, and Australia. Specially trained officers work with mental health professionals to respond to calls involving PMI. In many cases it is the civilian mental health workers who take the lead, with police there only to assist if absolutely necessary. These teams have shown good results in both reducing arrests and the use of force and in reducing hospitalizations as well, since they can make a more complete assessment and take steps to stabilize the person and connect them to appropriate outpatient services.

Outreach Teams

In some places, local officials face chronic problems from mentally ill people in public spaces. Some are homeless; others live in marginal housing or are unemployed and unengaged and spend much of their time on the streets. This population may at times experience acute mental health crises, but they are much more likely to come to the attention of police as a source of disorder, which may take the form of "quality of life" violations like public drinking and urination, disorderly conduct, or sleeping in parks, subways, or sidewalks. In some jurisdictions, officials have attempted to address this problem by developing police outreach teams. Some are designated as focused on homeless people while others deal more specifically with the mentally ill, but the functions overlap.

But why should armed police officers oversee outreach to the chronic and homeless mentally ill? Using armed police is expensive and brings few benefits. Trained mental health and social services outreach workers are perfectly capable of handling this job and, unlike police-based teams, are more likely to be able to build long-term relationships and gain trust, an essential component of outreach to highly isolated individuals with complex mental health and often substance abuse problems. The implied threat of coercive response that police pose drives such people further into isolation, not into proper care. Civilian teams are also cheaper.

Diversion Programs

There have also been efforts to divert PMI from incarceration. Police-based models such as the Law Enforcement Assisted Diversion program (LEAD) in Seattle, allow officers to identify people who are chronically involved in low-level criminality and disorder and place them in programs that try to address their underlying problem, whether it's a mental health or substance abuse issue or poverty driving them into black-market activities like sex work and drug sales.[23] These programs have reduced arrest and incarceration rates; they offer some new services to people in need and some relief for communities. But why do the police need to be the gatekeepers? Framing this as a policing issue bases access to needed services on how much the officer is motivated to resolve a public-order problem. A person muttering to themselves in disheveled and smelly clothing in a high-profile shopping district is more likely to gain the sustained attention of police than a suicidal, homeless teen hiding out under a bridge. Both need services, but police are much less likely to encounter the teen and less likely to treat that encounter as being driven by mental health issues. Mental health outreach workers are likely to see the suicidal teen as more acutely at risk and take steps to stabilize them.

Another important development has been the emergence of a wide array of mental health courts. The purpose of these specialized courts is to divert PMI from jail by connecting them with appropriate services, combined with oversight and the threat of possible incarceration for failure to comply with program goals and court directives.[24] Judges tend to take an active role in monitoring and rewarding progress; for some defendants, this represents a rare and important pathway to stability. These courts are not much cheaper to operate than regular misdemeanor criminal courts, but they reduce the number of people being sent to jail, which is tremendously expensive: because of high turnover, jails are much more expensive to operate than prisons, with per-bed costs reaching as high as $200,000 a year or more.[25]

These courts, however, rely on the constant threat of punitive sanctions. People who fail to follow through with case management plans can always be sent to jail, since a guilty plea is often a condition of receiving treatment. Also, they can only access the services the court provides if they have been arrested, meaning that many people in need of services remain unable to obtain them. As with the LEAD program, the focus is on abating nuisances and saving money rather than developing a rational system for delivering necessary mental health care.

Alternatives

We can never fully eliminate interactions between the police and PMI. There is indeed a need for more training of all officers, and even the participation of officers in some crisis-response scenarios. The situation we have today, however, represents a gross criminalization of mental illness. This system does not require that individual police officers be biased against PMI or regularly misuse their discretion—which studies show they usually do not.[26] It only requires that we have a fundamentally flawed mental health system that fails to provide adequate care to people—which we do. This means responsibility for dealing with people in crisis invariably falls on the police, whether they like it or not. Yes, crisis response teams, specialized courts, and improved training can reduce the impact of the criminal justice system on the mentally ill and the impact of the mentally ill on the criminal justice system, but these are not replacements for a rational, functioning mental health system.

Thoughtful police officers and leaders are well aware of this. Many view interactions with PMI as one of the least desirable and most fraught aspects of the job. Many are deeply frustrated by the revolving door of emergency room visits, jails, and police lockups, which never seem to solve the problem. Too often police are forced to arrest someone because a hospital, clinic, or other program is either unavailable or won't or can't accept them. Police officials are starting to speak up as well, like former Chief Michael Biasotti from New Windsor, New York. As chair of the New York State Association of Chiefs of Police, he backed measures to increase funding for mental health services, pointing out the irrationality of housing 350,000 PMI in prisons and jails. He notes that a real diversion program

> would be expanding services to the seriously mentally ill, and getting treatment before the police are at your door, before you are standing before a judge, and before you find yourself in jail ... Increased services mean less involvement with the criminal justice system and improved quality of life for those with mental illness and their families.[27]

Mike Koval, chief of the Madison, Wisconsin, police force, has spent years advocating for community-based mental health services in the wake of police killings of PMI. He realizes that even with enhanced training and specialized response, there are still limits to what the police can do: "The unique challenges presented in these calls are going to result in more tragic outcomes unless or until there is a commitment to provide more proactive, pre-emptive, and collaborative interventions BEFORE an individual's mental health issues have declined to critical levels."[28] He even got permission from the city of Madison to undertake litigation against the state for closing down a mental health clinic, arguing that the loss of its services diverts considerable police resources and money away from patrolling, as officers must now transport people longer distances.

According to the Florida Mental Health Institute, chronically mentally ill people are a major source of spending for the criminal justice system. Its study identified ninety-seven "chronic offenders" who, over five years, accounted for 2,200 arrests, 27,000 days in jail, and 13,000 days in crisis units, state hospitals, and emergency rooms. The costs to taxpayers for these people alone was nearly $13 million, or $275,000 per year per mentally ill person. In Miami-Dade jails, some 1,400 inmates take psychiatric drugs, making the corrections system the largest warehouse for PMI in Florida. Mental health care there costs taxpayers $80 million per year.[29] The Vera Institute of Justice found that incarcerating PMI costs two to three times what community-based treatment does.[30]

Instead of just funneling ever-increasing amounts of money into specialized police units and enhanced mental health services in jails and prisons, we need a major overhaul of our mental health systems. Billions of dollars have been cut from public mental health services in recent decades, as states have closed down expensive and poorly run hospitals but failed to fund community-based care. Instead of relying on forced treatment, we should be providing easy access to varied, culturally appropriate community-based services as needed. Even people with severe disabilities can live independently and with a limited impact on the community with long-term supportive care in a stable living situation. Some places are trying to move in this direction. Miami officials are working to turn a shuttered hospital into a rehabilitation hub for people with serious mental illnesses. The facility would provide safe drop-in spaces, treatment facilities, and access to short-term housing.[31] While this is a step in the right direction, it still doesn't provide long-term stable housing with medically appropriate support services. Part of the facility will also be used to house a mental health court—resources that could be better spent on housing and medical services.

Special attention is needed for services for those with severe problems such as schizophrenia, which, when untreated, can result in significant antisocial and even potentially dangerous behavior. Giving people medication and sending them to a homeless shelter or welfare hotel is not adequate. Without stability and support, patients are more likely to stop taking their medication. A safe, supportive housing environment is more likely to produce stability than incarceration or forced pharmacological treatment. For those who are currently homeless and off their medication, we need civilian outreach teams and access to safe drop-in spaces.

Finally, when people do experience a major mental health crisis, we should always attempt to approach that situation in the least confrontational way possible. Trained civilian responders should be the default preference. They pose the least threat to the PMI and are the least likely to escalate the interaction. Yes, these interactions can be dangerous, but people trained and experienced in dealing with PMI know these risks and have techniques for dealing with them. Even in state mental health hospitals that contain people with a history of violence, staff are generally able to manage patients with a minimum of violence. Force is used and is even sometimes excessive, but a well-trained team is much less likely to cause a death than an armed police officer.

5

Criminalizing Homelessness

While homelessness is not a crime, homeless people tend to have extensive contact with police, especially adult men and people with mental illness (PMI). Police are regularly called upon to provide social services, maintain order, and enforce the law with this population, resulting in arrests, referrals, and orders to "move along"—little of which does anything to help.

Policing the poor and homeless is nothing new. While modern homelessness emerged in the 1980s, earlier waves of mass homelessness in the nineteenth and early twentieth centuries also posed significant challenges for police. As waves of immigrants arrived in the late 1800s, cities were at times overwhelmed with people who were not able to find work and afford housing. This was less of a problem in boom times, but during financial collapses many were left unemployed and homeless. Apart from a few private charities, there was no social safety net, leaving many in desperate circumstances.

Police were expected to provide some care for this population, but primarily to reduce their impact on the public. In cities like New York, Chicago, Washington, and Boston, the basements of police stations were turned into nightly lodging houses. While these were often little more than filthy floors and a weak stove, they provided shelter from the elements. But the decision to place people in police stations, rather than other government buildings, indicated the police's role as general maintainers of public order and also the sense that this population represented a potentially dangerous social force.

Today, most cities provide some level of emergency shelter, especially for families, but the number of beds available is almost always inadequate. Some shelters hold a nightly lottery for available spaces; the losers are forced to bed down as best they can. Those that do bed down in public parks and other spaces run the constant risk of police harassment as local residents and business owners complain about their deteriorating "quality of life." Police routinely break up encampments driving people into more remote and isolated conditions that leave them more vulnerable to robberies, assaults, and the elements.

Even those with a place to stay at night are often turned out during the day, with little to do besides chase social services and look for work as best they can. Many have mental illnesses or substance abuse problems, or a combination of the two, which make their public presence in parks, subways, and sidewalks seem more menacing. Some engage in black-market activities; others are uninterested in abiding by middle-class standards of conduct and decorum or are simply unable to do so. As a result, police are often called to regulate their behavior. In some cases, a stern warning or an order to go elsewhere suffices. In other cases, a ticket may be written for littering, public urination, or other minor infractions. These tickets are rarely paid and usually result in lots of cycling through courts and jails and additional arrests as a rap sheet of minor offenses and unpaid tickets builds up. These tickets do nothing to improve a person's situation and are usually intended to drive people out of certain spaces more than change their behavior. Frequent incarceration disrupts their access to social services and undermines their employability, cutting off potential pathways out of homelessness.

When this strategy is unsuccessful, cities often turn to more intensive strategies and develop new laws to give officers "the tools they need" to take care of "problem populations." The National Law Center on Homelessness and Poverty has been documenting the rise of new laws that criminalize behavior associated with homelessness.[1] Their survey of 187 cities showed that 33 percent have citywide bans on camping in public, 57 percent ban camping in specific locations, 18 percent have total bans on sleeping in public, and 27 percent prohibit sleeping in specific locations. One-quarter have city-wide begging restrictions, 33 percent have citywide loitering bans, 53 percent prohibit sitting or lying down in designated zones, 43 percent prohibit sleeping in cars, and 9 percent have laws prohibiting sharing free food. The number of these laws is increasing. From 2011 to 2014 bans on camping have increased 60 percent, targeted sleeping bans 34 percent, city-wide begging prohibitions 25 percent, loitering and vagrancy laws 35 percent, sitting and lying laws 43 percent, and vehicle sleeping bans 119 percent. This is a resurgent problem across the country.

Seattle has taken the criminalization of homelessness to extremes. After experimenting with various new laws, they settled on a new "civil violation" approach. Whenever a homeless person was found to be committing any of a number of minor crimes that often go along with being homeless, they were not arrested but instead banned from a particular area, such as a park, a row of cheap motels, or even an entire neighborhood. In some cases the ban lasted a day, in others longer. For those caught violating the ban, the result was arrest and a longer and often more widespread ban. After several years, some people were banned from all city parks and a major portion of the city. Katherine Beckett and Steve Herbert argue that this is a return to the discredited medieval practice of banishment as a strategy for managing the poor and unwanted.[2]

Since these are civil rather than criminal orders, police are given almost total discretion in issuing and enforcing such bans. Beckett and Herbert document scores of cases in which police engaged in discriminatory treatment based on perceived social status rather than specific conduct. There is often no formal hearing, people have no right to a lawyer, and the burden of proof is very low. Generally police use these orders as they have other enforcement mechanisms: to move the problem off their beat and onto someone else's, further isolating and immiserating the people they target.

Cities large and small are reporting increases in the homeless population. New York, Los Angeles, and Seattle have all seen major jumps in people sleeping outside and in shelters in recent years. As a result, these and other cities are experiencing an increase in public disorder. Even the best-behaved people become an eyesore when living outside. Their food, bedding, and belongings give the appearance of decline. Urinating and sleeping in public are both unavoidable and criminalized, creating a terrible dynamic. It is also true that not all homeless people are well behaved. Mental illness and substance abuse contribute to disorderly and illegal behaviors that disrupt communities in ways that can make public spaces inhospitable and, in rare cases, dangerous.

Some efforts to remove homeless people through criminalization are clearly linked to economic development initiatives. Los Angeles's Safe Cities Initiative (SCI) was a bald-faced attempt to drive homeless people out of the historic Skid Row area to make way for gentrification.[3] Ironically, Skid Row itself was originally created as a kind of ghetto of social services for the very poor in order to keep them out of other residential neighborhoods. But as LA's downtown has become more developed and desirable, Skid Row has become a valuable area for real estate development.

The main stated goal of SCI was to reduce crime in a targeted fifty-block area through intensive broken-windows-oriented enforcement. Fifty additional police officers were assigned to the area, along with numerous specialized units. Homeless encampments were cleared away, thousands of arrests made, and many more citations issued. In addition, the police were used explicitly to drive people into social services through a variety of formal diversion programs and informal street practices. Forrest Stuart describes how police routinely treated people in programs more leniently than those they perceived to be "service resistant." In general, however, these programs were based on a variety of self-help and twelve-step approaches that rarely succeeded in part because there were no permanent housing, jobs, or sustained health services available. This dynamic contributed to a revolving-door phenomenon and plenty of victim-blaming for what is really a failed social safety net.

In the end, proponents claim that SCI had reduced the number of robberies in the target area by about fifty a year, at a cost of more than $6 million a year in policing and another $118 million in court and jail costs. In contrast, spending by municipalities, the state, and federal government on homeless services for all of LA County was only about $600 million a year. Yes, intensive and invasive policing displaces homeless people and perhaps even some crime, but it does nothing to reduce the overall homeless population.

In some cases, aggressive removal of homeless people can have deadly outcomes. In March 2014, Albuquerque police killed James Boyd while attempting to remove him from his unpermitted camp on open land near a suburban neighborhood.[4] Responding to a complaint from a resident concerned about Boyd's schizophrenic rantings, police encountered Boyd, who was holding a knife and threatening them. After a five-hour standoff that involved extensive negotiation from a trained crisis intervention team, Boyd was shot multiple times while he appeared to be gathering his things to go with officers, according to body-cam footage of the incident. The two officers who shot him were put on trial, the result of which was a hung jury and a decision by the DA not to seek a retrial. Boyd had a long history of involvement in the criminal justice system and treatment for severe mental illness.

In spring of 2015, the LAPD killed two homeless people. The first was Charly Leundeu Keunang, who was shot in the back during a struggle with officers who wanted to question him about a robbery.[5] Keunang was mentally ill, had been in prison, was on methamphetamines, and was awaiting deportation to Cameroon. A cell-phone video shows officers chasing him around a makeshift encampment in LA's Skid Row area and shouting commands at Keunang, who resisted them. At one point, an officer yells something about his partner's gun and then shoots him. Body-camera footage of the incident has not been made public, but sources who have seen it, as well as bystanders at the scene, deny that Keunang had obtained or was attempting to obtain the officer's weapon.

The second victim was Brendon Glenn, who had been homeless in the Venice Beach area for many years and was well known and liked by many residents, despite his alcoholism.[6] Police responded to a disturbance call and initially spoke to Glenn without incident. However, they later came upon him in a conflict with a bouncer and, during a struggle, shot him. A video from a nearby security camera shows that Glenn was unarmed and did not appear to pose a threat to officers or the public, prompting police officials to raise serious concerns about the incident and resulting in several protests and community meetings.

All three of the above-mentioned men posed regular threats to public order and in some cases public safety. The use of the police to manage those threats, however, was largely ineffective and ultimately deadly. These individuals were immune to threats of arrests and incarceration, which they had all experienced in the past. The criminal justice system, with its emphasis on punishment, could not address the underlying and intertwined problems of homelessness, mental illness, and substance abuse that drove their problematic behaviors, leaving police the unenviable task of "managing" them in a fruitless effort to reduce their impact on the rest of society.

The drive to criminalize homeless people remains strong. While many feel some compassion for those on the margins of society, there is also a high level of frustration at the declining conditions of some urban areas. These "quality of life" concerns play into the broader sense of insecurity felt by people who see their standards of living declining. Some are deeply concerned about having their social and economic status undermined by a growth in disorderly behavior. At the same time, many who are financially better off feel stressed as well because of ever-increasing housing costs. People in places like New York and San Francisco are paying up to 50 percent of their income on housing, and in some cases more. This creates a sense of social entitlement and financial insecurity that can drive even liberals to call on local governments to "get tough" on homeless people in their midst. My own research has documented the role of social activists with long histories of liberal activism calling for the removal of homeless encampments by police in New York and San Francisco.[7]

In addition, businesses feel tremendous pressure to displace panhandlers and those sleeping rough or acting strangely nearby. Managing this problem has been one of the drivers of the creation of "business improvement districts" that collect money from local businesses to enhance sanitation and security services and, in some cases, even create homeless services centers. In the worst cases, they have also been implicated in using force to illegally displace homeless people, panhandlers, and the mentally ill.[8]

The disorder associated with mass homelessness has played a role in the rise of more conservative urban politics, as well-meaning liberals—who call for social tolerance of disorder while long-term solutions are attempted but never realized—are replaced with neoconservatives who question the ability of government to solve economic problems and instead rely on aggressive policing to push homeless people out of public view. At the center of this dynamic is the deeply conservative "broken windows" theory. In general, broken-windows policing merely creates a revolving door in which homeless people are arrested, sent through the jail and court system and then released back into the community in the same condition they left it. This process rarely results in someone's stabilization. These agencies almost never have access to permanent housing or even long-term mental health or substance abuse services. As a result, rearrests are common. A recent study in New York City found that of the 800 people who spent the most time cycling through the jail system, over half were homeless. The top charges in these cases were petit larceny, drug possession, and trespassing.[9] Constantly rearresting homeless people for these offenses does little to alter their future behavior or reduce their impact on communities. And it certainly doesn't help to end their homelessness.

The cost of this process is exorbitant. New York City spent $129 million over 5 years to jail those 800 people. That's over $30,000 per person per year.[10] Supportive housing costs less. And that amount doesn't include the costs of emergency room visits, shelter stays, outreach efforts, etc. In 2013 the Utah Housing and Community Development Division reported that the cost of emergency room treatment and jail time averaged over $16,000 a year per homeless person, while the cost of providing a fully subsidized apartment was only $11,000.[11] A study by the University of New Mexico documented that providing people with housing reduced jail costs by 64 percent.[12] Researchers in Central Florida showed that providing chronically homeless people with permanent housing and support services would save local taxpayers $149 million in spending on jails and health care.[13] An in-depth case study conducted by researchers at the University of Southern California found that the total cost per person of public services for two years living on the streets was $187,288, compared to $107,032 for two years in permanent housing with support services, a savings of $80,256, or almost 43 percent.[14]

Criminal justice costs went from an average of over $23,000 to zero.

Many of the laws used to criminalize homeless people run afoul of existing law. Numerous anti-panhandling ordinances have been found unconstitutional because they violate the First Amendment right to freedom of speech in that they are soliciting donations.[15] Courts have thrown some cases out because they are unconstitutionally vague, leaving officers too much discretion in criminalizing innocuous as well as disorderly behavior. Cities often run into legal trouble when they sweep out encampments and in the process destroy people's possessions. The courts have made it clear that any seized property must be treated with care and held for someone to claim.[16]

The DOJ issued a legal opinion in 2015 that many of the anti-sleeping and camping statutes being enforced across the country may be illegal if people have no other viable alternative but to sleep in those restricted places.[17] Sleeping bans in particular are problematic when a city fails to provide adequate emergency shelter to those who seek it. Those left outside should not be criminalized for sleeping.

The criminalization of homeless people also violates the International Covenant Against Torture and the International Covenant on Civil and Political Rights,[18] which states that all people have a right to housing, that governments have an obligation to put the wellbeing of people above concerns about disorder and aesthetics, and that homelessness exerts a tremendous cost on those subjected to it. Criminalization efforts exacerbate that cost without housing any more people.

International human rights law also gives people the right to freedom of movement. Statutes that attempt to restrict homeless people's access to certain areas through loitering laws and probation conditions that restrict access to certain areas may violate this. Laws that have a discriminatory purpose and outcome in terms of race and property may also violate international treaties as well as the International Declaration of Human Rights. International law also provides some rights to squatters that may make sweeps of longstanding homeless encampments illegal if no alternative housing is provided.

In 2014 the UN Human Rights Committee raised significant concerns about the United States' adherence to the International Covenant on Civil and Political Rights.

> The Committee is concerned about reports of criminalization of people living on the streets for everyday activities such as eating, sleeping, sitting in particular areas, etc. The Committee notes that such criminalization raises concerns of discrimination and cruel, inhuman, and degrading treatment.[19]

This is an official finding about a treaty that the United States has signed and to which courts must thus adhere. It also lays out a framework for judging the criminalization of homeless people as cruel, inhuman, and degrading, which draws parallels with our constitutional ban on cruel and inhuman punishment as well as international restrictions on torture.

Even if criminalization was successful, legal, and cost effective, it would still be unethical. We live in an economic and social environment in which the market is unable to house people at the bottom of the economic order and government is unwilling to make up the difference. Given this reality, how can we justify treating homelessness as a criminal justice issue? The law appears to be applied universally, but this fails to take into account the fact that the poor are always under greater pressure to break it and at greater risk of being subjected to legal action. As Anatole France pointed out in 1894, "In its majestic equality, the law forbids rich and poor alike to sleep under bridges, beg in the streets, and steal loaves of bread."

There is an issue of substantive justice here. Even if the law is enforced equitably and without bias or malice, it still results in the incarceration of large numbers of people who are homeless, mentally ill, and poor, rather than hardened predators. Ultimately, the criminalization of homeless people should be understood as a way of managing growing inequality through increasingly punitive mechanisms of state control. The aggressive policing of homeless people may appear to be about improving the quality of life of middle-class residents, but to the extent that it does, it does so only by worsening the conditions of homeless people. In the process, it also relieves elected officials of the responsibility to embrace a transformative urban politics that focuses on the needs of poor people in terms of structural changes to housing and employment markets, as well as essential social services like health care.

Reforms

A number of police forces have created specialized outreach teams trained in dealing with this high need population. They are typically trained in conflict de-escalation, developing trust, and dealing with mental health and substance abuse issues, and are also informed about available services and referral procedures. Officers work in teams, often with civilian outreach workers, to contact and build relationships with homeless people in hopes of getting them into services and off the streets. One of the fundamental limitations of these programs is that they rarely have substantial services to offer and almost never have immediately available stable housing. This means that these teams, even when they include social workers, volunteers, or clinicians, still have a punitive quality. When a uniformed officer with a badge, gun, and handcuffs tells you not to camp here, it's an implied threat of future arrest, and in fact arrest, destruction of property, and displacement often follow over time. Professional outreach workers consistently report that long-term stabilization requires both trust and appropriate services. Without those, outcomes are frustrating for all involved, which often leads to renewed calls for get-tough policies and arrests.

Homeless Courts

The last twenty years have seen a huge growth in specialized courts. Organizations like the Center for Court Innovation have spun off youth courts, drug courts, mental health courts, veterans' courts, and homeless courts. At their best these courts are intended to connect people with services rather than cycling them through criminal courts and jails. To the extent that they accomplish these goals, they have some value.

The Homeless Court in Maricopa County, Arizona, "combines punishment with treatment and services in rigorous supervised rehabilitation programs which typically exceed the sentencing requirements of similarly convicted defendants adjudicated in the normal court process."[20] This approach makes clear that this is still a punitive process based on an assumption of individual culpability and irresponsibility. This particular court is only "for homeless individuals who demonstrate commitment to end their homelessness," despite a pervasive lack of low-cost housing. Yet the services the court mandates almost never include stable housing, much less permanent housing with support services. Instead, they keep people involved in a series of social service and court appointments that rarely resolve their underlying problems. And even when that does happen, this does nothing to expand the available supply of housing for those with very low or no income. In essence, they are rearranging who gets a particular unit, rather than addressing the structural lack of affordable housing.

The growing popularity of these courts and diversion programs raises another important concern: increasingly, the *only* way to access much-needed services is through the criminal justice system. These programs want to show success, and their success depends on having appropriate services. Since such programs rarely create significant new services, they instead try to obtain set-asides from existing programs, taking slots away from those who might obtain them through shelter case workers or other social-service providers. In some cases, for instance, courts put a hold on a certain number of emergency shelter beds in order to have slots for those who show up in court and need them. That means, however, that those beds are no longer available to anyone else in need. Someone who loses out on a bed in a voluntary lottery might later get arrested for sleeping in the park and then get the same bed from the court. This puts more resources and power in the hands of police and the courts to decide who deserves help, rather than relying on trained case workers.

Alternatives

Extensive evidence now exists that the ultimate solution to homelessness involves increasing pay for low-wage work and creating more affordable housing, with support services for those who need it. Emergency shelters, transitional housing, life-skills training, and forced savings programs do nothing to reduce the overall amount of homelessness. The housing market on its own cannot house the growing number of people who are left out of the formal economy or have a tenuous relationship to it. In such a situation, the state has no choice but to intervene directly.

Income Supports

As much as anything else, homelessness is about a mismatch between incomes and housing costs. Over the last forty years, wages have become increasingly polarized, a process that has only gotten worse since the 2008 fiscal meltdown. This process has driven more people into poverty and, perversely, has also significantly driven up the cost of housing in many parts of the country. There are more than 10 million extremely-low-income renter households in the United States but only 3.2 million rental homes that are available and affordable to them. As a consequence, 75 percent of extremely-low-income renter households spend more than half of their income on housing.[21] Over the last two decades, rent inflation has outpaced overall inflation and housing prices. This is especially true at the bottom end of the market, where supply is dwindling.

In addition, income supports from government in the form of welfare payments and the earned income tax credit have also failed to keep pace with housing costs. In many parts of the country, welfare benefits are well below the cost of housing even at the bottom of the market. A significant increase in such payments, or equivalent vouchers, could allow people to access the low-cost rental market. That influx of renters, however, would further drive up prices if no new housing is created. Governments, therefore, must either dramatically raise the value of transfers to stimulate new low-cost housing construction or provide the housing themselves.

Housing First

One of the lessons learned in the last twenty years is that the best way to get people off the streets and out of the shelters is to make immediate permanent housing available to them at very low or no cost, and to provide a range of optional support services to help them stay there. This is known as the housing-first approach, and it is growing in prominence. In the past, homeless programs focused on proving emergency and transitional shelter, in the belief that if you stabilized someone and got them a job or necessary benefits, they could then enter the housing market and obtain stable long-term housing.

This is not the case. This mismatch between low-wage work or government benefits and increasingly expensive housing makes the process untenable. Governments are going to have to intervene in housing markets by building large numbers of heavily subsidized units. The federal government could help by bringing back Section 8 subsidies on a large scale that could be pooled together to provide financing. But local and state governments have to *want* to build the housing, and right now many do not. Even New York's liberal mayor Bill de Blasio is insisting on using zoning bonuses and other incentives to get developers to include more affordable units in new construction projects. These units are never affordable to those currently living in shelters and on the streets, however, and such housing does not come with the necessary support service to help people maintain stable housing.

Virginia has been a major proponent of a housing-first approach, including rapid rehousing and permanent supportive housing. From 2010 to mid-2016, the state experienced a 31 percent drop in overall homelessness, including a 37.6 percent decrease in family homelessness. In 2015, it became the first state to end veteran homelessness.[22] The state of Utah was also an early adopter of a housing-first approach. Overall, officials are very happy with the results, which have significantly reduced overall homelessness and the number of chronically homeless people, who tend to have the most interactions with the police, courts, emergency rooms, and jails. While the state's claim of a 91 percent reduction in chronic homelessness appears overstated, the results are still impressive.[23] According to the director of Utah's Homeless Task Force, Lloyd Pendleton, "For the chronically homeless population, which represents about 10 percent of the homeless population ... when these individuals have a place of their own where they can be safe, the drinking and drug use decreases. Also, with effective case management support, we have found a positive supportive community is created."[24]

Community Remediation Process

Too often, shelters and other programs for homeless people come with significant restrictions such as requiring that they be clean, sober, and nonthreatening. These seem reasonable, but they leave lots of people out on the streets. In some cases the restrictions exceed practicality and veer into moralizing as well. Some religious-based service providers and even secular nonprofits continue to rely on a personal-responsibility model that blames homeless people, directly or indirectly, for their condition and demands that they demonstrate a willingness to abide by certain moral codes before receiving services. These codes can be especially restrictive and even discriminatory toward LGBTQ people.

Even if we began moving immediately toward a housing-first model, there would still be people waiting for a place to live for some time. And even when a full housing model is in place, there will always be people who fall through the cracks, so we need to give people a place to be that helps them stabilize their situation and reduce their impact on surrounding communities. The best way to do this is through a system of drop-in centers and emergency shelters focused on getting people off the streets without relying on police, the criminal justice system, or other punitive mechanisms—even people with mental health, substance abuse, and other behavioral problems. Such centers can have caseworkers, mental health services, counseling, and practical amenities like mail drops, health checkups, food, and clothing. Such places do exist and they are often quite successful and relatively low cost. But too often government support is inadequate or nonexistent. Cambridge, Massachusetts, had a community-based service provider called Bread and Jams that offered all of these things, as well as help with housing and job searches, benefits advocacy, health care, and policy advocacy. Unfortunately, it closed in spring 2014 because of inadequate funding, despite its role in stabilizing homeless people, improving their quality of life, and reducing the impact of homelessness on the surrounding community.[25]

Ideally, these spaces should also address the needs of local communities. Too often shelters and other services are plopped down in neighborhoods with little effort to work with residents in developing plans to reduce their impact. For example, in some cases communities complain that the shelter throws everyone out early in the morning, forcing them to roam the streets. The Mission Neighborhood Resource Center in San Francisco tries to address these kinds of concerns.[26] They offer a drop-in center with no restrictions, and act as a gateway to health care, social services, and shelters. They also do leadership development to help train homeless people to advocate for improved services and permanent housing. In addition, they work with the community to identify services that would reduce the impact of homeless people, such as access to showers and an outreach team that can respond to calls about people in distress on the streets, without having to involve the police.

We must move beyond the false choice of living with widespread disorder or relying on the police to be the enforcers of civility. In July 2015, a New York City police union called on its members and supporters to take pictures of homeless people creating a public nuisance as a way of pressuring city government to give the police a free hand in controlling their behavior through renewed criminalization.[27] The union was implying that the newly inaugurated Mayor De Blasio was "tying their hands" and therefore contributing to a decline in public civility. For this union, the only appropriate response was an increase in invasive and aggressive policing. This cannot be the answer. We know how to solve homelessness for most people on the streets, and we know how to reduce the impact of homelessness on communities without relying on police. We just need the political will to do it. As long as we ask the police to be the lead agency in dealing with people living on the streets, the outcomes will not be good. While the police can force people to move along, drive people into the shadows, or involve them in the criminal justice system, they do nothing to reduce the number of homeless people; police actions merely serve to further isolate and immiserate them at huge expense.

6

The Failures of Policing Sex Work

What Does It Mean to Criminalize Sex Work?

When we allow police to regulate our sexual lives, we inflict tremendous harm on some of the most vulnerable people in our society. Young people, poor women, and transgendered persons who rely on the sex industry to survive and even thrive are forced by police into the shadows, leaving them vulnerable to abuse, exploitation, and diminished health outcomes.

Residents and business owners often couch their concerns about sex work in terms of offenses to the moral order. They are concerned about exposing children to overt sex acts and the detritus of condoms and drug paraphernalia that often accompany the sex trade. Secondary problems include the harassment of women mistaken for sex workers, the propositioning of uninterested men by sex workers, and the disorder and even violence that can sometimes result from interactions between clients, prostitutes, and pimps. All have the potential to undermine quality of life and reduce property values, which means that complaints from property owners tend to drive policing. At a broader level, city officials express concerns about the spread of sexually transmitted disease and the nexus of drugs and organized crime in the sex industry, as well as the presence of juveniles and the abuses they and adult participants may experience from pimps and clients.

Recently, a raft of nongovernmental organizations (NGOs) have worked hard to raise awareness about the role of coercion and international trafficking in the supply of sex workers, especially juveniles. Many of these groups, as well as some religious, political, and community leaders, object to prostitution in primarily moral terms. Others contend that no one would choose prostitution of their own accord and equate sex work with coercion. These groups tend to take an abolitionist approach, arguing that all sex work should be banned, with punitive state enforcement action at the center of any such efforts. Many liberal feminists have embraced a prohibitionist stance out of concern for the wellbeing of women whom they believe end up in sex work because of childhood sexual abuse, while other feminists point to the ways this stance reproduces patriarchal attitudes and power relations.

There is also a strong tendency among police to view prostitution in highly moral terms. This can lead to minimizing the humanity of sex workers, because of their seemingly intractable involvement in behaviors police find personally offensive, or minimizing their agency in a kind of rescue mentality, in which police identify sex workers as victims in need of saving. When neither of these approaches improves the situation, a kind of anomic disinterest often emerges, in which prostitution is just another on-the-job problem to be managed with the least possible investment of emotional energy or regard for the outcome. Arrests are made, loiterers dispersed, and radio jobs handled. Does any of this make communities safer or improve the lives of sex workers? Overwhelmingly, the answer is no. Criminalizing sex work is notoriously ineffective and hurts sex workers and society at large. The prohibitionist approach assumes that strict enforcement of the law, whether it is directed at the provider or the client, will deter prostitution. The evidence, however, shows that even the most intensive policing efforts fail to produce this effect.

Up until the 1910s, overt red-light districts were quite common in American cities. While police often extorted bribes and at times sexually exploited sex workers, prostitution was effectively decriminalized within these zones and sometimes more broadly. Two factors combined to largely end that practice. The first was military authorities' desire to restrict prostitution during World War I, since in past wars, sexually transmitted disease had played a major role in undermining troop readiness. The second was the Progressive Era emphasis on restoring morality to the cities, which had been "polluted" by the massive influx of eastern and southern European immigrants. This took the form of a "white slave" narrative, in which prostitutes were described as unwitting victims of coercive and manipulative foreign men. Their goal was to "save" these women through prohibitionist policies similar to those against the "scourge" of alcohol.

Early enforcement actions included raiding brothels and intensive enforcement against streetwalking. Despite the helplessness implied by the "white slave" narrative, prostitutes were generally treated as criminal offenders and subjected to jail terms, constant police harassment, or worse. The police and government officials were successful in suppressing red-light districts, but prostitution activity went on unabated in more covert forms in bars, escort services, massage parlors and saunas, underground brothels, outcall services, VIP rooms in strip clubs, and many forms of streetwalking, with varying levels of visibility and risk.

Today, police employ a variety of tactics to manage sex work. Vice teams focus on both visible and covert prostitution. Those arrested for vice crimes are often pressured to provide information about brothels and other hidden sex work locations. Undercover officers investigate these locations as prospective clients, in some cases engaging in sexual acts in the process. This is followed by raids in which sex workers, managers, and in some cases clients are arrested and prosecuted. Vice officers also conduct street operations in which they pretend to be customers. Once a price and sex act are agreed upon, arrests are made in cars or hotel rooms, or on street corners. In some cases, those loitering in "known prostitution zones" are merely rounded up; the presence of condoms, "sexually suggestive clothing," transgender appearance, or a past arrest record are deemed sufficient evidence for arrest and prosecution.

In strip clubs, police enforce a variety of vague laws against obscenity that rely on sometimes arbitrary interpretations of "community standards": measuring the distance between patrons and dancers or inspecting the size and position of articles of clothing. In New York State, for example, women can dance topless but must be at least eighteen inches off the ground and five feet away from clients, and cannot receive tips unless covered. Undercover officers conduct regular inspections. Back rooms and VIP lounges present a special challenge, as officers must often pretend to be clients offering money for special services to uncover violations.[1]

Patrol officers are sometimes assigned to manage ongoing street-level prostitution activity in their assigned areas. They tend to rely on loitering and disorderly conduct laws to arrest or disperse suspected sex workers. Officers responding to a specific complaint will often be satisfied by a sex worker's promise to leave the area for the rest of their shift. Some make drug arrests, ticket cars for double-parking, or intimidate clients with threats of public exposure.

More extreme forms of enforcement, often undertaken in conjunction with city attorneys and local DAs, involve publicly outing clients or using civil forfeiture and commercial nuisance laws to shutter businesses and sue landlords for allowing sex work to occur on their premises. In some cases, DAs target repeat offenders with enhanced sentences, including felony charges. Seattle's "banishment" laws require that those arrested on prostitution charges, or in some cases just suspected of prostitution, remain out of specific areas for extended periods of time or face enhanced criminal penalties.[2] NGOs have also pressured local officials to target advertising venues, such as the pages of free weekly newspapers and online listings such as Craigslist, in an effort to control less visible forms of sex work. In 2015 the US Attorney's office in

New York raided the offices of Rentboy.com, a website where mostly male sex workers advertised their services. All the employees were arrested and the business shuttered, despite the absence of a single complaint from anyone using the site. The result was to drive these sex workers into more financially and physically precarious positions.[3]

The Rentboy case is especially important because of the vulnerabilities faced by lesbian, gay, transgendered, and other gender-nonconforming or unconventional sex workers. These sex workers are often at risk from clients, police, and predators and are more likely to operate at the margins of the sex trade. Transgender sex workers are routinely harassed by the police and face violent hate crimes. Too often, police assume that anyone openly transgender or gender-nonconforming must be engaged in sex work. In New York City, police routinely target transgender people for harassment and arrest based strictly on their appearance.[4] They are also much more likely to be the victims of violence. While sex workers in general are targeted for crime, these workers also suffer abuse from homophobes and others who object to their gender identity.

Despite decades of police enforcement, commercial sexual services remain easily available, from the $5,000-a-night escorts hired by Wall Street executives and elected officials to those who turn $20 tricks in inner-city alleyways. Even when individual sex workers move out of the profession as a result of police action, others replace them, and there is never a shortage of clients. At best, police can claim that their efforts limit the extent and visibility of the sex industry. It is true that concerted intensive police enforcement can sometimes drive streetwalkers from a specific location, but they move to more remote outdoor locations or indoor ones. This may provide some benefits for residents but does nothing to reduce the overall prevalence of commercial sex or improve the lives of sex workers themselves. Commercial sex has proven largely impervious to punitive policing.

Collateral Consequences

It's not just that criminalization is ineffective. It also hurts sex workers, the public, and the criminal justice system, contributing to the victimization of sex workers, the spread of disease, and the corruption of the police and justice system.

Policing has aimed not to eradicate prostitution but to drive it underground. This process leaves these workers without a means to complain when they are raped, beaten, or otherwise victimized, strengthens the hands of pimps and traffickers, and contributes to unsafe sex practices. When sex workers are forced to labor in a hidden, illegal economy, they have little recourse to the law to protect their rights and safety. Even when they are technically able to ask for police protection from violence, it is rarely forthcoming. Because of their social position and a history of disregard and abuse at the hands of police, these workers rarely see police intervention as being in their best interest. Sex workers have an interest in maintaining the anonymity of their clients; criminal prosecution and public embarrassment are bad for business. There are rarely credit-card receipts, photocopies of IDs, or surveillance footage that might be used to identify and prosecute offenders. Even when there is some evidence, victims are generally loath to open themselves up to additional police scrutiny for fear that they or their establishment might be raided.

In addition, sex workers have no ability to access basic workplace protections. They cannot complain about fire hazards or file complaints about stolen wages. They can't sue for theft of services or contractual breaches. The only tool they have is to withhold their labor, but even this may be constrained by coercive labor practices ranging from psychological manipulation to enslavement.

Criminalization also strengthens the hand of pimps, organized criminals, and traffickers. Because there are limited legal ways of entering most sex work and because of the criminal status of most of this work which can produce huge financial rewards, third parties play an important role in recruiting and coercing participants. Also, there is a value in being able to provide protection, secure hidden work sites, and organize cooperation from the police. These services are best provided by those already involved in illegal activity. All of this makes it difficult for workers to self-organize to participate independently in the sex economy. Property rentals, security services, and advertising must all be handled covertly, often through fictitious companies or other fronts. Even streetwalkers must contend with informally organized strolls, in which more regular and organized participants either drive off newcomers or force them into their own organizations. In some cases, pimps force sex workers into their "protection" as a way of guaranteeing their ability to ply their trade. Other pimps work in true partnership with sex workers, providing support and protection for a share of the earnings.

Exploitative pimps are motivated to coerce participation in sex work by the money, and because they know that workers have little legal recourse. Police often view these sex workers as offenders rather than victims and fail to take their requests for help seriously. Also, those who are pressured, coerced, or even voluntarily enter this work often come from very disadvantaged circumstances and may have mental health and substance abuse problems or have been the victims of childhood sexual abuse. All of this contributes to social isolation and vulnerability that makes them easier to control. Simplistic "rescue" efforts fail to deal with the depth of isolation and hardship facing these people. Sex workers who are offered counseling and drug treatment but not jobs and housing will often return to sex work, even in an abusive form, because they are not given a sustainable way out. Exploiters capitalize on this dynamic to keep them isolated and dependent.

International sex traffickers can also be empowered by poorly-thought-out prohibitionist police actions, which often involve deporting or incarcerating foreign women involved in sex work, a practice often driven by US policies.[5] In Thailand, for example, the US has pressured police to reduce sex trafficking—which is generally equated with the involvement of foreigners in sex work, regardless of whether they are voluntary or coerced. Women from Laos, Cambodia, China, and Myanmar are routinely swept up in police raids and forcibly repatriated. In addition, border crossings have been fortified to make entry more difficult. This means that voluntary migrants are more likely to turn to organized criminal networks for transportation, leaving them vulnerable to exploitation and coercion. It also gives these organized criminal groups more exclusive control of the flow of workers, which creates a powerful incentive to maintain a strong supply—through coercive means if necessary. This is especially true if the workforce is constantly being depleted through police action.

A similar dynamic is at work in parts of Europe and the United States. Voluntary migrant sex workers turn to smugglers and traffickers to gain access to these markets, leaving them vulnerable to high financial costs, fraud, abuse, indentured servitude, and in some cases even enslavement. This is also true of other service industries. Mexican and Central American "coyotes" frequently prey on female migrants, demanding sex and money as a condition of transport, sometimes forcing women into sex work to pay off debts or directly forcing them into prostitution.[6] Eastern European organized crime groups offer women access to American, European, and Asian sex work at very high costs that become a form of indentured servitude, as women must pay off the debts through sex work.[7] In some cases women are told they are being smuggled to perform domestic work, only to be forced into sex work.

The illegality of both sex work and drugs creates profit incentives for organized crime to link the two. Sex workers are sometimes given drugs or pressured to become drug dependent as a way of managing them. Others become enticed or coerced into sex work to maintain their drug habits. Clients are also often offered drugs as part of their sexual experience. Offering these two services in tandem is wildly profitable for organized crime, since the avenues of distribution and the provision of security from police and competitors often overlap.

Marginalization also contributes to unsafe sex practices. One of the most troubling is that police often regard possession of condoms as evidence of prostitution. Since streetwalkers often work in cars, parks, or other informal locations, the only way to ensure safe sex practices is to carry condoms. They must then weigh the long-term risks of disease against the short-term risks of arrest and prosecution. Clients will sometimes pay more for sex without condoms, and pimps can drive women to earn more in this way or risk abuse. Finally, while a few cities, such as San Francisco, have public health clinics for sex workers[8], many workers have difficulty accessing appropriate care because they lack health insurance and fear being stigmatized or criminalized. Finally, the police themselves have been implicated in demanding unprotected sex as a condition of avoiding arrest.[9]

Police Corruption

Police corruption plays a major role in the abuse and marginalization of sex workers and undermines public confidence in the police. Vice crimes such as gambling, prostitution, and substance abuse lend themselves to police corruption for a number of reasons. Police can enact harsh penalties, and those engaged in illegal activity usually have the resources to buy them off. Furthermore, enforcement is largely discretionary, so there is tremendous temptation for police to look the other way in return for bribes or actively pursue bribes as a form of "rent seeking," in which they use their position to maximize extorted earnings.

In many parts of the world, police corruption in relationship to prostitution is endemic, with most sex workers conducting financial and even sexual relationships with police.[10] It is considered an unavoidable cost of doing business for workers and part of the expected base salary for police, along with bribes to avoid traffic tickets and free meals and goods from local businesses. While these practices were the norm in American policing through the 1960s, their practice is no longer systematic. Increases in pay, greater public oversight, and corruption scandals such as the Knapp Commission helped to mostly end such practices at the systemic level. However, lower-level corruption remains widespread. Police are regularly arrested or fired for providing protection for brothels or making financial or sexual demands on individual sex workers, and it is not uncommon for sex workers to field financial and sexual demands from officers as a regular part of their work life.

In just the last few years, American police have been implicated in running and providing protection for brothels,[11] demanding sex from prostitutes to avoid arrest,[12] hiring underage prostitutes,[13] acting as pimps,[14] stealing from and assaulting sex workers,[15] and demanding bribes from prostitutes and their clients.[16] There is no way to know the full extent of these practices, but the problem is widespread and ongoing. A 2005 survey of sex workers found that 14 percent had had sexual experiences with police and 16 percent had experienced police violence, while only 16 percent reported having had a good experience going to the police for help.[17] Another study found that a third of the violence young sex workers experienced came at the hands of police.[18]

Reforms

Most reform initiatives that attempt to reduce the negative impact of policing on sex workers focus on shifting the burden of enforcement onto buyers and third-party purveyors. Others divert sex workers into court-mandated or social-services-driven treatment and rehabilitation regimes in an attempt to keep them out of jail and offer them pathways to economic self-sufficiency. These efforts include specialized courts, "john schools," new laws targeting clients, and other attempts to either deter clients or reform sex workers and their clients.

This can be seen most clearly in new legal regimes that decriminalize selling sexual services but criminalize buying or organized provision. The pioneer of this approach is Sweden, which in 1999 voted to decriminalize sex work but increased penalties for the trafficking and coercion of sex workers and the purchase of sexual services. This change was motivated by mostly liberal female legislators taking an abolitionist approach to prostitution on feminist grounds. They argued that all sex work is degrading to women (even though not all sex workers are women) and that all women involved in sex work have been coerced in some way—even if just out of economic desperation. Framing sex workers as victims made criminalizing them unjust, so instead they placed the burden on those who coerce women into the trade and those who demand their services.

This "Nordic model" also provides sex workers with access to social services, government benefits, and pensions. Since the law was enacted, there has been evidence of a decline in the overall number of prostitutes and an increase in the price of services. Interestingly, no one has actually been incarcerated for soliciting sex. The rise in prices suggests a drop in the supply of sex workers rather than a decrease in demand. The rhetoric of victimhood has also served to further stigmatize and socially isolate sex workers. Many sex workers report that they are voluntary participants and that criminalizing clients further isolates them. Because their clients are at risk of arrest, they must still work covertly. They still report feeling hunted by the police and driven into the margins of society.

In addition, some sex workers have lost custody of their children; others have been evicted by landlords concerned about being prosecuted for facilitating sex work. This means that women must often work alone, as opposed to their having an organized setting in which security and working conditions could be more easily controlled and improved. In the Netherlands and Nevada, where organized prostitution is permitted, workers are better able to organize to improve safety and working conditions.

In the United States, prostitution remains illegal except in rural Nevada, but there have been less-punitive approaches. In 1995 the City of San Francisco developed the First Offender Prostitution Program, in which clients could pay court costs and attend a "john school" to avoid prosecution. This is intended to educate clients about the harms that their practices produce for themselves, their families, communities, and sex workers through graphic lectures about the effects of sexually transmitted diseases and the coercion and exploitation experienced by some sex workers.[19] The hope is that once they know the true costs, clients will choose not to participate in this illicit economy.

In practice, these "schools" have a very punitive quality. Defendants are forced to attend or face criminal charges. The stern lectures have a moralizing bent. They also assume that men are unaware of the potential harms produced by their behavior. In fact, many men are well aware of the negative consequences of their actions, though they often suppress that awareness to suit their desires.

Like the Nordic model, this approach does little to improve the life options or working conditions of sex workers or address the underlying motivation for buying sexual services, which requires a much deeper conversation about the role of sex in society.

Several court-based diversion programs focus on pressuring and enticing sex workers to leave the trade. Their ability to participate in the court process is usually at the discretion of the local District Attorney, who can choose to prosecute instead. The court makes a needs assessment and orders participation in one or more therapeutic or rehabilitative programs, such as drug treatment or job training. In theory, these programs should offer a full range of services tailored to the specific needs of individual sex workers with the goal of providing them true pathways out of sex work, if this is what they want. Since sex workers who end up in the court system have complex needs and often traumatic histories, any rehabilitative effort should be long-term and anticipate setbacks and temporary program failures. Little of this is done in practice. Most programs have a very limited range of services including shelter referrals (not permanent housing), job training (not jobs), and outpatient mental health and drug treatment. They usually take an abolitionist approach that views women as victims to be rescued.

As a result, sex workers are rarely involved in the development of these programs. Christian rescue groups often receive contracts to provide many of the services and in some cases have been instrumental in establishing the courts and work with law enforcement to plan and execute raids. While some of the services can be very helpful, forced participation in religious counseling blurs the line between church and state and does little to improve the lives of sex workers. Fortunately, in some cases, groups with a history of sex worker membership or involvement—such as New York's Sex Worker Project—are involved in providing some small portion of the court-mandated services.

In 2013 New York created the first Human Trafficking Intervention Courts, designed to treat sex workers as victims rather than criminals. Molly Crabapple profiled the utter futility and abuse of this system for *Vice* in 2015, showing that police practices remain essentially unchanged, with the vast bulk of enforcement targeting women in the street trade and often dragging in other poor women of color who were just in the wrong place at the wrong time.[20] The courts themselves offer only minimal services. In many cases the penalties from these courts were actually higher than for a regular court, as women were forced to go through days of counseling and community service rather than just paying a small fine and getting on with their lives. The issue of trafficking is almost totally absent: the workers are never asked if they were trafficked and the entire focus is on controlling their lives through moral suasion and forced counseling.

Since these programs are only available after an arrest, the police still have tremendous discretion in determining who is a sex worker and whether they should be put into the criminal justice system. This leaves open the possibility of strong bias toward arresting those in the street trade and sex workers of color. In Brooklyn, which has a Human Trafficking Intervention Court, 94 percent of those arrested for street prostitution are African American. In addition, these courts maintain all the temptations of corruption, in which police officers can extort sex or money from sex workers in exchange for avoiding arrest and placement in the court.

Recidivism rates for participants in these programs are slightly better than for those jailed and fined. However, most participants do go back to sex work, even those involved in abusive relationships with pimps. More importantly, these courts seem to have little impact on the total population of sex workers. Since demand is maintained and economic and social vulnerabilities remain unaddressed, there is a never-ending supply of new workers. In some cases they help those who are aging out of prostitution or are ready to leave abusive situations, but they seem much less effective in diverting those with high earning potential. Sex workers who are not being coerced often see the programs as demeaning, misguided, and largely irrelevant.

With the rise in awareness about human trafficking has

come an explosion in efforts to "rescue" women and girls in sex work by governments and NGOs. These "abolitionists" operate on the assumption that all sex workers are there involuntarily. This approach is driven by religious conservatives embracing a moral framework of sexual indiscretion followed by moral redemption, and by conservative feminists, who look to the state to advance the interests of women through punitive means ("carceral feminism," as coined by Elizabeth Bernstein[21]) or market-based rehabilitation programs while overlooking larger systems of economic and cultural domination. Proponents define sex workers as women who are victims in need of saving and in some cases support full criminalization of female sex workers.

This framework may be best known in the United States in relation to conservative religious efforts to "save" prostitutes through on-the-job interventions, often captured on video. Films like *The Abolitionists* portray moral crusaders working with local police to identify victims and perpetrators. Many, like Operation Underground Railroad, focus on rescuing child sex workers and victims of coercion and international forced trafficking. They pose as clients and then try to talk sex workers into leaving the trade by joining their programs, which typically offer emergency housing and some social support services along with a heavy dose of religious mentoring.

Internationally, these groups often work with local authorities to do large brothel raids, in which foreign workers are deported to their home countries and local workers are forced into social services and training programs. Sometimes these "rescued" women are willing participants in sex work and fight to escape. Others are forced into sweatshop-like conditions, primarily in extremely low-paid garment work. In Thailand, women are held for a year in rehabilitation camps, where they are required to learn sewing and other trades in hopes that they will accept low-wage work instead of much higher-paying sex work. The sex workers' rights group

Empower Chiang Mai has documented numerous incidents in which "rescued" sex workers were abused by police, held in detention, and deported.[22] Needless to say, many of those "saved" return to sex work.

Under the George W. Bush administration, these groups found a welcome reception. In 2002, Congress passed the Global AIDS Act, which barred the use of federal funds to promote, support, or advocate the legalization of prostitution. Governments that wanted funds for AIDS prevention were barred from even exploring the possible benefits of legalized prostitution regimes in reducing HIV transmission rates; nonprofits were required to take a public stance against prostitution and trafficking in any form—which generally included noncoercive migration of sex workers. This made it very difficult for groups to build trusting relationships with sex workers or openly help them organize for mutual aid and political power. In addition, it has often played into local anti-immigrant sentiments, in which visible sex work is blamed on an influx of immigrant sex workers. As a result, enforcement often targets migrant workers without regard for their reasons for doing such work, the means of their arrival, the conditions of their work, or the dangers of illegally crossing borders.

Domestically, the Trafficking Victims Protection Act of 2003 conflated all prostitution with forced trafficking, despite the objections of sex-worker organizations. The act was intended to punish traffickers rather than sex workers themselves. The FBI and local law enforcement were pressured to set up anti-trafficking initiatives using new federal money. Unfortunately, enforcement modalities appear largely unchanged. FBI raids typically result in arrests of a small number of traffickers and large numbers of sex workers. The act also created special visas for trafficking victims willing to aid law enforcement in prosecuting their traffickers; the vast majority of these go unused.

The law also pushed local and state governments to create

anti-trafficking laws that conflate prostitution with trafficking in important but inaccurate ways. Alaska's 2012 law equates trafficking with advertising or working collectively. As a result, individuals who have advertised on Craigslist have been arrested, as have massage parlor and brothel owners—even in the absence of any evidence of coercion, much less forced international migration. These laws intensify the criminalization of sex workers and make sex work less secure. In the end, those arrested are generally subjected to the same pointless revolving-door justice.

Alternatives

Both traditional and reformist approaches to policing sex work have failed to alter the basic landscape of commercial sex. The basic level of supply and demand has remained largely unaltered by crackdowns, street sweeps, diversion programs, and rescue operations. It's time to completely rethink the use of punitive mechanisms for managing the social and individual harms associated with sex work. There is no one strategy for doing this, but many countries and localities are experimenting with new approaches. Some combine a harm-reduction approach with efforts to legalize or decriminalize prostitution. Police are largely taken out of the process; their role is reduced to dealing with truly coercive situations and other serious criminal behavior. None of these approaches is without problems, and they may not be transferable to every location. Instead, they are guideposts on the road to developing local solutions in conjunction with communities and sex workers themselves.

The goal of any new approach to sex work should be to take the coercion out of the process while understanding that, whether you personally find it distasteful or not, sex work will continue. Therefore, we should endeavor to improve the lives of sex workers and offer them voluntary pathways out of a job that can be difficult, demeaning, and even dangerous. While those who fit the idealized image of the college student paying her way through school with sex work before going on to a successful "legitimate" career are a small sliver of the market, many choose this work over low-paid employment in sweatshops, diners, hotels, and kitchens. All of these workplaces can also be demeaning, dangerous, and even sexually exploitative—just ask domestic workers in Singapore, *maquiladora* workers in Mexico, or hotel maids in Manhattan. In upstate New York, Susan Dewey found that almost all the sex workers she interviewed had previous employment and that most cycled between sex work and low-paid service work. Most preferred sex work because of the potential for financial windfalls, whereas service work was "exploitative, exclusionary, and without hope of social mobility or financial stability.[23]"

Brazil has largely decriminalized sex work. Adult sex work is legal, though operating a brothel is not. In practice, organized brothels exist fairly openly in many cities, including the central business districts of Rio de Janeiro and São Paulo. Different establishments offer services to different classes of clients. The street trade is somewhat minimal because there are so many indoor work environments; it is often specialized—such as catering to elderly clients around Praça da República—and is largely ignored by police. Sex workers catering to women and gay men are also more or less open and rarely subject to police action. There is also a strong aversion to pimps among police and in the general culture, and they are involved in only a small and marginal part of the market. This market is remarkably unregulated. There are no licensing or health check requirements, and widespread competition has helped to undermine abusive practices, though the low end of the business is still fraught with unpleasant and dangerous working conditions. Sex workers can go to the police for help when dealing with abusive customers or pimps. Brazil's deregulated approach is no panacea; there are underage prostitutes working in many areas, especially as part of the sex tourism sector in resort areas, and safe sex practices are not always ubiquitous. There is also constant pressure to criminalize parts of the industry on behalf of real estate interests, moral entrepreneurs, and local officials concerned about their international image in connection to events like the World Cup and Olympics.

Organized prostitution in brothels has been legal in rural Nevada since 1974. Workers (all female) are part of the formal economy, paying taxes and participating in Social Security. They are treated as independent contractors. They are required to pay the house a percentage and have regular health checks. The house provides clean workspaces, security, and administrative support. Numerous studies show a high degree of worker satisfaction, low levels of violence, and long work histories. There have been no allegations of forced or underage prostitution. Most workers report having previously worked in other kinds of employment, but find sex work more remunerative. Despite the consistently positive findings of researchers, the urban areas of Nevada have resisted legalization, and politicians and moral entrepreneurs frequently challenge the law. In 2014, Senate majority leader Harry Reid accused state legislators of cowardice for failing to criminalize sex work as part of a "modernization" effort to attract businesses to the state, prompting some brothel owners to point out that widespread illegal and coerced prostitution hasn't been an impediment to business in the rest of the country.[24]

Sex work is formally decriminalized in parts of Germany, Belgium, and the Netherlands. Red-light districts operate openly in cities and are highly regulated.[25] Women have full rights as workers and police enforcement is largely limited to underage and coerced sex workers, including international trafficking, and there is very little evidence of these; usually when they do arise it is in underground establishments. Sex businesses are generally zoned into specific areas; even some public strolls are allowed. Violence is largely unheard of in the regulated areas, and police respond to calls for assistance. While organized crime has been somewhat displaced by open competition, the limited number of venues and a significant underground trade allow it to remain a substantial and problematic part of the industry.

New Zealand has fully decriminalized prostitution in public and in organized settings, subject to local regulation. Government health and safety workers regularly inspect work premises; sex workers participate in national social benefit schemes and are protected by employment and labor laws. A similar system exists in parts of Australia as well. Violence and trafficking are largely nonexistent, as are underage and coerced sex work. The low cost of licensing and cooperative local governments mean that the underground trade is minimal. In some cities brothels can advertise. Organized crime seems to be largely absent; sex workers are mostly local women who report a high degree of satisfaction with their work lives. Public support, which was divided when the law was changed in 2003, has increased in recent years, prompting conservative governments to leave the system in place despite calls from moral reformers. In 2008, the New Zealand Prostitution Law Review Committee found that sex workers reported feeling safer, better able to negotiate safe sex practices, and more willing to report abuses to the police. They also found no evidence of increases in the number of minors involved in the sex trade.[26]

From Mexico to New Zealand to rural Nevada, allowing and regulating sex work reduces harm to sex workers, their clients, and communities, with very little role for the police. Legalized sex work has dramatically reduced the role of organized crime and police corruption and in many cases allows for greatly improved working conditions in which sanitation, safety, and safe sex practices are widespread and reinforced through government oversight. Civilian health workers rather than police are the primary agents of regulation, encouraging greater cooperation and compliance. This approach also undermines the view of sex workers as helpless victims in need of saving, which is degrading, stigmatizing, and simply inaccurate.

Do these approaches encourage sexual commerce by giving it the patina of legitimacy? Perhaps. But if the central social concerns of coercion and disease are being managed more effectively than under prohibition, isn't that a success? We should embrace these approaches as a starting point for policies that directly address social harms rather than moral panics. While commercial sex work will always have harm attached to it, so do legal sweatshops. In fact, the subordinate position of women in our economy and culture is the real harm left unaddressed by prohibition. Despite the lofty goals of abolitionists, as long as they are denied equal economic and political rights and equal pay for equal work, women will be forced into marginal forms of employment. As long as women and LGBTQ people are poor, socially isolated, and lack social and political power; as long as runaway and "throw away" kids have no place to turn but the streets, they will be at risk of trafficking and coercion. Neither the police nor the "rescuers" seem keen to address these social and economic realities.

7

The War on Drugs

The War on Drugs is the most damaging and ineffective form of policing facing us. Whether we date this war from the 1914 Harrison Act, President Reagan's famous all-out offensive, or President Clinton's massive expansion of federal drug crimes in the 1990s, there is no evidence that our country's drug problems have been improved by driving millions into prison. Since 1982, drugs have become cheaper, higher quality, and more widely available than ever before. Millions of Americans have tried them; high-school students have easy access to them. While ending the War on Drugs by itself won't transform policing, it would be a major positive step toward radically redefining the role of police in society and improving racial justice.

Illegal (and legal) drugs produce significant harm, no question about it. Thousands die from overdoses, many more become unable to work, and even more suffer from addictions that impede their personal and family lives. Illegal drug use in its current forms is also a source of property crime and violence, and a factor in the spread of diseases like HIV and hepatitis C. But there is a mountain of evidence that shows that most users suffer no significant harm, and that most harms that do occur could be reduced by ending, not expanding, the War on Drugs. Unfortunately, police and political leaders continue to embrace a politics of prohibition that flies in the face of decades of evidence and common sense.

The reality is that no amount of police intervention will ever stamp out drug use. People are deeply committed to it. In 2014, 27 million Americans said they had used illegal drugs in the last month.[1] When we include legal mind-altering drugs the number reaches 70 million; when we include regular use of alcohol, it reaches 130 million—or about half the adult population.

The rise of two currently popular drugs shows the counterproductive nature of the drug war in improving public health. As early as the 1930s, amphetamines were legal, easy to obtain, and popular among everyone from depressed housewives and overnight truck drivers to dieters. The US and other militaries distributed amphetamines during World War II to boost the performance of soldiers in combat. In the 1960s, employers and moral crusaders raised concerns about their recreational use and restrictions were put in place, requiring a prescription and limiting medical usage. As a result, a huge black market has emerged for methamphetamine, which is totally unregulated in terms of purity or potency. Methamphetamine has more side effects, which can be more pronounced than those of amphetamines. Its illegal, unregulated production creates dangerous byproducts that have led to poisonings, house fires, and explosions.[2]

The current increase in heroin use, especially overdoses, is directly tied to prohibitionist policies and the deregulation of the pharmaceutical industry. In 1995, the Food and Drug Administration (FDA) approved a prescription opioid called OxyContin, kicking off a boom in the use of prescription opioids. Sales of OxyContin grew from $45 million in 1996 to $3.1 *billion* in 2010. The manufacturer, Perdue Pharmaceuticals, told doctors that this new opioid formulation was less likely to be addictive and that they should prescribe it aggressively to reduce pain.[3] Unfortunately, many patients became addicted and a huge black market in the pills developed. Eventually the Drug Enforcement Agency (DEA) and Food and Drug Administration (FDA) realized this and took steps to tightly control the availability of the drug. Millions of people who were now dependent on it could no longer get it legally. Instead, they had to pay very high prices on the black market, or switch to heroin, which is much less expensive and much more dangerous. People who were taking medically regulated pills shifted to totally unregulated street heroin, which can vary in strength and contain impurities and additives—which is what produces the vast number of overdoses. Indeed, Oxy overdoses only began to spike after the pills became harder to obtain. In addition, heroin is more likely to be injected, leading to the spread of disease, abscesses, and other complications. It has also been suggested that the ongoing prohibition of marijuana has contributed to this crisis. There is growing evidence that marijuana is effective in some forms of chronic pain management.[4] Prohibitionist policies, including restrictions on research, have led doctors to rely on opioids in circumstances where marijuana might be used, thus eliminating the risks of addiction and overdose posed by opioids.

The prohibition efforts of the twentieth century were not about improving public health; they were about political opportunism and managing "suspect populations." The first major prohibitionist measure was the Harrison Act of 1914, which created legal restrictions on opium, heroin, and cocaine, all of which had been widely available in patent medicines and other forms. Arguments in favor of restricting these drugs had a profoundly racial character. Opium, which was associated with laborers from China, was largely ignored until it became popular with upper- and middle-class white women, who were obtaining it in "shady" Chinatown opium dens. Racial purists and xenophobes were alarmed by white women mixing with Chinese opium users and sellers, fearing a breakdown in the social distance between them. During this period, Chinese workers had no legal rights in the US court system and were subject to extreme exploitation and racial hatred. The prohibition of opium gave police a tool to justify constant harassment and tight social regulation of this "suspect" population.[5]

Similarly, those who railed against cocaine did so in anti-black terms. Plantation foremen had given it to enslaved workers to stimulate work and reduce hunger. Now cocaine was vilified because black people were taking it of their own accord. Prohibitionists raised the specter of drug-induced attacks on white women, and many accusations of rape and concomitant lynchings were tied to the drug. There was also a widespread fear in the South that blacks on cocaine had superhuman strength and couldn't be stopped with .32-caliber bullets, then the standard police issue, prompting the widespread adoption of.38 caliber bullets.

Marijuana had been used along the Mexican border for many decades without much concern. However, there was a significant upsurge in migration following the Mexican Revolution of the early twentieth century. States passed anti-marijuana laws, giving police a legal pretext to search and question migrants and create a climate of fear. In the North, marijuana was criminalized after becoming more popular among African Americans in the big cities. Its close association with jazz and black culture led to a moral panic. These twin forces came together nationally with federal prohibition in 1937.

Intensive drug prohibitionism was tied to conservative nativist politics. Johann Hari describes the exploits of the nation's first drug czar, Harry Anslinger, who from 1930 to 1962 waged a never-ending battle focused primarily on immigrants and people of color.[6] He was personally involved in arresting and harassing jazz legend Billie Holiday and may have directly contributed to her death in police custody in 1959. Using junk science and political intimidation, he forced doctors and officials to embrace prohibitionism despite robust medical evidence to the contrary. He also helped drive the adoption of international treaties that allowed for a greater federal role in drug control and spread the prohibitionist ideology internationally.[7]

The modern War on Drugs really began with Richard Nixon, who saw it as a way of inserting the federal government more forcefully into local law enforcement. This was part of his "Southern Strategy" to win over historically Democratic Southern whites in the wake of desegregation and the civil rights movement.[8] Rather than refighting a lost battle, Nixon appealed to white Southerners by using the language of law and order to indicate his desire to keep blacks in check through expanded law enforcement powers. Since most criminal law is handled at the state level, Nixon settled on drug enforcement as his avenue. He could justify federal involvement in what had been primarily a state matter because drugs often cross international borders and state lines and because the United States is a signatory to international drug prohibition treaties. In addition, he knew that racial fear and animus had always played a central role in drug enforcement. Nixon's chief of staff, H. R. "Bob" Haldeman, infamously wrote in his diary about the way President Nixon "emphasized that you have to face the fact that the whole problem is really the blacks. The key is to devise a system that recognizes this while not appearing to."[9] Nixon's chief domestic policy advisor, John Ehrlichman, also said in an interview with Dan Baum that the War on Drugs was a political lie:

> The Nixon campaign in 1968, and the Nixon White House after that, had two enemies: the antiwar left and black people. You understand what I'm saying? ... We knew we couldn't make it illegal to be either against the war or black, but by getting the public to associate the hippies with marijuana and blacks with heroin, and then criminalizing both heavily, we could disrupt those communities. We could arrest their leaders, raid their homes, break up their meetings, and vilify them night after night on the evening news. Did we know we were lying about the drugs? Of course we did.[10]

Health officials in the Nixon administration had favored a decriminalization approach and the use of methadone and other harm-reduction strategies, until Nixon overruled them with his politically motivated expansion of intolerance, prohibition, and criminalization.

Ronald Reagan expanded Nixon's framework ideologically and practically. His wife Nancy led the ideological charge with her "Just Say No" campaign, which applied the naive idea that people just needed a helpful reminder to summon the willpower to resist drugs. This head-in-the-sand approach to the problem was suitably ridiculed. Its effects, however, were more substantial. The Reagan ideology was that drugs were a problem of poor willpower and the absence of suitable role models and parental supervision, undermining calls for treatment and decriminalization. President Reagan oversaw congressional actions that dramatically expanded the federal government's role in local crime control and increased the number and seriousness of drug offenses at the federal and state levels. He expanded the role of the military in drug interdiction efforts, as well as those of the DEA and other federal law enforcement agencies.[11]

Many people tend to end the story of the emergence of the War on Drugs there, but in fact Bill Clinton played a major role in expanding the drug war. His crime bills increased the number of death penalty offenses for drug trafficking, created three-strikes provisions, dramatically expanded funding for the DEA, and allocated $8 billion to construct federal and state prisons. He also set aside more than $8 billion to hire police. Drug incarcerations didn't really start to spike until 1992, and almost all of that increase was for possession rather than distributing or manufacturing drugs.[12]

Today, half of all federal prisoners are incarcerated for drug crimes, as are about a third of all state prisoners. We now spend upwards of $50 billion a year fighting the War on Drugs.[13] In addition, the drug war has transformed policing:

the explosion in SWAT teams and other militarized forms of policing, asset forfeiture abuse, racial profiling and racist enforcement patterns, expanded powers to search people's homes, persons, and automobiles without warrants, the criminalization of young people of color, police corruption, and the development of a warrior mindset among police. While some of these changes are part of larger trends, they have been accelerated, reinforced, and exacerbated by the drug war.

While most scholars point to the drug war's erosion of the Fourth Amendment's protections against unreasonable searches and seizures, journalist Radley Balko discusses the role of the Third Amendment, which prohibits the quartering of troops in people's homes.[14] That amendment symbolizes the limits of the powers of the state to encroach into the privacy of people's homes. Balko describes case after case where SWAT teams have used "no-knock" warrants to stage large-scale armed invasions of people's homes on flimsy evidence, in search of mostly low-level drug dealers and users. These raids have killed suspects, police, and totally innocent people mistakenly targeted by police. Raids have been conducted based on erroneous information from confidential informants, who are motivated by cash payouts from police. In addition, Balko shows how SWAT teams physically and mentally abuse people, destroy their property, and kill their pets. SWAT teams and similar paramilitary units are also used in large-scale drug sweeps of neighborhoods and housing projects and even random patrols of "high-crime" neighborhoods.

One of the ways these teams have been financed in recent years is through asset forfeiture laws, which typically allow police forces to keep assets they seize in drug raids and investigations.[15] This gives departments a strong financial incentive to pursue the drug war aggressively and allows for the almost completely unchecked and unregulated expansion of paramilitary units. These laws are also pernicious because of the huge potential for abuse. Asset forfeiture laws allow for civil proceedings as opposed to criminal ones, which means the burden of proof is much lower and the legal action is against the property in question, not the individual. In most cases there is a clear presumption of guilt. There is also a problem of disproportionality: even small quantities of drugs for personal use can lead to the loss of a car or home.

Many police forces have become so entranced by this easy money that they undertake a wide array of drug "fishing expeditions" in hopes of finding valuables to seize. There have been numerous cases of traffic stops in which people are searched and the presence of cash above a few hundred dollars is by itself taken as evidence of drug involvement—leading to the cash being confiscated on the spot, even if no drugs are found and no criminal charges brought against the owner of the money. The owner's only recourse is to prove in court that the money was not drug-related, a Kafkaesque perversion of justice.

Not only has money been criminalized, so has anything that could be perceived as drug-related, opening the door to corruption and racial injustice. Broad laws against "paraphernalia" target pipes, scales, and other materials that have other uses but *could* be used for drug distribution or consumption. In Philadelphia there is a law prohibiting retailers from selling small plastic baggies if there is reason to believe they might be used for drug distribution. Narcotics officers then have a pretext to raid corner markets in communities of color.[16] The mostly minority store owners were often arrested and in some cases had their businesses seized or were so burdened with fines that they went bankrupt. Eventually, owners came forward with videotapes showing that police conducting raids were also emptying cash registers into their own pockets and carting off loads of merchandise, some of which ended up in the hands of informants.

Corruption

It is impossible to fully catalog the abuses of authority, thefts, bribes, and drug sales committed by US police every day in the War on Drugs. The extremely profitable black market ensures that there will always be a strong incentive for dealers to bribe the police to look the other way, and for police to protect, steal from, or become drug dealers.

Most of the major police scandals of the last fifty years have had their roots in the prohibition of drugs. The Rampart Scandal in Los Angeles involved officers abusing their authority and engaging in brutality toward drug dealers in Los Angeles and eventually involved the stealing of drugs from evidence rooms and selling it on the streets. The book and movie *Prince of the City* detail the corruption of narcotics detectives in New York who traffic in drugs to get information from informants, take bribes, and steal money and drugs from dealers.[17] Similar practices were uncovered in the late 1990s by the Mollen Commission and its investigation of the "Dirty Thirty" precinct in Harlem.[18]

More recently, drug scandals have emerged in numerous police agencies, including the DEA. For example, in March 2015 alone:

- The Fresno (California) Police Department's second in command was arrested by FBI and ATF agents for dealing oxycodone, marijuana, and heroin.[19]
- In Scott County, Tennessee, a deputy sheriff was arrested for burglarizing drugs from the police evidence room.[20]
- An NYPD officer was arrested in Florida after he was caught in a drug sting attempting to buy $200,000 worth of cocaine.[21]
- A Miami-Dade police lieutenant pled guilty to aiding cocaine smugglers and planning the execution of rival dealers.[22]

- A Winston County, Alabama, deputy was sentenced to more than three years in prison for extorting a local woman into cooking methamphetamine for him to distribute.[23]
- An FBI agent who spent years working on drug enforcement pled guilty to sixty-four counts of stealing heroin from evidence bags for his own use.[24]
- A police officer from Titusville, Florida, was sentenced to ten years in prison for dealing cocaine.[25]
- The DEA released a report detailing how agents assigned to Colombia had for years been having sex parties paid for by local drug cartels.[26]

The arrest of officers is so common that the organization StoptheDrugWar.com publishes weekly reports of police arrested on drug charges.[27]

Racial Impacts

Racialized patterns of enforcement are at the core of a great deal of drug war policing. While there is clear evidence that drug use and dealing are evenly distributed across race lines, most drug enforcement happens in communities of color and poor, white rural areas.[28] When a white person is caught with drugs, they are much more likely to receive probation or get diverted into treatment than nonwhite defendants. One of the best-publicized examples of racialized enforcement is the controversy around "driving while black," which led to court battles and reform efforts in New Jersey and other states in the 1990s. Repeated complaints from black motorists that they were being stopped on state highways for no reason and pressured into consenting to searches led to complaints and eventually lawsuits from the NAACP, ACLU, and other groups, forcing a federal investigation and a consent decree in which the police promised reforms. After years of technical reforms, however, many of the same racially disproportionate outcomes persist.[29]

Drug policing is almost exclusively undertaken in poor mostly nonwhite communities. Across the country the vast majority of people in prison for drug offenses are black or brown: over 90 percent in New York State. In *Hunting for Dirtbags*, Lori Beth Way and Ryan Patten spent hundreds of hours riding with regular patrol officers in one East Coast and one West Coast city. In both cities, officers from all different parts of each city spent a significant part of their workday looking for easy drug arrests in poor minority neighborhoods, even if they weren't assigned there. The most ambitious officers were the worst offenders, since they felt they needed high arrest numbers to help them get more desirable placements in specialized units.

Most street-level drug policing is discriminatory and ineffective.[30] For example, Baltimore police must contend with major drug markets but are largely unable to make any dent in dealing or use. Instead, they have been reduced to managing the symptoms in counterproductive ways. Former Baltimore police officer Peter Moskos writes that the typical procedure is to ignore it unless there is a specific complaint. If someone is at the location of the complaint when police arrive, the officers tell them to "move along." Usually no arrest is attempted, because police know that the person standing there is a facilitator who doesn't have drugs on them. The person generally just walks around the block and then returns to business as usual. Moskos reports that in his experience, even in major concerted drug raids involving specialized units and extended investigations, no one was ever prevented from getting drugs for more than a couple of hours. A staggering 10 percent of Baltimore residents have used an illicit drug in the past year, and nearly a third of all arrests in the city are for drug crimes.[31] This realization led former Baltimore mayor Kurt

Schmoke to come out strongly against the drug war at the 1988 US Conference of Mayors. He continues to argue that we should treat drug use as a problem of health rather than criminal justice.[32] He's not alone. Across the country, law enforcement officials are calling for an end to the drug war. There's even a new organization, Law Enforcement Against Prohibition (LEAP), made up of current and former police and prosecutors who have seen firsthand the ineffectiveness and harm of the drug war.[33]

Rural policing is not exempt from this dynamic. Take the case of Tulia, Texas, a town of five thousand where a sheriff brought in a hired informant to orchestrate a series of drug raids in 1999.[34] Based solely on the word of a paid informant, the sheriff made several arrests. Almost no drugs were found, but he used the threat of long mandatory sentences to get people to incriminate others. Additional raids resulted in the arrests of forty-six people, forty of whom were black; the other six had close ties to the small local black community. Most pleaded guilty to low-level charges, despite having no drugs found on them or in their homes. Fortunately, some persisted in claiming their innocence. Their lawyers found that the hired informant had been responsible for false arrests in other jurisdictions, that the descriptions of the alleged dealers did not match those arrested, and that some defendants had clear alibis for the times when alleged drug transactions were said to have occurred. Eventually, the charges were dropped against almost all the defendants, including several who were already imprisoned. The city ended up paying out $6 million in legal settlements and the paid informant was convicted of perjury. The white sheriff who orchestrated the whole affair and the local prosecutor who won the convictions remained in office.

Right to Privacy

The Fourth Amendment was originally conceived to prevent the state from engaging in gross and indiscriminate invasions of people's homes and privacy. The insatiable drive to "find the drugs," however, has given rise to a range of judicial rulings and legislative inventions that have eroded that right. Federal courts have consistently expanded the powers of the police to randomly stop people, search their possessions, spy on their homes, tap their phones, go through their garbage, and investigate their personal finances.

In March of 2016, the *Washington Post* reported on the use of warrants based on "officer training and experience" to justify searches.[35] In most of the cases this was based on the police obtaining an address off an old arrest for drugs and then raiding the house in hopes of finding more. They found that 14 percent of all warrants served in DC had this quality and that 99 percent of them were served on African Americans. Of those, 40 percent yielded nothing; in many cases the person listed on the warrant no longer lived there. Of the others, almost all of them found only drugs for personal consumption.

A variety of "good intention" provisions have undermined the exclusionary rule, giving police a great deal of latitude. The fact that most of these home invasions produce only small amounts of drugs, and in many cases none, seems of small concern to a judiciary obsessed with expanding police power. This is the ideological victory of the drug warriors, who have succeeded in their effort to portray drug dealers as the root of all evil. No penalty is too harsh and no method too extreme if it means getting another dealer off the streets.

In one tragic example, an NYPD officer killed Bronx teenager Ramarley Graham in his home because he was suspected of marijuana possession. The police wanted to question Ramarley and when he fled, officers pursued him into his home by battering down the door. Once inside, an officer fired on him while he was attempting to flush marijuana down his toilet. The officer had no warrant and no objective reason to suspect that Graham was dangerous. But the War on Drugs has normalized such actions to the degree that neither local nor federal prosecutors brought charges against the officer.[36] Clearly, Graham's life and his right to be free from police intrusion into his home *did not matter*.

Michelle Alexander argues in *The New Jim Crow* that the War on Drugs, more than any other single development, has led to the mass criminalization and incarceration of young people of color.[37] While men have borne the greatest burden of this, black women are the fastest-growing segment of the prison population, and this is tied primarily to drug enforcement. Furthermore, most people caught up in the drug war are low-level offenders arrested for possession in street-level "buy-and-bust" operations (pursuant to a search of sometimes questionable legality), and are targeted as part of a growing system of paid informants, or are implicated by others facing draconian mandatory minimum sentences.[38] Our prisons are not filled with drug kingpins, nor are they filled with saints. Mostly they are filled with people enmeshed in a massive black market that provides jobs and incomes for millions who have little access to the formal economy.

Because it is an underground market, it is at times violent. Most drug-related crime is not about people on drugs committing crimes because of their altered state of mind. Instead, it takes two primary forms: property crime to fund drug habits, and business disputes. In an illegal market, you can't go to court: if someone cheats you, your options are to accept the loss or resort to violence. In addition, the large amounts of cash on hand make drug buyers and dealers inviting targets for thieves, who know that their victims will rarely complain to the police.

Health Effects

The drug warriors always justify their expanding power with tales of the lives lost to drugs, but prohibition actually undermines health outcomes for drug users. Since drugs are illegal, there can be no regulation of their purity or potency. Dangerous additives and unpredictable dosages lead to overdoses, infections, abscesses, and poisonings. Heroin overdoses now claim the lives of more than ten thousand people a year, a 500 percent increase since 2001.[39] When heroin of consistent quality is available by prescription, as was the case in much of the United States in the late 1910s and early 1920s and in the United Kingdom up until the 1960s, overdoses fell to almost zero. Doctors saw opioid addiction as a medical problem that responded best to medical treatment, which typically led to a reduction in use and the elimination of infections and overdoses. It was only zealous drug war politics that led to the rejection of this approach.

Criminalization makes it hard for drug users to complain about adulterated products or even share information with other users and interferes with access to treatment. Most heavy drug users who are arrested receive no real drug treatment and are expected to go clean on their own while incarcerated, leading to adverse health effects and even death. Prohibition also forces people to share needles and other drug paraphernalia; the second most prevalent method of HIV transmission in the US today is injection drug users sharing needles. (The situation is even worse in Russia, where overdoses and HIV infection rates have skyrocketed thanks to punitive drug policies.[40]) This is also a major cause of hepatitis C transmission. While a few needle-exchange programs have found support, police typically look on them with disdain and frequently target participants for surveillance and harassment. Most states, however, continue to restrict access to clean needles in the misguided belief that this will somehow reduce drug use.

International Effects

The US government typically supports the draconion drug policies of other countries. It is the driving player in maintaining international treaties that criminalize drugs and prevent countries from even experimenting with legalization regimes.[41] The most dramatic effects of this policy can be seen in Mexico, where drug cartels are fighting a brutal battle for control of the lucrative domestic and North American drug markets.[42] Major cities like Tijuana and Ciudad Juárez have been turned into gruesome battlefields, with daily body counts feeding into a national total of more than seventy thousand deaths since Mexican president Felipe Calderon launched his own drug war in 2006. Police across the country are now in the direct employ of the cartels, transporting drugs, weapons, and cash. Journalists, politicians, or residents who speak out against the violence and corruption are routinely killed and their mutilated bodies left in public places as a warning to others.

The Hollywood film *Sicario* lays out a frightening scenario in which the CIA takes an active role in managing the players in Mexican drug cartels to reduce violence along the border, through targeted executions and collusion with different factions. While this is a fictional account, the CIA has a long history of involvement with drug dealing to advance other interests, such as the Vietnam War counterinsurgency, the dirty wars of Central America in the 1980s, and the "weapons for hostages" Iran-Contra deal. Historian Alfred McCoy details this sordid history in his book *The Politics of Heroin: CIA Complicity in the Global Drug Trade.*[43]

The US policy of deporting anyone arrested on drug charges has also had a destabilizing effect on several Central American countries. So many young people tied to gangs and drugs in the US have been deported to places like Guatemala and Honduras that these countries have become centers in the international drug trade and are experiencing explosive growth in their own violent drug gangs. The consequent violence has given rise to right-wing politicians promising a range of get-tough *mano dura* strategies, as documented in Oscar Martinez's book *A History of Violence: Living and Dying in Central America.*[44] This explosion of violence and repression has served to escalate migration to the US, most tragically by unescorted minors fleeing the violence of home only to be preyed upon by thieves, human smugglers, and ultimately the US immigration enforcement system.

Reforms

There is a growing awareness that we cannot incarcerate our way out of the problems associated with drug use. A 2015 report from the Pew Charitable Trusts found that the harsh drug laws of the 1980s and 1990s did nothing to reduce drug use rates or even recidivism.[45] As a result, there have been an increasing number of experiments with alternatives to conventional strategies of punishment and incarceration. Some have involved reducing the penalties through changes in laws and enforcement practices. Others have embraced alternative sentencing regimes that attempt to divert people into various treatment approaches. Unfortunately, what most of these approaches share is a reliance on police as gatekeepers. Drug courts, diversion programs, and various forms of decriminalization all place police in a central role that usually involves deciding who gets jail and who gets treatment, while maintaining a fundamentally punitive and moralizing approach to drugs.

Drug Courts

At their best, drug courts take a therapeutic approach, relying on the threat of punishment to drive people into treatment.

Typically, a defendant is asked to plead guilty to an offense and then, instead of being incarcerated, is given a recovery plan that the court oversees. The court makes direct referrals to specific treatment programs and then metes out punishments for failure to comply with the treatment regime. This can involve short-term "shock incarcerations" of a week or more to get people to "take their treatment seriously," or longer sentences based on the original charges. Some people spend years cycling between stints in jail and in treatment.

Outcomes for those who successfully complete a program from the court are somewhat better in terms of recidivism and relapses than for those in the regular criminal justice system, leading the Center for Court Innovation and other boosters to declare them an evidence-based success story.[46] The real picture, however, is more complicated and less positive. When we look at the overall population of people initially assigned to drug courts—a more accurate grouping—the results are not good. As many as 70 percent of people assigned to these courts do not in fact complete their programs. And for that 70 percent, the outcomes are actually much worse than for those in the regular criminal justice system because they have higher relapse and incarceration rates.[47] In one study of New York Drug Courts 64 percent of those who failed to complete the program were rearrested within 3 years.[48]

It also turns out that the courts don't save taxpayers any money. They are much more expensive to operate than other courts, and while a few people are successfully diverted, many more end up spending more time in jail.[49] There is also a net-widening effect: drug courts meld together punitive and therapeutic approaches in very counterproductive ways that extend rather than reduce the role of the criminal justice system in the lives of drug users, creating what sociologist Rebecca Tiger calls an "outpatient incarceration" effect.[50]

A medical approach to heroin, as discussed above, allows for some normality. People on these treatments can go back to work, live with their families, and generally experience a gradual reduction in usage. It also keeps them off the streets and reduces the need for theft, removing them entirely from the criminal justice system. Instead, most judges order immediate abstinence, often in jails, with no medical treatment for the intense symptoms of withdrawal.[51] This is usually followed up with an outpatient treatment program. In many cases, the person immediately returns to the streets and begins using again. This dangerous cycle increases the likelihood of overdosing and, in a few cases, has resulted in deaths that might have been avoided.[52] This may also be a violation of the Americans with Disabilities Act, which specifically lists addiction as a disability; courts should not be denying people access to medically proven treatments for their conditions.

The treatment programs themselves are also problematic. Some are little more than court-mandated twelve-step programs, suffused with an ethos of moral reform and punishment in which people are berated, harassed, and threatened for violating any of a host of minor rules.[53] Often this is driven by a mindset that people will only get off drugs if they "hit bottom," are confronted with their failures, and then experience a moral reawakening. Medically driven strategies with track records of success are derided as enabling addiction. The research, however, shows that coerced treatment, humiliation, and belittlement are incredibly counterproductive in ending addiction.

Even when these courts do offer useful services, access to them is driven by engagement with police: to access court-ordered services one first has to be arrested. Second, as noted above, the resources that the courts rely on are not new ones; people who end up in court are merely moved to the front of the line, displacing others. In New Jersey, there is a severe shortage of drug treatment beds and, increasingly, the only way to access one is by being arrested and sent to a drug court. According to state senator Joseph Vitale (no relation to the author), "if you are arrested you can get drug court, you can get into the system. If you don't commit a crime, in many cases, you can't get access to inpatient care."[54] Finally, these courts only serve people with "drug problems," which means they exclude the large number of people arrested on drug charges who are not themselves drug users. They go straight to prison—one reason why drug courts have had little impact on overall imprisonment rates.

In the end, these courts have few resources to help addicts. The Drug Policy Alliance[55] and the Justice Policy Institute[56] have called for us to rethink our reliance on these courts to deal with drug problems, arguing instead that the criminal-justice model should be replaced with a robust public-health and harm-reduction response.

Decriminalization

Many states and localities have tried to reduce the burden of drug enforcement by decriminalizing one or more drugs.[57] In the 1970s, eleven states eliminated criminal penalties for personal marijuana possession. The hope was that this would prevent police from getting involved in a mostly innocuous activity. In New York, the law was changed in 1977 to make marijuana possession a "violation," which is similar to a traffic ticket. There may be a fine and court appearance, but no arrest. For many years this policy was effective in dramatically reducing the number of low-level marijuana arrests. However, the law left public use or display of marijuana as a crime and this proved to be a crucial weakness by the 1990s. As New York embraced broken-windows policing, the NYPD reprioritized marijuana arrests as part of a strategy of asserting strict control over the public lives of young people of color. In conjunction with the widespread use of "stop, question, and frisk" practices, the police were stopping a growing number of young people and in many cases asking them to "empty their pockets." While this is not technically a lawful order, police used various forms of coercion to pressure people to comply. If the person produced marijuana and showed it to the officer, they were arrested for public display of the drug, a misdemeanor. As a result, marijuana possession arrests jumped from almost nothing to fifty thousand a year, resulting in the incarceration of hundreds of thousands of people.[58]

Fortunately, after years of public pressure, the NYPD has mostly stopped this practice. However, they still issue "summonses," which require an appearance in court and often a fine. This means many people have to miss work or school and pay fines they can often ill afford. Too often, people fail to appear and a warrant is issued for their arrest, meaning the prospect of incarceration. Decriminalization programs that leave open the role of police in making discretionary decisions or that otherwise tie people up with the criminal justice system still create a heavy burden on individuals and communities, primarily of color.

More extensive and systematic decriminalization programs have shown more positive results. In 2001, Portugal decriminalized all drugs and dramatically shifted its enforcement practices to a harm-reduction model. The results have been mostly very favorable. Most drug use is now treated as a health problem. Doctors can prescribe drugs, personal possession is no longer a crime, and police are no longer involved in trying to stop low-level dealing. Needle exchange is available and opioid addicts are offered replacement drugs such as methadone. Studies have found significant reductions in heroin addiction, overdoses, and disease transmission.[59] In 1999, Portugal had the highest rate of HIV infection among injecting drug users in the European Union; by 2009, the number of newly diagnosed HIV cases among drug users had decreased substantially. There is some indication of a minor increase in lifetime usage rates, though this may be due to more truthfulness in reporting as social and legal stigmas decline. In addition, the problems of excessive use of incarceration, police corruption, and harassment of addicts has declined. What remains, though, is the illegal importation of drugs, which is tied to international organized crime. Police continue to pursue interdiction efforts, seizing large quantities of drugs, which keeps the door to police corruption open.

Alternatives

The use of police to wage a war on drugs has been a total nightmare. Not only have they failed to reduce drug use and the harm it produces, they have actually worsened those harms and destroyed the lives of millions of Americans through pointless criminalization. Ultimately, we must create robust public health programs and economic development strategies to reduce demand and help people manage their drug problems in ways that reduce harm—while keeping in mind that most drug users are not addicts. We also need to look at the economic dynamics that drive the black market and the economic and social misery that drive the most harmful patterns of drug use. Harm-reduction, public-health, and legalization strategies, combined with robust economic development of poor communities could dramatically reduce the negative impact of drugs on society without relying on police, courts, and prisons.

Harm Reduction

One of the best-known harm-reduction strategies is needle exchanges. These programs allow IV drug users to bring in used needles and exchange them for clean ones. This has proven to be an incredibly successful strategy in reducing the transmission of disease. When needles are scarce, people share them, which increases the risk of transmission of HIV, hepatitis C, and other serious infections. Arguments that needle exchanges enable users have no factual basis. People with heroin addictions are not going to quit overnight because they can't get needles, nor is the availability of needles going to encourage a non-user to start using drugs. These are spurious arguments driven by a moral absolutism that is completely divorced from reality.

Another harm-reduction strategy is supervised injection. Supervised injection facilities give addicts a place to inject drugs where medical personnel are on staff who can administer lifesaving treatments such as Naloxone quickly if needed. These facilities can also help people access treatment for existing medical conditions as well as addiction, and reduce the presence of discarded needles in public places. Such centers exist in several European countries and Canada and are being explored in several parts of the United States.[60]

Drug treatment on demand is another strategy. Right now, most drug users face long waits for medically supervised inpatient drug treatment. They are expected to deal with their addictions alone for weeks, months, or years after requesting help. Too often users are no longer interested in treatment when it becomes available, or die in the meantime. Making treatment available when people are ready for it would reduce the burden of addiction on families and communities.

Finally, we should look to public education and public health messaging. Unfortunately, the bulk of public education efforts occur within a punitive and moralizing framework. The most popular program, DARE, is run by police and has never been shown to have any positive effect in youth drug-use rates. Newer programs are often for profit and rely heavily on drug-testing regimes in which they or others have a financial stake. Public-health messaging must acknowledge the obvious and pervasive appeal that drugs have for young people and explain the real risks. Telling kids to "just say no" doesn't work. Many will try and even regularly use drugs; we should make that use as safe and temporary as possible. Driving them into the shadows encourages riskier behavior, isolates them from help, and entangles them in a criminal justice system that will only terrorize, stigmatize, and demonize them.

Legalization

Legalization and regulation can take several forms; the benefits include eliminating dangerous black markets, providing purer and safer drugs to those who use them, and collecting taxes that can be used to strengthen communities and individuals to reduce the demand for drugs and black-market employment.

The US has begun experimenting with the legalization of marijuana and, so far, the results look promising. Colorado has implemented its system without incurring a breakdown in civilization. Crime has not taken hold and usage rates seem largely unchanged. Local police in Denver and other cities report strong support for the results so far. Even minor upticks in crime or usage would be a small price for ending prohibition. Most likely, they would reflect a sorting-out period rather than a long-term trajectory. It's also worth noting that the benefits of marijuana legalization may in fact be much less than those of legalizing other drugs, since marijuana usage poses so few health hazards.

There are many potential methods for legalization. One is to follow the example of Colorado, in which possession for personal use and even low-level sharing are legal and sales are regulated and taxed. This could be done for all drugs, with controls on purity and restrictions on sales to minors. A less regulated form or legalization might be one in which people can buy drugs on an open and unregulated market or go to a doctor and request a prescription for maintenance doses, which would be especially important for opioid users. Any system, however, would have to accommodate recreational use that comes with medical risks. Yes, people would be able to go and buy cocaine or ecstasy on a Friday night before going to a party or a club. And yes, some of them may suffer negative consequences for that, just as they currently do from consuming alcohol and tobacco. The reality is that the system we have in place now does nothing positive about these harms.

People will be concerned about public intoxication, disorderly behavior, and driving under the influence of drugs. Those can be real harms and police have tools to sanction such behavior. But, as Michael Reznicek points out, legalization opens the door to the possibility of reasserting informal social controls on problem behavior.[61] By bringing drug use out of the shadows, families, friends, and others will be in a stronger position to set limits on the behavior of users. Social norms are always more powerful and effective than formal, punitive ones. Look at the alcohol abuse rates and problem behavior in places like Italy and France. Public drinking there is widespread and almost completely unregulated, even for minors, but public intoxication and alcoholism are mostly absent.

Economic Development

Many people involved in the drug industry don't really have a drug problem; they have a job problem. Many others have drug problems that directly stem from the economic conditions they struggle with. There is no way to reduce the widespread use of drugs without dealing with profound economic inequality and a growing sense of hopelessness.

African American and Latino neighborhoods have suffered devastating declines in employment levels and overall economic wellbeing. Private-sector employment has largely dried up and what remains is low-paying and contingent, with little chance for advancement. At the same time, austerity has undermined the public-sector employment and social programs that constitute the few remaining avenues for stability in these communities. Buying power for the jobs that remain is declining as employee contracts fail to keep pace with inflation.

Rural white areas are also under considerable stress. Here, too, living standards are headed straight down as manufacturing jobs are mechanized or move overseas and wages and social programs stagnate or decline. For too long, the only economic assistance many in these areas could hope for was the opening of a new prison. Even when private-sector employment becomes available, low, nonunion wages have become typical, combined with dangerous and demeaning working conditions. These conditions have fueled the rise of methamphetamine use and dealing. Researchers like William Garriott have shown that use and dealing are concentrated among the under- and unemployed and those working in dirty, dangerous, and repetitious jobs with low pay and poor working conditions.[62] Strict enforcement, forced treatment, and police-driven public education campaigns have been a total failure, because people's underlying economic circumstances remain unaddressed. Until we do something about entrenched rural poverty, this trend will continue. Unemployment and bleak prospects drive people into black markets, which become the employers of last resort.

We need to invest in developing the human capital of people in these areas and find meaningful employment in developing infrastructure and improving the environment. We also need to take a tough look at how multinational agribusinesses have transformed the rural landscape in ways that degrade the quality of the food we eat, the livelihoods of rural people, and the natural environment.

Groups like Black Youth Project 100 in Chicago are working to develop economic strategies to improve the economic wellbeing of poor communities of color, so that they are not dependent on black markets. They demand increased public-sector hiring, a livable minimum wage, and real social supports, especially for children and families. The issue of reparations must also figure into this conversation. As Ta-Nehisi Coates points out, the history of American wealth generation is a history of the exploitation of black people—from slavery to the present.[63] That past cannot be ignored in any effort to come to terms with inequality. Some of the resources for overcoming that legacy could come from the billions we now spend on fighting the drug war and the taxes we could collect from legalized drugs.

8
Gang Suppression

Malcolm Klein, in his book *Gang Cop,* tells the story of "Officer Paco Domingo," a composite of dozens of gang officers. Officer Paco sees the gangs on his beat as a source of serious criminality and attempts to control them through aggressive and punitive interactions that often skirt the law. In a typical interaction, he confronts a group of teenagers hanging out on the corner and searches them without any reasonable suspicion or probable cause. He interrogates them about what they're doing there, then orders them to disperse. He might handcuff them, make them lie on the ground, and order them not to look at him. His goal here is not law enforcement; it's control and humiliation. Gang cops like Officer Paco believe that intimidation is what dissuades young people from gang activity. The dynamic between street gangs and the police looks a lot like a war between competing gangs, with each side using constantly increasing terror to try to show who is toughest.

After a relative lull in the 1970s, gangs have become larger, more numerous, and widely distributed across the United States. While Los Angeles and Chicago remain outliers in the intensity and extent of gang activity, other cities are gaining ground, giving rise to a wide variety of police-centered suppression strategies at the local, state, and national level. Hundreds of cities and many states now have dedicated gang units that concentrate on intelligence gathering and intensive enforcement. Many states have also added enhanced legal penalties that play a role in mass incarceration. Despite these efforts, gangs remain alive and well, continually renewing their membership. While the bulk of crimes committed by active gang members involve low-level drug dealing and property crime, violence plays an important role in the cohesion of gang identities, and protecting territory from rivals is at the center of much of this destructive behavior.

Police gang units emerged as a national trend in the 1980s. By 1999, half of all police agencies with over 100 officers had such units. By 2003 there were estimated to be 360 such units, the vast majority of which had been in place for less than ten years.[1] At the national level, the FBI has established 160 Violent Gang Safe Streets Task Forces staffed by nearly a thousand federal law enforcement personnel.[2]

Gang units tend to take on two main functions: intelligence gathering and street suppression. A few units maintain a largely intelligence-gathering function, channeling information about gang activity to enforcement units in patrol, narcotics, and other divisions. Most, however, are directly involved in suppression. Tactics include both long- and short-term investigations and random patrols. They harass gang members constantly on the street and in their homes and target them for frequent arrest.

These gang units tend to become isolated and insular. Their specialized function and intelligence-gathering aspect lend them an air of secrecy and expertise that they cultivate to reduce outside supervision or accountability. In addition, a strong group loyalty often emerges, similar to that seen in SWAT teams, in which experience, training, and the specialized nature of the work contributes to an "us against the world" attitude. Officers often come to believe that they are the only ones who understand the nature of the problem and the need for heavy-handed tactics to deal with young people who openly defy their authority. They see police executives who embrace community policing and preventative measures as empty suits handing over neighborhoods to the gangbangers and deride non-law-enforcement efforts as empty-headed coddling of hardened criminals.[3] In addition, these units often come to play a role in perpetuating the politics of gang suppression. As part of an effort to maintain funding, they spend a lot of their time speaking to community groups about the threat gangs pose and the need for more suppression efforts. This tends to be one-way communication; these units rarely take input from communities about where and how to carry out their activities. Instead, it is usually part of a self-serving effort to win more resources and keep up the moral panic about youth violence and gangs, as well as to channel all related concerns into continued aggressive policing.

There are a lot of misunderstandings about the nature of gangs, which have come to play a role in the way that police handle them. Strategies that seek to "eradicate" gangs often fail to consider exactly who the targets for such action are, or the effect on those targeted and on the community. Officials often use language that dehumanizes gang members, such as one LA sheriff's captain who said, "Everyone says: 'What are we going to do about the gang problem?' It's the same thing you do about cockroaches and insects; you get someone in there to do whatever they can do to get rid of those creatures."[4] This kind of language opens the door to civil and human rights abuses and is unlikely to result in long-term reductions in gang activity.

This is exactly what has happened in Los Angeles. For years, the LAPD has embraced a series of suppression measures designed to root out gangs. In the 1970s, the department developed specialized antigang units first known as TRASH (Total Resources Against Street Hoodlums) and later sanitized into CRASH (Community Resources Against Street Hoodlums). In 1987, after a series of horrific gang killings, Chief Daryl Gates initiated a massive crackdown called Operation Hammer in which CRASH units, with the support of other units, carried out sweeps of communities with gangs, with little regard for legal standards or whether those arrested had anything to do with gangs or crime. In one weekend in April 1988, a thousand officers made almost 1,500 arrests, only 103 of which resulted in charges. Officers raided an entire low-income housing development that they erroneously believed was an epicenter for gang-related drug dealing. When no actual gangs or drugs could be found, officers ripped open walls, destroyed furniture and personal belongings, and spray-painted threatening messages like "LAPD Rules" and "Rollin' 30s Die" on the walls. Dozens were arrested, humiliated, and had their property destroyed, but no one was ever convicted of a crime.

By 1990, fifty thousand people had been arrested in such sweeps. Current LAPD chief Charlie Beck points out that these sweeps "undermined the moral authority of the police."[5] Gang members may have been a source of problems in these communities, but they were still a part of them. They had mothers, cousins, uncles, and friends who viewed the sweeps as the arbitrary, abusive, and disproportionate actions of an occupying army. Many became more sympathetic toward gangs and the young people facing the brunt of this enforcement activity. All the while, crime rates continued to go up—as did excessive-force lawsuits against the police. By the late 1990s, CRASH units had become insular, brutal, and unaccountable. The Rampart Scandal of 1999 unveiled a pattern of corruption and criminality. Dozens of officers were accused of false arrests, unlawful shootings, beatings, and even robbery and drug dealing. Joe Domanick, in his expose of the post–Rodney King LAPD, details the intensity of this corruption and the utter lack of accountability. Excessive force was routine; so were coverups. Shootings and other incidents were only ever investigated by supervisors within CRASH, who often led the effort to make events appear justified on paper. Accounts and paperwork were routinely fabricated in the name of sticking it to the gangbangers. It was within this atmosphere that Rafael Pérez and others began stealing drugs from the Rampart Division evidence room and reselling them on the streets. When investigators cornered Pérez, he implicated dozens of others in illegal killings, coverups, robberies, and drug dealing. Hundreds of prior convictions had to be overturned; many officers were disciplined or forced to retire; some were incarcerated; millions in damages were paid out.[6]

While police have some useful firsthand knowledge, they too are subject to pressure by politicians and the public, whose views are shaped by sensationalist media coverage as well as movies and television. Communities directly affected also have some immediate knowledge, but they too are remarkably unclear about the exact role of gangs versus unaffiliated youth and tend to have their views skewed by extreme events, which often then become associated with any group of young people hanging out together in public spaces. A group of middle-school kids who hang out together and paint graffiti may be perceived as dangerous, even if they rarely go beyond vandalism and perhaps shoplifting supplies. While more organized gangs often have certain symbols or styles of clothing, these may be difficult for many to distinguish. A lot of property and violent crime are committed by young people, and much of it happens in poor communities, especially black and Latino ones; wealthier kids are generally less likely to get caught and more likely to be dealt with informally or leniently if apprehended.[7]

The police tend to see most youth criminality in gang neighborhoods as gang-related. They also tend to view gangs as highly organized, directed by central leadership, central to local drug markets, and comprised of hardened criminals.[8] This comports closely with their suppression orientation, which has been amplified by the growth of gang databases, sentencing enhancements, and injunctions.

Even in the most gang-intensive communities, only 10 to 15 percent of young people are in gangs; research consistently shows that most involvement is short-lived, lasting on average only a year. While some become intensively involved and identified with their gangs, many more have a looser connection and drift in and out depending on life circumstances. Rarely does leaving result in serious consequences. A new child or job are generally sufficient explanation for not being on the streets any longer.[9]

Suppression efforts mostly focus on established members of whom the police are aware. Police assume that these members play a central leadership role in initiating and directing illegal activity, with younger members playing a support role. They believe that getting rid of leaders will disrupt and destabilize the gang, causing it to either dissipate or at least be less violent. The reality is that for every "shot caller" or "old head" that's locked up, there are many more to take their place. The whole idea of one or two leaders directing gang activity is itself a misunderstanding of the horizontal nature of gangs, with many people playing shifting and overlapping leadership roles at different times and in different circumstances. Just as importantly, much of the violence committed by gang members is performed by younger members hoping to prove themselves, who have had no previous contact with the police and are not in gang databases or under surveillance.[10]

Another central misconception is that arrest and incarceration will break the cycle of violence and criminality. The fundamental premise is that young people will either be intimidated by the threat of arrest and incarceration or that removing them from the streets will reduce the number of young people active in gangs and other illegal activities. There is very little evidence to support these ideas. Young people seem largely immune to this deterrent effect. Juveniles rarely make such rational cost-benefit calculations. Instead, they tend to make impulsive decisions, think in very short time horizons, and believe that they will not get caught. Many report that they expect to have very short lifespans and focus on achieving respect and social acceptance on the streets rather than considering the impact of arrests and incarceration on their future. It could also be argued that, for some, despite the threat of punishment, the gang may still be the "rational" decision in circumstances where legitimate economic opportunities are scarce and there is a need for protection in one's neighborhood.

Nor do arrests incapacitate gangs. Many are intergenerational, and there are always more young people to fill the shoes of those taken away. Destabilizing existing dynamics of respect and authority can create a power vacuum that encourages more crime and violence as people jockey for prestige. There is also evidence that intensive gang enforcement breeds gang cohesion. The constant threat of police harassment becomes a central shared experience of gang life and contributes to a sense of "us against the world," in an ironic converse of the police mentality. Gangs often thrive on a sense of adventure; boasting and fraught encounters with the police become central aspects of gang identity. One way to gain respect is to stand up to police harassment in subtle ways, like flashing gang signs or giving them the eye as they drive past. This use of bravado to gain respect can only be accomplished if police are there as an oppositional force.[11]

What's more, the many young people incarcerated by this process are now burdened with a criminal record that makes them less employable. They are generally drawn into prison gang activity, which tends to be even more violent than street gangs. Finally, they have often been abused by guards and other inmates. All of this contributes to hardening a criminal identity. Since all but a few of those incarcerated come back to the community at some point, relying on this approach sets these young people and their communities up for failure.

We can see this play out in places like Oakland, California, where young people are subjected to punitive probation and parole policies, policing, and school discipline. Wherever they go they are hounded by government officials, who treat them as always-already criminals. The effect is what sociologist Victor Rios calls the "youth control complex," which undermines their life chances by driving them into economic and social failure and long-term criminality and incarceration.[12]

Many cities have doubled down by developing new tools of punishment and suppression such as multi-agency task forces, gang sentencing enhancements, and gang injunctions. The center of these innovations is California, which has extensive gang activity and has also been at the heart of mass incarceration politics and policy over the past thirty years.

San Diego's Jurisdictions United for Drug Gang Enforcement (JUDGE) targeted gang members believed to be involved in drug dealing. They intensively monitored those with a past drug arrest and arrested more than 80 percent of them in a two-year period. Ninety-seven percent of those arrested were black or Latino. Much of the enforcement focused on probation violations; almost half of those targeted spent six months or more in jail or juvenile facilities. Four years after the program ended, two-thirds of those targeted had been rearrested, usually multiple times. Evaluators of the program noted the high recidivism rate as a clear indication of failure and went so far as to say that the program may have done more harm than good, as incarceration is more likely to lead to additional offenses than drug treatment, improved educational access, and employment are.[13]

Multi-agency task forces, in which local and federal officials work together to develop major cases against gangs, have seen similarly dismal results. In drug cases this involves low-level buy-and-bust operations to develop informants, who then provide information on drug dealers. These dealers are then targeted and whoever is caught is asked to provide evidence against others in the gang. Strong loyalties mean that often people refuse to cooperate or name others outside their group. Rarely do these investigations move higher up the drug distribution chain; generally they have no effect on the availability of drugs or the cohesiveness and impact of local gangs. Susan Phillips points out that incarcerating earners further destabilizes families and communities.[14]

Nevada and California have developed sentencing enhancements that add many additional years to sentences based on loose definitions of gang membership. Anyone the police want to assert is affiliated with a gang can find an extra decade added to their sentence. Neither state has seen a reduction in gang activity; the enhancements have further overpopulated state prisons without providing meaningful relief to youth or their communities.

Gang databases are another problematic area of intervention. California has a statewide database populated with the names of hundreds of thousands of young people, the vast majority of whom are black or Latino. Officers can enter names at will, based on associations, clothing, or just a hunch. There are very few ways of getting your name removed from the list; many people do not even know whether or not they are on it. In some neighborhoods, inclusion on the list is almost the norm for young men. Police and courts use the list to give people enhanced sentences, target them for parole violations, or even target entire neighborhoods for expanded and intensified policing. The Youth Justice Coalition in Los Angeles has documented cases where information in the database has been shared with employers and landlords, despite legal requirements that the database not be publicly accessible.[15]

These databases have made possible another new tool: the gang injunction. These are civil injunctions brought by local authorities to try to break up gang-related activities on a broad scale. Rather than targeting individuals for criminal prosecution, they criminalize membership in—or even association with—gangs. San Jose's injunction prohibits "standing, sitting, walking, driving, gathering, or appearing anywhere in public view" with someone suspected of being a gang member. Some injunctions name specific individuals; others are directed at a gang and anyone believed by police to be associated with that gang is covered, even without prior notification. Those that violate the injunction are subject to criminal prosecution for contempt of court, which is a misdemeanor punishable by up to six months in jail. By 2011, the city of Los Angeles had brought forty-four injunctions targeting seventy-two gangs. People can be penalized for associating with family members and lifelong friends—sometimes without realizing it. People who have long since left gang life but remain in a database may find themselves or those they associate with criminalized for walking down the street together. Ana Muñiz argues that one of the primary functions of these injunctions is maintaining racial boundaries by tightly constraining the behaviors and movements of black and brown youth.[16]

Little systematic evaluation of these injunctions has been done, and the studies that exist are far from conclusive. However, most show either no effect or a very short-lived one in which, after a year or two, crime rates return to their previous levels. In one study, the ACLU found that crime activity near an injunction in Los Angeles was merely dispersed and may actually have increased.[17] A gang injunction targeting two neighborhoods in Oakland was withdrawn after residents and criminal justice reform groups such as Critical Resistance showed that it did not make these neighborhoods any safer. Even local police officials admitted that the injunction had been ineffective and undermined police-community relations more broadly.

Social-media-based gang-suppression efforts take guilt by association to a new level. The most notorious is Operation Crew Cut in New York City. In 2012, the NYPD doubled the size of its gang unit to 300 officers and began creating fake social media profiles and using them to monitor the activities of people as young as twelve who are suspected of involvement in crime. They attempt to trick these young people into accepting friend requests, often by creating fake profiles using photos of attractive young women, to gain access to secure information. The investigators then use this access to track who is friends with whom in order to draw up extensive lists of "known associates." These associates then get designated as members of a particular gang or crew. The police can then use conspiracy laws and other measures to round up large numbers of young people under the banner of gang suppression without concrete evidence of criminal behavior, just a social media connection to someone suspected of a violent crime.

This is exactly the wrong direction. Law professor Babe Howell argues that New York City's expanded emphasis on gang suppression is being driven by the legal and political pushback against "stop-and-frisk" policing. She says that when police lost the ability to engage young people of color through street stops, they developed new but similarly invasive gang policing techniques under a new name. In both cases, black and brown youth are singled out for police harassment without adequate legal justification because they represent a "dangerous class" of major concern to police.[18]

Reforms

Efforts to take a more nuanced approach to gang and youth violence attempt to closely target youth believed to be at high risk of crime and use social support services to try to steer them off the streets. The two best-known models have been the Spergel Model and "focused deterrence." Irving Spergel at the University of Chicago developed a comprehensive model for gang intervention that has received extensive support from the Office of Juvenile Justice and Delinquency Prevention.[19] The model calls for a robust mix of suppression strategies and social services. At its best, it involves collaboration between law enforcement, schools, social service providers, and local communities, with an aim toward developing the most appropriate tools to address local conditions. Some plans involve intensive enforcement toward young people using coordinated teams of police, parole, and prosecutions while also attempting to provide family support, job training, and socialization skills development.

"Focused" or "targeted deterrence" initiatives function in much the same way. Developed by criminologist David Kennedy and first implemented in Boston in 1996, they attempt to stop gun violence through intensive and targeted enforcement combined with support services and appeals from community stakeholders to stop the violence. Ideally, this model begins with a community mobilization effort in partnership with local police. The goal is to send a unified message to young people that gun violence will no longer be tolerated. If it occurs, they use every resource at their disposal to apprehend the assailant and to disrupt the street life of young people involved in crime, across the board (this is called "pulling levers"). The hope is that young people will choose to avoid violence, so that they can concentrate on socializing and low-level criminality free of constant police harassment. This is based on evidence that a great deal of shooting was not drug-related but involved tit-for-tat revenge shootings by warring factions. The key is to break that cycle. To achieve this, police develop "hot lists" of young people they believe are more likely to engage in violent crime, based on a host of sometimes secret factors like prior arrests, involvement in foster care, and even school performance. The young people are called into meetings with local police and community leaders and threatened with intensive surveillance and enforcement if the gun violence doesn't stop. These "call ins" are made possible in part because many of these young people are on probation or parole for past offenses. There is usually an effort to develop some targeted social services to offer education and employment opportunities.[20] In New York under the banner of Operation Ceasefire, if violence does occur after a call-in, the entire population of young people is targeted for aggressive prosecution on any arrest, even if they were not part of the call-in and had no knowledge of the initiative.

These models are very similar and rely primarily on intensive punitive enforcement efforts. While focused deterrence is more concerned with gun violence, both models rely heavily on traditional gang suppression efforts of investigations, arrests, and intensified prosecutions. The social services offered tend to be very thin, involving some counseling and recreational opportunities but rarely access to actual jobs or advanced educational placement. Life skills and socialization classes do nothing to create real opportunities for people, instead reinforcing an ethos of "personal responsibility" that often ends up blaming the victims for their unemployment and educational failure in communities that are poor, underserviced, segregated, and dangerous.

Research on these programs does show some meaningful declines in crime that can even last for years. Overall, though, the results are thin. Most reductions are small, occur in only a few crime categories, and don't last very long. They also continue to reinforce a punitive mindset regarding how to deal with young people in high-crime, high-poverty communities, most of whom are not white. It is certainly true that violent crime is heavily concentrated among a fairly small population of young people in specific neighborhoods. It makes more sense to target them than to indiscriminately stop and frisk pedestrians or to arrest hundreds of thousands of young people who have either done nothing wrong or are engaged in only minor misbehavior. Despite the claims of the broken-windows theory, there really isn't a strong connection between the two groups.

The targeting is problematic, because police fail to understand the often amorphous nature of gang membership and the fact that one prior offense doesn't necessarily mean a strong long-term commitment to crime. This is also a profound invasion of privacy: people are subjected to intensive police surveillance based on a perceived risk factor rather than any specific criminal or even suspicious behavior. This "predictive policing" is just another form of profiling of young men of color. Most young people who engage in serious crime are already living in harsh and dangerous circumstances. They are fearful of other youth, abusive family members, and the prospect of a future of joblessness and poverty. They don't need more threats and punishment in their lives. They need stability, positive guidance, and real pathways out of poverty. This requires a long-term commitment to their wellbeing, not a telephone referral and home visits by the same people who arrest and harass them and their friends on the streets. Bill Bratton, in his first stint as NYPD commissioner, pointed out that police officers are not social workers: they're not trained for it, nor prepared for it, and that's not their role. Why would they be suited for engaging these young people as mentors or life-skills trainers? They aren't.

In addition, deterrence theory rarely applies to the young people being targeted. As noted, they are driven by emotions and short-term considerations and impulsiveness, not carefully calculated long-term risk assessments. Violence among this group is often driven by fear, anger, and humiliation, not calculations of material gain.[21] Threats, intimidation, and incarceration merely intensify those feelings of low self-esteem and, yes, humiliation. In the end, focused deterrence is really a continuation of the punitive practices already employed.

Some police officials who have spent years using punitive methods have begun to question them and look for alternatives. Joe Domanick shows this process playing out in Los Angeles. LAPD chief Charlie Beck, for example, has come to embrace a more community-centered approach. Beck had been an active participant in Daryl Gates's Operation Hammer, but began to see that without community support, they could accomplish little of long-lasting consequence. He began to reach out to organizations and young people who were already out on the streets trying to reduce the violence as "gang interventionists." The LAPD had treated these groups with suspicion or even revulsion in the past. Many are former gang members who had spent time in jail. Police saw them as too close to the street and too critical of the police to be trusted. Beck came to understand that this was exactly what made their work possible. Beck brought them into discussions for the first time. The most concrete outcome was police support for the role of violence interrupters.[22]

In the end, though, this was primarily about securing community support for more nuanced but still primarily punitive law enforcement. What remained was a still-dysfunctional system of law enforcement and largely unconnected youth programs. Advocates, such as Connie Rice at the Advancement Project, understood this but were unable to get the city council to realign its emphasis despite putting together an extensive report, *A Call to Action: The Case for a Comprehensive Solution to L.A.'s Gang Violence Epidemic,* which documented the failures of the suppression model and the dysfunction of existing efforts.[23] Today, the overall focus of the LAPD remains on suppression, with some nods to the role of community-based gang interventionists. In fact, in 2014, the LA Youth Justice Coalition developed a plan to redirect 1 percent of the LA County law-enforcement budget toward social programs for youth, including community centers, youth jobs, and violence interrupters.[24] That 1 percent would generate around $100 million a year, a rhetorical intervention that has yet to bear fruit.

Alternatives

Redirecting resources from policing, courts, and jails to community centers and youth jobs is crucial to the real reforms needed to reduce juvenile violence. We are spending billions of dollars annually to try to police and incarcerate our way out of our youth violence problems while simultaneously reducing resources to improve the lives of children and families.

It makes much more sense to reduce racialized segregated poverty, provide troubled kids with sustained treatment and support, and provide communities with tools to better self-manage their problems without the use of armed police. First, we must have a real conversation about the entrenched, racialized poverty concentrated in highly segregated neighborhoods, which are the main source of violent crime. It is true that crime has declined overall without major reductions in poverty or segregation, but the crime that remains is concentrated in these areas. Unlike aggressive policing and mass incarceration, doing something about racialized poverty and exclusion would have general benefits for society in terms of reducing poverty, inequality, and racial injustice.

In a bit of an overgeneralization, Elliott Currie argues that we need three things to reduce youth offending: "jobs, jobs, and jobs."[25] Most young people would gladly choose a stable, decent-paying job over participation in the black markets of drugs, sex work, or stolen property. The United States is more segregated today than ever before. It allows up to 25 percent of its young people to grow up in extreme poverty, something that just isn't tolerated in other developed countries. It is from that population that most serious crime originates. The research on whether a short-term increase in the supply of youth jobs (often temporary and low-paying) reduces crime has shown mixed results. What remains to be tested is what would happen if there were a sustained increase in decent-paying jobs over several years. Such an increase might be able to overcome the educational and even cultural dynamics that contribute to black-market participation and violence.

Not every young person in these neighborhoods is ready and able to work, even if jobs were available. So the second plank is doing something to improve stability for these young people, so many of whom have been subject to soul-crushing poverty, abuse, and violence. What's remarkable is not how much crime they commit but how *little* they do, given this extreme deprivation. For years, the proponents of austerity and neoconservative tough-on-crime politics have claimed that social programs and treatment don't work. Of course no single program by itself can end serious crime; too often, in their scramble for resources, supporters of these programs make overly ambitious claims that set them up for failure. Midnight basketball by itself won't bring an end to crime any more than Police Athletic Leagues will. In many cases, the programs that do get funding tend to deal with those young people with the fewest needs. But most programs avoid those who need help the most; those that do serve them tend to have the best results, but only when they involve a sustained, comprehensive approach that deals with both their problems and those of their families.[26] Such "wraparound" services have to be at the center of any youth-violence reduction program.

Finally, we need to build the capacity of communities to solve problems on their own or in true partnership with government. The primary face of local government in poor communities is the police officer, engaged primarily in punitive enforcement actions. Why not build community power and put non-punitive government resources to work instead? Michael Fortner argues that African Americans played an important role in ushering in the era of mass incarceration and overpolicing by demanding that local government do something about crime and disorder.[27] What this analysis misses is that many of these same leaders also asked for community centers, youth programs, improved schools, and jobs, but these requests were ignored in favor of more police, enhanced prosecutions, and longer prison sentences. It's time to revisit this equation.

Communities often have good ideas about how to reduce crime through nonpunitive mechanisms, when given access to real resources. One model for pursuing this is community-based restorative justice. In this model, community members, through a representative body, are asked to assess the risks of taking some offenders back into the community instead of sending them to prison.[28] They use some or all of the resources that would have been spent on incarceration to develop rehabilitation and prevention programs. One study found that New York State was spending more than $1 million a year to incarcerate people from a single square block in Brooklyn—and there are many such "million-dollar blocks."[29] Most communities could find ways to spend that money that would achieve much better results than those produced by heavy-handed policing and mass incarceration. Jobs programs, drug treatment, mental health services, and youth services would all help reduce crime and break the cycle of criminalization, incarceration, and recidivism.

At the same time, this model would engage offenders in restitution and harm-reduction projects to help repair the damage they have caused. Abandoned houses that are sites of drug dealing and violence could be rehabilitated to provide stable housing. Older youth could be trained to mentor younger ones about how to resolve disputes without relying on violence, stay in school, and prepare for a difficult job market.

So much of the youth gang and violence problem stems, as David Kennedy's research points out, from a sense of insecurity.[30] When young people are constantly at risk of victimization, they turn to gangs and weapons to provide some semblance of protection. Communities need help in exercising informal controls to try and break this dynamic. There is no one solution to this, but active, positive adult involvement in the lives of these young people would be a major step in the right direction. This would require developing the capacity of parents to be more involved, which means looking at the structure of working hours and the high costs of childcare.[31] Often parents are unable to supervise their children adequately because of the intense demands of multiple jobs with erratic schedules. We also need to invest in drug treatment and mental health services to address the difficulties some parents face in managing themselves, much less their children.

Youth workers, coaches, and school counselors can all play a role in mentoring and monitoring young people. In too many cases, however, we are replacing them with more police. When communities demand more police, those resources have to come from somewhere else, and too often they come from schools and community services. This all squares nicely with austerity politics, where social programs are slashed to make way for tax cuts for the rich and enhanced formal social control mechanisms.

Another way to empower communities is to invest heavily in public-health-oriented prevention programs that operate at the neighborhood level. Often undertaken under the banner of "Cure Violence," these programs try to send strong anti-violence messages to young people, engage them in pro-social activities like after-school art and job training programs, and hold workshops in nonviolence conflict resolution.[32] They also employ outreach workers as violence interrupters, who can talk to young people from a shared position. The power of that connection for building credibility cannot be overstated. These workers are trying to break the cycle of violence through rumor control, gang truces, and ongoing engagement with youth out on the streets.

Some places are trying to move in this direction. Minneapolis has a "Blueprint for Action to Prevent Youth Violence," a multi-agency effort involving government, nonprofits, and community members.[33] Unlike gang-suppression efforts, it's housed in the health department rather than the police department. The blueprint brings people together to discuss existing problems and programs and tries to coordinate their efforts and prioritize funding for new services and initiatives. It's a flexible real-time process that responds to conditions as they change. The two main drawbacks are a lack of resources and a lack of buy-in from the police department. This creates a dynamic where young people who are involved in programs and positive activities are still being harassed and arrested by the police.

These programs are not a panacea. Research on their effectiveness is limited and shows mixed results. That is because they need the other parts of the solution to be in place as well. Without community-level changes in employment opportunities, adequate social services for young people with serious life problems, and improved educational structures, no one program can end the violence. There must be a holistic approach that begins by reducing our reliance on the criminal justice system and building political power to demand more comprehensive and less-punitive solutions.

9

Border Policing

Until the late nineteenth century, the US had no formal immigration restrictions. The border was essentially open, with only customs controls directed at shipping. In 1882, after 200,000 Chinese laborers immigrated to build the railroads and perform farm labor in the West, Congress passed the Chinese Exclusion Act to prohibit their further immigration. Much of the language used in debating the act was explicitly racist and consistent with local bans on the right of Chinese people to own property and appear as witnesses in court.[1] Proponents referred to Chinese immigrants as a "Mongolian horde" and "Johnny Chinaman" and accused them of being immoral and lazy. Small informal units were mobilized to limit unauthorized entry of Chinese immigrants, mostly along California's border with Mexico. The only restrictions on white immigration during this period banned those who were criminals, infirm, or politically radical. Anarchists were specifically banned in 1903, with Italians targeted for particular scrutiny.

With the rise of mass immigration in the late nineteenth and early twentieth centuries came growing nativist resentment. Throughout this period, groups such as the Immigration Restriction League and the American Party organized around ideas of racial purity, cultural superiority, and religious prejudice to demand an end to open immigration. This was finally achieved in 1924 with the passage of the National Origins Act, which established nationality-based immigration quotas for the first time. To enforce these quotas, Congress created the US Border Patrol.

The new Border Patrol focused on limiting unauthorized immigration from Mexico. Most enforcement was at designated border crossings, with only a few "linemen" patrolling in between. In practice, individuals and even vehicles needed only to venture a few miles from a formal checkpoint to cross. During Prohibition, illegal cross-border trucking was a major concern for California farmers, whose fields and fences were often damaged, but they received only minimal help from the Border Patrol. Part of the reason for weak enforcement was the strong desire for Mexican workers among growers in Texas and California, who vehemently opposed restrictions on their access to cheap labor.[2] The enforcement that did occur was often profoundly racist, with overt brutality and extrajudicial killings.[3] Historian Kelly Hernandez describes revenge killings and reckless shootings of border crossers.

During World War II there was a great need for farmworkers. The Border Patrol largely ignored Mexican immigration while keeping an eye out for possible enemy combatants, though almost none were discovered. The US government developed the Bracero Program to try to regularize migrant farm work.[4] Employers were obligated to provide decent wages and working conditions, and migrants received official permits to work in the United States. Enforcement was lax, and wages and working conditions were quite poor and well below the standards set for other workers. Women, children, and domestic workers were not covered by the program, so unauthorized immigration continued. In addition, many employers refused to use the new program, especially in Texas. Farmers and ranchers resented federal intervention in their longstanding labor systems, which often amounted to peonage. Workers who complained or organized against low wages and abysmal conditions were simply handed over to the Border Patrol for deportation.

Throughout the early 1950s, the number of people apprehended by the Border Patrol doubled.[5] In 1954 it launched

"Operation Wetback" to try to stem the tide through intensive border enforcement and raids in cities and on ranches, forcing more employers to utilize the Bracero Program. More than a million people were deported. In the end, the farmers and ranchers relented, especially after workplace protections were reduced and heavy penalties for worker organizing enacted.

The title of the operation, however, speaks volumes about the mindset of federal officials and the Border Patrol. US border enforcement has been primarily about the production of whiteness and economic inequality. The border has never been truly closed to poor immigrants. They have been allowed in, with tight regulation, or officially denied entry but in practice allowed to enter in large numbers, with few legal protections from employer exploitation and abuse. Each of these systems places immigrants in a degraded economic position where their rights to organize are denied and they are forced to work in substandard conditions for low wages.

One of the fastest expanding areas of policing in the past twenty years is border policing. Today the Border Patrol is part of the Department of Homeland Security. In 1992 there were just over four thousand Border Patrol agents; following the attacks of September 11, 2001, that number increased to ten thousand; today it stands at more than twenty thousand, making it larger than the ATF, FBI, and DEA combined.[6] The Border Patrol is aided by local and state police and a variety of federal agencies, including the National Guard, the US military, and Immigration and Customs Enforcement (ICE). In fiscal year 2012, the federal government spent more than $18 billion on immigration enforcement—more than all other federal law-enforcement spending combined.[7] Under the Trump administration, these numbers are likely to increase dramatically with the hiring of more officers and the building of more walls.

Border policing has always been highly racialized. Foreigners to be kept out or allowed in only under degraded circumstances are always defined as outside the American mainstream, and this is generally accomplished by appeals to race. Martha Menchaca's *Recovering History, Constructing Race* describes how racial hierarchies were first established in the border region by the Spanish elite and later by American settlers looking to justify their expropriation of Native and Mexican lands.[8] Even some longstanding Mexican Americans have attempted to achieve whiteness by encouraging the exclusion of new immigrants who undermine their attempts to equate themselves with Americanness—though, by embracing a racialized system of exclusion, they reinforce a racial caste system that in turn defines and treats them as less than full citizens.

From early on, the Border Patrol has engaged in racial profiling. They have argued that "looking Mexican" is sufficient grounds for stopping, questioning, and demanding identification. In 1973 the Supreme Court codified these practices in *US v. Brignoni-Ponce*,[9] in which it upheld the right of the Border Patrol to use racial profiles as the sole basis for vehicle stops and forced identifications. This is based in part on the 1953 federal law that gives Border Patrol agents the right to suspend constitutional protections within a hundred miles of the border and stop, search, and ascertain the immigration status of any person, whether or not they have any probable cause or even reasonable suspicion. The ACLU maintains that this is a violation of the Constitution.[10] They also point out that Border Patrol abuses have been reported far away from the border as well. In 2008, US senator Patrick Leahy was stopped at least 125 miles from the border, ordered out of his vehicle, and forced to produce identification. When he asked under what authority the agent was operating, the agent pointed his weapon at the senator and said, "That's all the authority I need."[11]

The current intensification of border enforcement began in the early 1990s, under the Clinton administration, with the launching of Operation Gatekeeper in California, Operation Hold-the-Line in Texas, and Operation Safeguard in Arizona and the passage of the Illegal Immigration Reform and Immigration Responsibility Act of 1996 (IIRIRA). Within a few years, funding for what was then the Immigration and Naturalization Service (INS) doubled, as did the number of Border Patrol officers. These operations represented the first real effort to close the southern border.[12] It involved several new initiatives, including significantly increasing the amount of fencing, immediately deporting immigrants living in the US for a long list of major and minor criminal infractions, creating immigration courts in border areas to facilitate quicker processing and deportation of captured migrants, and creating a massive system for identifying migrants through biometric data collection. The latter two initiatives became the basis for ramping up criminal prosecutions of migrants for crossing the border without authorization.

This process intensified after 9/11. Even though President George W. Bush had campaigned on a platform of more open borders, he oversaw additional fencing, increased Border Patrol hiring, and the intensification of the criminalization of migrants. As a result, the policy shifted from what was euphemistically called "catch and release" to one of "capture and hold." For decades, most migrants caught crossing the border were asked to waive their right to a hearing to challenge their deportation and then quickly returned to Mexico, spending as little time in custody as possible, which was generally advantageous for both the migrant and the US government. Now, an ever-growing number of migrants are being prosecuted. A first offense of illegal crossing is punishable as a misdemeanor; a second offense of illegal reentry, however, is now a felony that could result in years of incarceration. In addition, immigrants convicted of other crimes are now being sentenced and incarcerated for their full terms in a US prison before being deported.

In 2005, with massive new funding and infrastructure, the Border Patrol began to implement a series of zero-tolerance "capture and hold" policies under "Operation Streamline." Over the ensuing ten years more than 400,000 migrants were prosecuted for improper entry and over 300,000 for the felony of reentry.[13] The Trump administration has pledged to expand this practice. The US government has spent $7 billion on this approach, with much of the money going to private, for-profit prisons. Despite the prosecution and incarceration of three-quarters of a million people at the border, they found no deterrent effect on migrants, who are driven by profound and desperate poverty and the desire to unify families.[14] They also interviewed judges and lawyers and found widespread opposition, with most characterizing it as a politically driven policy lacking any legitimate policy achievements.

In addition, Operation Streamline has corrupted the federal court system. Judges and court personnel near the border cannot keep up with the massive volume of defendants, which has reduced their ability to properly handle these cases or adjudicate other matters. *Texas Monthly Magazine* found that the two busiest federal court districts in the country are in Texas, and that the courts are dealing with the load through mass prosecutions.[15] Dozens of defendants are routinely ushered into court together, often without any real legal representation, are asked to plead guilty, and are then either deported or incarcerated. In 2009, the Ninth Circuit Court of Appeals stepped in and demanded that defendants at least be asked individually about their pleas and their ability to understand what was happening. But that ruling merely slowed down the process without changing its basic character. Even though apprehensions along the border have been declining for decades, nearly 40 percent of all federal prosecutions are now related to immigration. Even prosecutors, who remain committed to a punitive framework, see that this system fails to deter migrants. One noted, "We prosecute people because they have committed violations of statutes enacted by Congress that reflect what our norms are ... We mete out punishment according to some systematic process. If some people are deterred by it, good. If not, I'm not surprised."[16] This statement lays bare the bind in which the entire institution finds itself. Police, prosecutors, and judges all see the futility of criminalizing a population driven by extreme hardship to seek out a better life across the border.

Today there are seventy-five thousand noncitizens in US prisons, about half of whom are there for immigration violations.[17] Many are held in for-profit private prisons. ICE uses forty-six such facilities to hold 70 percent of all immigration detainees, despite repeated reports of abuse, overcrowding, and inadequate medical services.[18] In addition, ICE subcontracting opportunities have encouraged a boom in jail and prison construction across the Southwest. Both local jurisdictions and these corporations have a financial stake in maintaining high rates of detention, further perverting the politics of immigration. In addition, large numbers of migrants are held in local jails on immigration detainers or awaiting transport. Conditions in these facilities, whether public or private, are inadequate. In 2010, the *New York Times* documented widespread problems with the delivery of health care services;[19] according to a 2016 report, eight people have died in recent years of preventable causes such as diabetes, because of inadequate health care.[20]

During the great migration of unaccompanied youth from Central America over the last few years, tens of thousands of children have been held in detention and many forced to appear in court without representation, creating a legal and humanitarian crisis. Thousands of families with small children have been held for extended periods in immigration detention while awaiting deportation or immigration court proceedings. These conditions are deplorable, especially for children. The US courts have recognized the inappropriateness of this, especially given that these families pose almost no safety risk. Despite repeated court rulings, the federal government continues to hold families with children in custody.

In addition, the US has issued about a million detainer orders, requesting local and state police to hold someone suspected of being in the country illegally. These detainers ask local police and sheriffs to be the front line of immigration enforcement. Beginning with the border buildup of the 1990s, local police were offered the opportunity of receiving the official authority to enforce federal immigration law. This authority, under section 287(g) of the IIRIRA, has created a huge dilemma for local police, who have been pressured to participate but in many cases view that cooperation as counterproductive to good policing. Most police believe that, to be effective, they need the cooperation of the community. It is community members who report crimes, provide information, and act as witnesses. In areas with high rates of unauthorized immigrants, fear of police is already very high. If people believe that they or their friends, family members, co-workers, or neighbors may be at risk of deportation, they will be gravely reluctant to bring any issues to the attention of police.

That is why many cities have either refused to participate in 287(g) or designated themselves "sanctuary cities" that refuse to cooperate with immigration enforcement efforts. Unfortunately, these declarations are sometimes rather hollow.[21] New York City has a sanctuary statute, and the NYPD does generally avoid involvement with immigration matters. However, for many years, corrections officials cooperated, even renting jail space to federal officials. More recently, they have moved those operations out of jails, so immigration officials merely station themselves in the courts and apprehend people after their court appearances. Under Obama, ICE tended to focus this effort towards those convicted of violent felonies. Under the Trump administration, any crime might trigger such proceedings, leading to widespread concerns that the hundreds of thousands of "broken windows" arrests that occur each year for minor infractions like jumping the subway turnstile might put many more people at risk of deportation.

In addition, 287(g) is part of a process of enhancing police power by blurring the lines between civil and criminal enforcement. Normally police are required to ensure people's constitutional rights when they suspect them of a criminal violation. Since most immigration violations are technically civil, the same protections do not apply. This means that police, sometimes under the guise of immigration enforcement, can enter people's homes without a judicial warrant and hold people in custody without the opportunity to post bond.

Pushback from many local jurisdictions led to a reduction in 287(g) agreements under the Obama administration, but the Trump administration has attempted to ramp up these agreements and bring sanctions against cities that refuse to participate or engage in other "sanctuary city" practices designed to impede increased deportations.

ICE is another major part of border policing. While most of its work involves inspecting people and goods at official border crossings, it is also tasked with apprehending undocumented migrants once they are in the United States. ICE also runs the detention facilities used to process, detain, and incarcerate migrants. In 2003 ICE created Fugitive Operations Teams intended to focus on finding migrants who have committed serious crimes. Over the last decade and a half, the number of these units has risen from eight teams in 2003 to 129 today, at a cost of $155 million a year.[22] These units were created to get serious criminals off the streets and out of the country, which is likely to make them a focus of increased funding under Trump. In practice, however, they engage in fishing expeditions in which they enter homes and workplaces on flimsy evidence and undertake dragnet type tactics that ensnare primarily noncriminal migrants. DHS's inspector general reported that the information used to plan and justify these raids is "grossly inaccurate."[23] The Migration Institute documented that, from 2003 to 2008, about three-quarters of those arrested had no criminal record. In 2007, despite spending over $100 million, these teams arrested only 672 people with serious criminal histories.[24] In more recent years, the percentage of serious arrests has declined even further, quotas have been established, and the number of units increased. In 2012, these teams arrested 37,000 people, the vast majority of whom had no history of violent crime.[25]

ICE also created a Worksite Enforcement Unit in 2006 that conducts heavily armed raids of workplaces and reviews employee lists looking for possible undocumented migrants, who are then intimidated into agreeing to deportation without a hearing or access to a lawyer. The Obama administration claimed to have shifted the focus to targeting employers, but employee audits led to mass firings of legal and undocumented workers. Of almost a hundred thousand prosecutions in 2009, only thirteen were of employers.[26]

The border is also the front line of the failed War on Drugs. The US employs a "supply-side" strategy of denying people access to drugs through interdiction and criminalization. Interdiction involves using the Border Patrol, Coast Guard, US military, and ICE to interrupt the flow of drugs into the country. It has failed. A recent report showed that 80 percent of the people arrested on drug charges by the Border Patrol were US citizens.[27] These arrests are occurring at border crossings, at checkpoints, and during immigration raids and are mostly for marijuana. There is speculation that drug seizures are being driven by the dramatic decline in border crossers and that the agency needs to justify its huge size and budget by seizing drugs instead.

The massive enforcement buildup has made the border a much more dangerous place. Since the crackdowns began in 1996, thousands have died trying to cross in ever more remote desert areas of Arizona and New Mexico. In some years as many as five hundred people die of heat, exposure, and dehydration.[28] They must rely on the criminal underworld of "coyotes" who charge thousands of dollars to facilitate passage but often fail to deliver and in some cases kidnap, rape, and kill those who pay them. Migrants in these circumstances are more likely to be coerced into carrying drugs. In many places a trip through the desert on foot can last days and require more water than a person can carry by hand. Some individuals and organizations have set up water stations along the border, only to see them sabotaged by anti-immigrant vigilantes.

There has also been a dramatic expansion in the number of deportations, which have more than doubled over the last decade to close to a half million a year. Barack Obama deported more people than all previous presidents combined. In the past, the government was reluctant to break up immigrant families if a member of the family was a US citizen. In fact, family reunification was one of the major sources of legal immigration in the postwar period, in keeping with the ideology that immigrants involved with family life are more likely to adjust to American culture and values. Now, we routinely tear families apart in truly heartless ways. There are currently more than five thousand children in foster care whose parents have been deported without them.[29] Young adults who came to the US as very young children have been deported alone to countries that are totally alien to them, where they have few, if any, family connections, and in some cases don't even speak the local language.

Many of these people are deported to Central America, where they end up in homeless shelters or sleep on the streets and often fall in with criminal gangs. This tragedy is compounded by the fact that many of these young people and their families fled Central America to avoid the violence of drug gangs in the first place—and, as noted in the previous chapter, US deportations played a major role in the expansion of such gangs in the first place. Many new deportees are forced either to join with these criminal enterprises or be victimized by them. Since some fled to avoid such a choice in the first place, they too often become victims in the failed US politics of immigration suppression. In July 2016, twenty-five US senators asked President Obama to stop deporting people fleeing the violence in that region, citing eighty-four documented cases since 2014 of people being killed after being deported, primarily in El Salvador, Honduras, and Guatemala. As Senator Edward Markey of Massachusetts put it, "We should not be sending families back to situations where they can be killed. That's just un-American."[30]

The Border Patrol has also become actively involved in securing major national events like the Super Bowl as part of the War on Terror.[31] Todd Miller describes how agents provide high visibility and high-tech security at such events and simultaneously fan out to bus and train stations to conduct intensive immigration checks of travelers who are completely disconnected from such events, much less international terrorism. Miller also highlights the troubling practices of detaining and searching US citizens because of their political, academic, and journalistic activities. Agents have watchlists; people on these lists can be arrested and interrogated and have their electronic possessions seized when crossing the border. The journalist and filmmaker Laura Poitras was detained multiple times after she worked with whistleblower Edward Snowden and produced a film called *My Country, My Country,* which criticizes US policy in the Middle East. American scholars of Islam and the Middle East have been accused of terrorism, detained without lawyers, and had their personal and electronic possessions searched and seized without a warrant. In none of these cases was there any question about their citizenship.

The Border Patrol has never had any effective accountability mechanism. While it is technically subject to internal investigations and congressional oversight, prosecutions and disciplining of officers are rare. In May 2010, Mexican national Anastasio Hernandez-Rojas died in Border Patrol custody after resisting officers at the San Ysidro crossing.[32] He was beaten and tasered while handcuffed and died a short time thereafter. A five-year investigation by the FBI, DOJ, and DHS found no criminal wrongdoing, despite a video reminiscent of the 1993 Rodney King beating in which a prone Rojas is surrounded by more than a dozen officers while being Tasered. Since then the Southern Border Communities Coalition has documented fifty additional deaths at the hands of Border Patrol agents.[33] While many of these cases involved migrants using violence, others involved reckless pursuits on sea and land, casual disregard for the lives of migrants, and excessive use of force. Since 2005 only three Border Patrol agents have faced indictments for excessive use of force, two from local prosecutors and one from the Department of Justice. In that later case, agent Lonnie Swartz faces murder charges for killing a twelve-year-old Mexican national by shooting him through a fence while he was allegedly throwing rocks at agents from the Mexican side of the fence in 2012. After four years, the case remains delayed and videos of the incident are sealed.[34] Neither of the other previous cases resulted in convictions. In 2014 the American Immigration Council found that, out of 809 official complaints against BP agents, only thirteen resulted in any discipline.[35] In the most serious case, one officer was suspended; the rest received little more than reprimands. President Obama's main effort to add accountability was to propose $5 million for body cameras.[36]

The water gets even muddier when military troops are involved. In 1997, US Marines working as lookouts and snipers with the Border Patrol in rural West Texas mistook a goat herder for a drug trafficker and killed him.[37] Investigators harshly criticized the Marines and Border Patrol for sending troops to the border with no training or preparation. A state grand jury refused to indict the marine who pulled the trigger, but the government paid the Hernandez family a settlement of a million dollars.

For decades, National Guard troops have played a variety of support roles along the border, from building roads to staffing radar stations and providing lighting. None have been involved in fatal incidents, because they're not involved in direct border enforcement or law enforcement tasks. This is changing, however. In 2014, then–Governor Rick Perry ordered the Texas National Guard to the border at a cost of $12 million a month to "enforce state law."[38] This involved thousands of heavily armed troops, with little or no civilian law enforcement training, in domestic law-enforcement operations. This seems to contravene the spirit, if not the letter, of the Posse Comitatus Act, which outlaws the use of the military for domestic law enforcement. Texas Governor Greg Abbott recently reauthorized the deployment as a "deterrent" to potential migrants and drug smugglers. But many local officials rankle at the militarization of the border and the criminalization of migrants. According to Hidalgo County Judge Ramon Garcia, "There is no public safety crisis here. These are not drug dealers. These are not terrorists. These are human beings looking for something better than what they had."[39]

Low-level misuse of funds and corruption remain a problem. Since 2003, the DHS has been increasingly pulling local police into the job of border enforcement. While 287(g) asks for police cooperation in identifying criminal aliens, Operation Stonegarden directly subsidized local police to undertake a variety of border enforcement activities, including money for overtime pay and special equipment for drug raids, pursuing suspected illegal migrants, and patrolling the border. There has been almost no oversight of how the money is spent. The

Arizona Daily Star uncovered massive overtime payments to officers, sometimes in excess of their base salaries, leaving local taxpayers to come up with dramatically higher pensions as officers retire and collect based on these inflated salaries.[40]

A growing chorus of right-wing politicians has championed high- and low-tech ways of closing the border. We are familiar with Donald Trump's exhortations to "build a wall," but this is not new. The US government has been trying to build a wall along the southern border for many decades and has little to show for it, other than massive fiscal profligacy and the deaths of migrants pushed into ever harsher and more remote terrains. There is no logistical way to build an effective wall between the US and Mexico. The terrain is too difficult, the cost too great, and the ways around it too many. For one thing, 40 percent of all people in the country illegally come by plane and overstay one of a variety of visas.[41] Walls can't just be built and left to do their thing. They must be staffed and maintained. Any wall can be breached, climbed over, or tunneled under if no one is watching. That would require a vast army along the fence, which would undoubtedly contribute to more unnecessary deaths. More than 700 border tunnels were discovered between 2006 and 2014, and further wall building will undoubtedly stimulate more tunnel building.

The US is plowing billions into electronic border-protection initiatives.[42] As early as the late 1980s the US was attempting to use technology to pinpoint enforcement efforts. Over the next ten years, the Intelligent Computer Aided Detection and Integrated Surveillance Intelligence System programs spent hundreds of millions of dollars for a system that in the end was deemed "functionally inoperable."[43] Undeterred, Congress gave Boeing a billion dollars over the next several years to build the Secure Borders Initiative net. After years of cost overruns, mismanagement, operation failure, and critical Government Accounting Office reports, the program was completely scrapped.

In the wake of 9/11, funding for such initiatives became widely available. Hundreds of millions have been spent on sensors that measure ground vibrations, infrared movement, and sounds of human activity to alert Border Patrol units that someone may be crossing. Much of this technology is ineffective; even when it works, units must be available to respond. Additionally, the US is using large numbers of planes, helicopters, and drones to patrol the border and has experimented with balloons to search for unauthorized aircraft crossings, though occasionally some break free from their tethers and cause extensive damage.

Reforms

While the inauguration of President Donald Trump withered much of the will to reform border policing, there are still efforts to rethink how we manage the need for migrant workers, who have become central to several parts of the American economy.

Some argue for a return to a system of foreign worker authorization similar to the Bracero Program. While this program did reduce the flow of unauthorized immigration and created some regularized employment for Mexico's poorest workers, it did not stem all illegal immigration and did little to improve the living standards of either American or Mexican workers.

Part of the problem is that migrant workers are not limited to agricultural work; migrants work in a variety of construction, production, and service industries, including construction, food processing, domestic work, and cleaning. What the Bracero Program did was guarantee a stable low cost and compliant work force for agricultural producers who wanted to keep wages extremely low. The program allowed employers to blacklist anyone who complained or attempted to organize. Today's migrant farmworkers are not covered by minimum-wage laws, have few enforceable workplace protections, are routinely exposed to dangerous chemicals, and receive only the most minimal access to housing, health, education, and welfare services. A new Bracero Program won't fix that; it will merely institutionalize it. If we want to raise the standard of living of agricultural workers, we have to allow them to organize, pay them higher wages, and enforce necessary health and safety standards. If US citizens could make higher wages doing this work, more of them might choose to do it. As it stands now, employers prefer to hire undocumented migrants precisely because they know that organized resistance is much less likely among this population.

Unions have at times made the mistake of thinking that excluding new migrants, legal or undocumented, would automatically improve conditions for US workers. While it's true that strikes have been broken by bringing in undocumented scab workers, in many cases this is not what really happens. Instead, employers regularly rely on racial minorities who are authorized to work, consciously taking advantage of the racial antipathies that they themselves have worked hard to create in order to keep workers divided and playing one group against another. It is very hard for unions with predominantly white memberships to tell black workers, whom they've historically excluded, not to cross a picket line. Increasingly the AFL-CIO has come to realize that the only hope for improving the lives of working people is to foster broad solidarity rather than antagonism. While many union locals retain anti-immigrant sentiments, the AFL-CIO's official position is to protect the rights of all workers regardless of immigration status and to encourage organizing along those same lines. Heavy-handed immigration policing will not build a workers' movement; it will shatter it.

One of the mistakes that Trump supporters make is imagining that their own economic conditions will be improved by continuing to exploit foreign lands while excluding those who suffer as a result. That analysis assumes that the wealth generated by that process will somehow trickle down to American workers. The last twenty years have taught us that these global economic arrangements do not include national allegiance on the part of corporations or sharing wealth within national economies. The wealth of the United States has increased dramatically in the last two decades, but all of that growth has gone exclusively to the richest 10 percent. The rest of us have seen wages and government services decrease. Our standard of living is not declining because of migrants but because of unregulated neoliberal capitalism, which has allowed corporations and the rich to avoid paying taxes or decent wages. It is that system that must be changed.

In 2010, the DOJ's Office of Community Oriented Policing Services (COPS) funded the Vera Institute to study best policing practices in communities with large numbers of immigrants. It surveyed hundreds of departments and focused on eight principles: get to the root causes of crime, maximize resources, leverage partnerships, focus on the vulnerable, engage in broad outreach, train both law enforcement and the community, monitor success and failure, and sustain programs that work. Embedded in these principles is the idealized notion of community policing, critiqued in earlier chapters. This approach places police at the center of solving community problems by enhancing their resources, broadening their reach, and shaping community action and perceptions through outreach and training based on policing priorities.[44]

There is certainly value in having police speak multiple languages, respect cultural differences, and focus on the needs of those most victimized. However, in the Vera study there is very little discussion of the profound conflicts of mission in policing these communities, it is listed, for instance, only one mention of sanctuary cities. In several examples, police are applauded for hiring civilians as translators and community outreach educators. But why should these resources be attached to and under the control of the police department? These should be core functions of local civilian government and exist independently of law enforcement.

If we want immigrants, documented or not, to be more integrated into society, more likely to report crime, and better able to defend themselves from predators, we should instead look to end all federal immigration policing, remove social barriers in housing and employment, and acknowledge their important role in revitalizing communities and stimulating economic activity.

Alternatives

Border policing is hugely expensive and largely ineffective, and produces substantial collateral harms including mass criminalization, violations of human rights, unnecessary deaths, the breakup of families, and racism and xenophobia. Unfortunately, both dominant political parties have embraced its expansion, whether as part of a system of restricted and managed legalization or as part of a fantasy of closing the border. Rather than debating how many additional Border Patrol agents to employ, we should instead move to largely de-police the border. Borders are inherently unjust and as Reece Jones points out in his book *Violent Borders,* they reproduce inequality, which is backed up by the violence of state actors and the indignity and danger of being forced to cross borders illegally.[45]

Until the Clinton administration, unauthorized cross-border migration was widespread, yet it did not lead to the collapse of the American economy or culture. In fact, in many ways it strengthened it, giving rise to new economic sectors, revitalizing long-abandoned urban neighborhoods, and better integrating the US into the global economy. When the EU lowered its internal borders, there were fears that organized crime would benefit, local cultures would be undermined, that mass migration would create economic chaos as poorer southern Europeans moved north. None of this happened. In fact, migration decreased as the EU began developing poorer areas within Europe as a way of producing greater economic and social stability.

We could do the same thing in North America, but instead have largely done the opposite. The North American Free Trade Agreement had devastating consequences for agricultural production in Mexico, displacing and impoverishing millions.[46] The end of state-subsidized corn farming in Oaxaca led to the collapse of the rural economy there, driving hundreds of thousands to attempt to migrate to the US. Similar processes are widespread in Mexico.[47] Drug-related violence that further contributes to the stream of migrants from Mexico and Central America is also directly related to historical and current interdiction efforts of the US War on Drugs.[48] By opening the doors to capital and goods but not people, we have created tremendous pressure to migrate. Instead, we should be opening the borders and working to develop the poorest parts of the United States and Mexico. This would create economic and social stability and development that might reduce the extent of migration. The $15 billion a year we spend now on border policing could go a long way toward that goal. It turns out that most people would rather stay in their own cultural setting than migrate if given the opportunity.

Ultimately, we must work toward developing a more internationalist ethos and analysis. The reality is that people in Central America and Mexico are poor partially because of US economic policies. By consistently subverting democracy, we have helped create the dreadful poverty in those places. In 2009, the US government backed a coup against the democratically elected left-wing government in Honduras. That government is now torturing, executing, and disappearing environmental and labor activists.[49] This was just the most recent in a long string of foreign direct and indirect interventions in the politics of Central America, including Ronald Reagan's backing of dictatorships in El Salvador and Guatemala as well as of the Contras' attempt to overthrow the leftist government in Nicaragua.

Once we understand migration as a global process driven in large part by the policies of our own government, we in the United States should feel obligated to end those practices and open our doors to those fleeing them. Migrants are human beings who are no better and no worse than Americans and should enjoy the same rights and opportunities. As the group Immigrant Movement International notes, migrants have as much right to international movement as "corporations and international elites"; "the only law deserving of our respect is an unprejudiced law, one that protects everyone, everywhere. No exclusions. No exceptions."[50] We should be working to improve the conditions where people come from and allowing them access to the opportunities we have. We cannot and should not rely on ever more intensive, violent, and oppressive border policing to manage problems that we ourselves helped create.

10

Political Policing

The police have always been political. The roots of political policing lie deep in the desire of kings and queens to maintain power in the face of the shifting allegiances and interests of nobles and foreign powers. Today, states portray their police forces as value-neutral protectors of public safety, but in reality, states continue to monitor and disrupt all kinds of political activity through surveillance, infiltration, criminal entrapment, and repressing protest. The continued existence of these practices poses a major threat to any effort to change the basic role of the police and, more broadly, to achieve the goals of racial and economic justice.

In a dictatorship, it is easy to see that the police are a threat to democracy and the forces of civil society, fulfilling a primarily political function; crime control is always secondary. Repressive regimes in the postcolonial countries of Africa and Latin America rely on uniformed and secret police to harass, intimidate, and murder their political opponents. So-called civilian police in places like El Salvador[1] and Guatemala[2] are riven with a history of torture and extrajudicial killings. Dictatorships in Brazil and Argentina "disappeared" tens of thousands of labor leaders, artists, and political opponents in the 1970s.[3] Today, even semidemocratic regimes still rely on the police for primarily political functions. Nigerian police, for example, are notoriously ineffective at crime control. Most units are poorly paid and trained and frequently rely on torture, extortion, and unlawful detentions.[4] But in semidemocratic Nigeria, political intelligence and riot control units tend to be the most desirable and prestigious assignments and are regularly implicated in the suppression of social movements and opposition political groups as well as vote-rigging and voter suppression.

India, while more democratic, has a police force primarily concerned with political management. After independence from Britain, it retained colonial forms of policing, with their emphasis on political surveillance and riot control to suppress industrial actions, ethnic conflicts, peasant uprisings, and guerilla movements such as the Naxalites. Efforts to deal with crime and everyday public safety have been consistently sidetracked in favor of beefing up intelligence-gathering and developing more sophisticated systems of suppressing political activity. The only units to receive extensive training and resources are intelligence and riot control divisions.[5] Corruption and low wages for regular units remain endemic. Rural police are usually under the control of local agricultural elites, who rely on them to maintain control over the vast rural poor, especially the lowest "scheduled" castes and ethnic minorities. Police are routinely implicated in atrocities against such groups. Everyday policing is characterized by the release of politically connected or rich suspects and the torture and imprisonment of those unable to secure their release through bribes. Police are specifically authorized to spy on opposition political parties and do so with great thoroughness. Organizations must receive prior approval from the police for demonstrations and even meetings and conferences that might draw international participation.[6]

The origins of this kind of policing run deep in the colonial centers that bred it. We can see this clearly in the context of the transition from autocratic to more modern liberal policing in the nineteenth century. The imperial powers of Europe each had secret police that spied on, interrogated, imprisoned, and at times tortured political opponents and infiltrated and subverted the movements of workers, ethnic minorities, and even liberal reformers. France has had several forms of policing going back to the Middle Ages.[7] As the size and complexity of Paris increased, it was necessary for the *ancien regime* to extend and professionalize its mechanisms of social control. In 1666, Louis XIV created a Lieutenant of Police whose chief duties were to provide intelligence to the crown and maintain public order, including suppressing riots and political movements, but this organization failed to predict or prevent the uprisings that led to the French Revolution.

After the revolution, the new Ministry of Police became more civilian, but no less political. Despite a rhetorical emphasis on enforcing the law, the police became a tool of whichever faction was in power, focusing primarily on *la haute police*, or the high policing of politics. Under Napoleon, the police were further professionalized and integrated more clearly into a modern legal system capable of providing daily intelligence reports of conditions across the country, which were forwarded to him during his foreign military adventures. The military Gendarmerie policed the countryside, while municipal police were responsible for the cities. At the center was a massive intelligence operation, the Directory, engaged in political intrigue, surveillance, and censorship. Today both the rural gendarmerie and national police play a central role in domestic intelligence gathering, giving rise to the saying that "French citizens are free to do as they choose—under police supervision."[8]

However, policing in liberal democratic settings has been no less political. The British police, whose origins are discussed in detail in chapter 2, regularly engage in surveillance and subversion of domestic political movements. During the 1960s and 1970s, they infiltrated labor unions, universities, and peace organizations, pressured members for information about subversives and foreign agents, and raided them to seek political information. In 2011, during the Occupy Wall Street movement, police in the City of Westminster circulated a notice to local businesses and individuals asking them to report any signs of the presence of "anarchists" to the police counterterrorism desk immediately—side by side with notices about Al-Qaeda.[9] In the absence of any evidence or even allegation of criminal activity, the police routinely collect information on political activists whose philosophy runs counter to existing political arrangements.

The 2011 incident was tied to Project Griffin, which was designed to "advise and familiarize managers, security officers, and employees of large public and private-sector organizations across the capital on security, counter terrorism, and crime prevention issues."[10] These projects involve a disturbing trend in which local police are asked to provide security updates for the private sector about the threat of demonstrations—essentially political threat assessment. Such briefings tend to report past criminal and terrorist activity, vague assessments of broad international trends or micro-reporting of loose bits of unconnected and distant tidbits, such as a suspected terrorist in Pakistan being found with a map of the London subway on his laptop.

Police infiltrators in the United Kingdom have targeted peace, animal rights, environmental, and anarchist groups, and undercover detectives have had sexual relationships with women in these movements. There are some estimates that more than a hundred women have been victimized.[11] In at least one case the relationship produced a child, resulting in a settlement of close to $1 million.[12] That agent, Bob Lambert, was implicated in planting and setting off explosive devices in department stores selling fur coats, in order to deepen his acceptance into the extremist wing of the animal-rights movement and justify continued police infiltration and disruption—the very definition of an agent provocateur.[13]

Political Policing at Home

Despite our concerns about political liberty, the US police have a long history of similarly abusive practices. The myth of policing in a liberal democracy is that the police exist to prevent political activity that crosses the line into criminal activity, such as property destruction and violence. But they have always focused on detecting and disrupting movements that threaten the economic and political status quo, regardless of the presence of criminality. While on a few occasions this has included actions against the far right, it has overwhelmingly focused on the left, especially those movements tied to workers and racial minorities and those challenging American foreign policy. More recently, focus has shifted to surveillance of Muslims as part of the War on Terror.

In 1908 the Justice Department created the Bureau of Investigation (BOI), which was headed by J. Edgar Hoover in 1924. Hoover turned the BOI and later the FBI, created in 1935, into a massive domestic intelligence-gathering operation with files on millions of Americans including politicians, political activists, and celebrities. The rise of modern federal intelligence gathering was driven initially by concerns over anarchists and "reds," who were implicated in waves of strikes, bombings, and assassinations in the early part of the century, from the assassination of President McKinley in 1901 to the bombings of the Los Angeles Times in 1910 and Wall Street in 1920, leading to a wave of reprisals targeting anyone with anarchist affiliations, Wobblies, and in many cases Italian labor activists of any political stripe.[14]

In the wake of the Russian Revolution, a massive wave of "red scare" gripped the country. Revolutionary groups did exist across the US, but their influence was largely ideological rather than organizational. They produced numerous newspapers and leaflets, but had little connection to actual unions. This did not prevent the Justice Department from collecting files on them. Hoover's BOI claimed to have a card catalog with over 200,000 entries of suspected "reds." Following a wave of suspicious bombings in 1919, surveillance turned to subversion, despite the fact that Hoover's own records made clear that none of these organizations was involved in orchestrating violence, or were in any position to stage an armed insurrection. The two "most dangerous" anarchist groups surveilled had a total membership of 37.[15]

Attorney General A. Mitchell Palmer launched a major national campaign to disrupt any movements sympathetic to socialism, communism, or anarchism in 1919. He relied on new, more restrictive immigration laws that allowed for the deportation of anyone espousing the violent overthrow of the US government. He argued that anyone who was a member of an organization that supported the Soviet Revolution was making such an espousal, even when the group formally adhered to a strategy of nonviolent political change.

These became known as the Palmer Raids, which began with the rounding up and deportation of a few hundred left writers and activists, including Emma Goldman in 1919, even though she was a naturalized American citizen. In January 1920 Palmer, working with local police, undertook a massive campaign of arrests, interrogation, false imprisonment, and deportation. Thousands were arrested including large numbers of US citizens. Journalists were specially targeted, files seized, and papers closed down. Many were held for weeks in basements and building hallways with no access to bathrooms, food, or lawyers. Many others were beaten or tortured, and in one instance a prisoner "jumped" out of a window and died.[16] Buffalo's police chief was quoted as saying, "It's too bad we can't line them up against a wall and shoot them."[17] The Massachusetts secretary of state said, "If I had my way I would take them out in the yard every morning and shoot them, and the next day would have a trial to see whether they were guilty."[18]

In the end, the raids were found to be utterly illegal, but not before hundreds were deported, organizations disrupted, and lives destroyed. While the avowed focus was on preventing armed revolution, the real target was the disruption of the burgeoning labor movement. In addition, Palmer singled out groups that supported equal rights for African Americans for public attack, such as the Communist Party, which, to his horror told "Negros" that they had the right to strike.[19]

In the wake of the abuses of the Palmer Raids, the FBI was initially somewhat constrained in its political activities—focusing primarily on intelligence gathering. American concerns about an over-powerful state meant that there was some limited oversight of their activities by Congress, which placed some checks on their most egregious practices. They continued, however, to play a role in identifying and intimidating "known communists" during the McCarthy period. In the 1960s, the FBI's Counter Intelligence Program, or COINTELPRO, is now known to have kept files on millions of lawful activists and engaged in the active disruption of movement organizations through false letters, infiltrators, and the use of agents provocateurs.[20] Notable figures like Martin Luther King had their phones tapped. FBI agents often attended meetings either covertly or overtly to take notes for intelligence files and used their conspicuous presence as a form of intimidation. They planted informants within organizations to collect information, but also to sow dissension, make false allegations against people, and at times, suggest violent courses of action to entrap and discredit organizations and their leaders.

Unfortunately, there were few checks on the activities of local police. Frank Donner in his exhaustive history of local "Red Squads" shows how America's large police forces dedicated significant resources to political policing, and that this policing was closely tied to far right politics, private business interests, and corruption.[21]

As immigration and industrialization transformed the economic and social landscape in the late nineteenth and early twentieth centuries, local police were increasingly involved in suppressing workers' movements. Up until the 1930s there was no real right to form a union or strike in the US. Union activists were routinely fired, driven out of town, and sometimes killed by either company agents or police. Strikes were put down through threats, the use of scabs, and when necessary, violence. Early in this period, much of this work was done by private security companies such as the Pinkertons, who were implicated in numerous beatings, shootings, and infiltrations of unions including the Homestead strike of 1892, in which guards and workers squared off in a gun battle that killed several on both sides, prompting the calling out of the local militia who crushed the strikers and their union. By the 1930s the Pinkerton agency had over 1,300 spies embedded in various unions in an effort to disrupt their activities on behalf of employers.

In most places, local police played a major role in suppressing strikes. Often this was done through a process of political corruption in which police were beholden to local elected officials who did much of the hiring and firing of police, especially at the top ranks. In many places in the nineteenth and early twentieth centuries, police were directly appointed by local politicians on the basis of political services and substantial bribes. These local officials were often beholden to large employers through bribery and political favors. When these employers were faced with labor unrest, they need only call on local police to suppress the strike, break up meetings, and intimidate and brutalize alleged "ring leaders."

As labor unrest and violence grew near the turn of the century, special squads were formed in most major cities. Much of the initial focus was on alleged anarchists, who were believed to play the most militant role in labor strife and were associated with numerous bombings and assassinations. Police began keeping large systems of files on suspected anarchists and other labor radicals. The Wobblies of the International Workers of the World (IWW) were among the most frequent targets of surveillance and harassment. Meetings were disrupted and suspected anarchists were often arrested, sometimes on trumped up charges, as in the case of Sacco and Vanzetti, who were executed in 1927.

In the aftermath of the Bolshevik Revolution, attention turned to "reds," as communist agents and sympathizers became the primary obsession of employers, political leaders, and police hoping to find a way to suppress the growing labor movement. Red Squads flourished after World War I. They generally operated in secret and in close collusion with local employers and Hoover's BOI. In many cases, detectives who helped to break up strikes were given large unreported cash bonuses from employers, just one of the many forms of corruption to emerge from this system of secretive political policing. Employers also often provided cash to pay for informants and infiltrators. This system blurred the line between public and private interests and undermined the core ideals of an independent police under the control of elected civilian governments.

Throughout the 1940s and 50s, Red Squads played an important role in the blacklisting of anyone suspected of ties to communism. While the FBI played a role in this process, it was largely supplanted by local police, who increasingly shared information with each other and provided information directly to congressional committees working to expose communists inside government and the labor movement. In 1956, a new independent agency, the Law Enforcement Intelligence Unit, was created to share files among police agencies concerning organized crime and political activity. Though funded in part by federal grants, they maintained that they were a private entity and thus not subject to any kind of government oversight or accountability. This agency still exists.[22]

A major source of data for Red Squads were volunteers, usually tied to ultra-nationalist groups like the American Protective League, American Legion, and Catholic activists driven by Cardinal Spellman's anti-communist crusades. These groups were sometimes given resources to expand their efforts, were often used as muscle to shut down meetings and beat and intimidate suspected communists, and were even given access to the files collected by police. The dissemination of this information was often crucial to the blacklisting process as these activists shared the information with local employers.

By the 1960s, the focus shifted to the civil rights movement, peace activists, and radical students. Red Squads again developed massive systems of files to keep track of the growing movements. While the vast majority of participants in these movements were nonviolent, police used the fact that people were arrested and that violence occurred in connection with these movements to justify surveillance and eventually active subversion; this despite the fact that the arrests and violence were often the result of discriminatory police action, rather than actual criminal wrongdoing.

While the federal Counterintelligence Program (COINTELPRO) worked to subvert the civil rights movement, it was police in Los Angeles, Chicago, New Orleans and other cities who staged raids of Black Panther chapters, killing and imprisoning many of its local and national leaders. It was local police who violently suppressed anti–Vietnam War demonstrations in Chicago, New York, and Washington and beat and imprisoned civil rights activists in Birmingham, Selma, and Montgomery, Alabama.

In 1971 a group of activists broke into an FBI office in Media, Pennsylvania, and uncovered COINTELPRO, including documents showing attempts to get Martin Luther King to commit suicide through sexual extortion.[23] Through a series of high-profile congressional hearings, local investigations, as well as numerous lawsuits that followed, the public began to learn more about the secret networks of police spies. Some departments were forced to hand over files; others destroyed or attempted to hide them.[24] As recently as 2016, the NYPD claimed to have lost a room full of documents ordered preserved by the court about its spying operations in the 1960s and 1970s.[25] Through a series of court orders, local laws, and federal intervention, many Red Squads were shut down and others were given much tighter constraints on their actions. Court settlements resulted in restrictions and oversight. Intelligence units were required to restrict their activities to cases where there was actual evidence of criminal activity being planned or committed, with approval required to undertake undercover work or hire informants. In some cases, independent auditors were empowered to review files. Photographing and videotaping people involved in lawful protest activity or participating in political gatherings were restricted.

These reforms, while important in exposing and limiting the extent of political policing, were temporary and incomplete. Part of the problem is that any criminal activity is sufficient to trigger an investigation. Since civil disobedience actions have become a mainstay of social movement activity, almost all social movements participate in some form of technically illegal activity. Intelligence units continue to view monitoring political activity as part of their mandate.

Since 9/11, however, police have rehabilitated their intelligence-gathering infrastructure under the cover of terrorism prevention. In New York, the NYPD went to court to try to water down its consent decree, the *Handschu* agreement that placed significant restrictions on surveillance practices; the court allowed it to resume photographing demonstrators, even though there is almost no conceivable connection between protest and terrorism. They were also allowed to use informants and undercover agents with little to no oversight. NYPD agents collected broad intelligence against activists protesting the Republican National Convention in New

York in 2004, including organizers, independent journalists, and well-known organizations with no history of violence. Those who were arrested were subjected to interrogation about their political beliefs, organizational affiliations, and social networks. After the New York Civil Liberties Union exposed the practice, the NYPD voluntarily agreed to stop it.[26] However, in 2015, activists arrested as part of the Black Lives Matter movement reported similar standardized political interrogations.[27]

In 2010, the ACLU found hundreds of incidents of police spying on legal political and protest activity in thirty-three states since 2001.[28] In 2003, Oakland police infiltrated an anti-police-brutality organization and played an active role in planning and coordinating events, including the route of a march. This represents a fundamental conflict of interest and abuse of police power and crosses the line from passive observation into active manipulation. The impropriety is compounded by the fact that the target of these demonstrations was the police themselves.

Joint Terrorism Task Forces and Fusion Centers

One of the major formations of political policing is Joint Terrorism Task Forces (JTTF). Created in the 1980s, these units combine federal and local law enforcement to look for terrorist threats. Since such threats are rare, they appear to have shifted their role to monitoring political activity. JTTFs function with no public oversight, especially at the local level, which has caused at least two major cities, Portland, Oregon and San Francisco, to pull out. After 9/11, Congress eliminated many restrictions on political spying. While there is some history of political violence from fringe elements of the environmental and animal-rights movement, the scope of surveillance seems sweeping and indiscriminate—though the true scope is unknown, since we must rely on rare legal actions or leaks to find out about it.

In 2002, it was learned that the Denver Intelligence unit had a binder with a "JTTF Active Case List" that included information about the American Friends Service Committee, the Colorado Campaign for Middle East Peace, Denver Justice and Peace Committee, and the Rocky Mountain Independent Media Center.[29] In 2003, the *Wall Street Journal* reported that the Denver JTTF added "anarchists" and other "political extremists" to the FBI's Violent Gangs and Terrorist Organization Files.[30] In 2008, the ACLU uncovered that the Maryland state police had spied on local death penalty and peace activists for years, classifying fifty-three individuals and twenty organizations as terrorists. The list was circulated to the local JTTF and surrounding local and federal law enforcement agencies. Nothing in any of the surveillance files indicated any illegal activity.[31]

On September 24, 2010, as part of a JTTF investigation, FBI agents raided the homes of several people active in opposing US policies in Palestine and Colombia and who had participated in planning demonstrations at the Republican National Convention in Saint Paul, Minnesota, in 2008. The search warrants focused on obtaining information from computers and other sources of alleged "facilitation of other individuals in the United States to travel to Colombia, Palestine, and any other foreign location in support of foreign terrorist organizations including the FARC and Hezbollah."[32] Twenty-three people were subpoenaed to testify before a grand jury, but all refused. No criminal charges or specific accusations of criminal activity have emerged, leading to claims that the raids were politically motivated.[33]

Despite having evidence that turned out to be linked to actual violent attacks, JTTFs have played a limited role in preventing attacks or prosecuting terrorists. In the year before Major Nidal Malik Hasan shot thirteen people to death in

Fort Hood, Texas, the JTTF was aware of his extremist views and ties to Pakistan but took no action against him.

Another post-9/11 form of political policing is fusion centers, created to help federal agencies share information about potential terrorist threats (the focus has shifted to cover "all hazards/all crimes" and to include state and local partners, private-sector interests, and the military).[34] As with JTTFs, there are no clear lines of accountability[35] and according to a US Senate Report, little indication that they have prevented any terrorist activities.[36] They have, however, been at the center of both conflating political activism with terrorism and in coordinating intelligence on nonviolent political movements. In 2008 the ACLU of Massachusetts obtained a fusion center document on standard operating procedures that authorized surveillance and intelligence gathering of public meetings absent any connection to criminal behavior. Even a single, anonymous speech act or social media post advocating illegal activity (including civil disobedience) could trigger a full investigation.[37]

In 2009 and 2010, two fusion centers listed supporters of third-party candidates, including those backing libertarian Ron Paul, as potential threats, linking them to the militia movement.[38] The Pennsylvania Homeland Security office was found to be using paid consultants to monitor environmental, peace, and gay rights groups and then reporting the findings to local businesses, including the Hershey Company and oil and gas companies engaged in the politically fraught fracking business. Some of the reports compared these nonviolent political organizations to Al-Qaeda. The contract agency involved was also under contract to provide private security to many of the same companies.

Fusion centers have also been implicated in monitoring the Occupy movement and coordinating local efforts to end it. A report by the Center for Media and Democracy found that "Terrorism Liaison Officers" were monitoring and reporting on the activities of Occupy Phoenix, including attending meetings and demonstrations, infiltrating the organization, and following social-media activity. Major cities' chiefs of police, the Police Executive Research Forum, and fusion centers across the country were actively gathering daily head counts. The documents also show that they had access to "Stingray" cell phone surveillance equipment, facial recognition, and massive data-mining software that could pose a huge threat to the privacy of political activists and their organizations. These intelligence agencies prepared regular reports for banks and other financial institutions targeted by the Occupy Wall Street movement. Because of the loose association between Anonymous and Occupy, their reports on hacking threats sometimes included Occupy social media activities, conflating illegal hacking with social media organizing.[39]

The Partnership for Civil Justice Fund also uncovered, through litigation, evidence that the FBI treated Occupy as a "terrorist threat" even before it undertook its first action. While there is insufficient evidence to support claims by Naomi Wolf and others that the federal government organized or coordinated the local efforts to shut down Occupy, it is clear that federal intelligence agencies, working with local law enforcement, were actively gathering and sharing information about the movement with each other and with financial institutions.[40] In the end, the decision to break up Occupy encampments in hundreds of cities was made by local political leaders and carried out by local police, though the timing and tools used to accomplish them may have grown out of federally-coordinated information sharing.

Entrapment

Police have fought the War on Terror nationally and locally through widespread surveillance, entrapment, and inflaming public fears, with little increase in public safety. Whistleblower Edward Snowden, with the help of journalist Glenn Greenwald, helped to expose the true extent of government spying, which violates constitutional principles and existing laws.[41] Americans have come to understand that their telephone and electronic communications are not secure and that this is being done in collusion with major communications corporations. The government has yet to produce a single terrorism case from this surveillance.

In 2004, the NYPD arrested twenty-four-year-old Pakistani immigrant Shahawar Matin Siraj for plotting to bomb the Herald Square subway station in Manhattan. Lawyers say Siraj was entrapped by a paid police informant facing drug charges, who spent months hatching the plot and pushing the idea of a bombing. Siraj had "no explosives, no timetable for an attack, and little understanding about explosives." According to Human Rights Watch, the NYPD's own records showed that he was unstable and "extremely impressionable due to severe intellectual limitations."[42] When asked to participate in the plot, Siraj replied that he had to ask his mother first and never actually agreed to participate, according the NYPD's own assessment. Nevertheless, he was convicted and sentenced to thirty years in prison.

In 2011, Rezwan Ferdaus was arrested by the FBI for participating in a plot to blow up the Pentagon and US Capitol. He was targeted by an FBI informant who infiltrated his local mosque, coaxed Ferdaus into the plot, and supplied him with fake weapons, although it was clear he had a mental disability. As the plan unfolded, Ferdaus's condition deteriorated dramatically. He lost control of his bladder and began to suffer from seizures and extreme weight loss. Eventually his father had to quit his job to care for him. Despite this, Ferdaus was convicted of supplying material support to terrorism and was sentenced to seventeen years in prison. These cases were hailed as proof that police were winning the War on Terror.

The NYPD undertook a massive secret spying operation run by its "Demographics Unit," targeting Muslim and Arab communities throughout the city without any specific probable cause. Documents obtained by journalists Matt Apuzzo and Adam Goldman described undercover operatives dispatched to mosques, cafes, community centers, and college campuses to search for hints of extremist viewpoints and to learn the social, cultural, and political layout of these communities.[43] Comings and goings at places of worship, snippets of conversations in local bookstores, and the social activities of student clubs were regularly reported. On my own campus at Brooklyn College, an undercover officer posed as a recently converted Muslim and ingratiated herself with Muslim students and their clubs, attending weddings and social events, only to be discovered because of her involvement in an unrelated investigation. Leaked documents indicated that police informants traveled with these clubs and reported on their membership, activities, and guest speakers, despite the complete absence of any history or evidence of criminal activity. The program never generated a single lead related to terrorism. The New York Civil Liberties Union sued in 2013, alleging that the program violated people's right to free religious association and denied them equal protection under the law;[44] as recently as 2015, however, the NYPD continued to carry out surveillance of Muslims without proper authorization.[45]

These practices are counterproductive and substantially undermine the credibility of police. Most real information about extremist violence is obtained by community members reporting on people they fear are up to no good. However, when whole communities feel discriminated against, abused, and mistrusted, they are less likely to come forward for fear that their role will be misunderstood or that well-meaning but mistaken tips will hurt the innocent rather than sparking an honest investigation. In the words of the ACLU, this type of policing makes us both less safe and less free.

Crowd Control

Protest policing in the United States is generally organized around strategic philosophies of how to manage protest activity. In the 1960s and early 1970s, the police operated under a philosophy of "escalated force," meeting militant protestors with overwhelming force.[46] In response, a new doctrine of "negotiated management" emerged that called for the protection of free speech rights, toleration of community disruption, ongoing communication between police and demonstrators, avoidance of arrests, and limiting the use of force to situations where violence is occurring.[47]

Today, however, two major forms of protest policing predominate; both severely restrict the right to protest. The police in New York City and some other jurisdictions insist on "command and control" techniques, in which they micromanage all-important aspects of demonstrations in an attempt to eliminate any disorderly or illegal activity.[48] This approach sets clear and strict guidelines on acceptable behavior, based on very little negotiation with demonstration organizers. It is inflexible and frequently relies on high levels of confrontation and force in relation to even minor violations of the rules. This does not represent a return to escalated force because it attempts to avoid the use of force through planning and careful management of the protest. When this fails force is used, but only in the service of reestablishing control over the demonstration. This is a highly managed system, not characterized by uncoordinated uses of force or police riots as seen in the 1960s, in which police supervisors were seen chasing after their officers to try to keep them from beating protestors in the streets.

Another form of protest policing, the "Miami model," emerged nationally in response to the disruptive protests at the World Trade Organization meetings in Seattle in 1999. It is named for the Miami Police Department's handling of protests at the Free Trade Area of the Americas meetings in 2003. This style is characterized by the creation of no-protest zones, heavy use of less lethal weaponry, surveillance of protest organizations, negative advance publicity about protest groups, preemptive arrests, preventative detentions, and extensive restrictions on protest timing and locations.[49] This set of tactics is reserved for groups that the police believe cannot be controlled through micromanagement, such as those who do not apply for permits and threaten direct action or civil disobedience not coordinated with the police. Such groups are arrested while lawfully gathering and held in detention for long periods while awaiting arraignment, often in poor conditions. They are also likely to be the subjects of extensive police surveillance and to be accused of planning violence. They are often met with high levels of force in the form of "less lethal" weaponry such as pepper spray, tear gas, and rubber bullets. The Miami model has also been driven in part by the broad militarization of civilian policing, as described in previous chapters.

Some argue that militarized riot control is merely prudent preparation—for example, in Ferguson, Missouri. Shouldn't authorities take whatever steps they can to protect life and property? There are two major problems with this line of thinking. First, it is not at all clear that these measures advance public safety; second, the right to protest cannot be abridged because of the threat of illegal activity or even the commission of violence nearby. All this militarized posturing failed to prevent widespread looting and property destruction in Ferguson. Neither local police nor the National Guard could adequately protect local businesses. What they could do was attack protestors and the media with tear gas and smoke grenades. Law enforcement officers were distracted from the real threat: the few dispersed individuals and bands of people attacking local businesses and further inflaming tensions and undermining the credibility of local police. In addition, it is quite possible that the militarized response of police immediately after the shooting of Michael Brown, and their continued aggressive posturing, contributed to the outbreaks of violence and property destruction. People subjected to tear gas and baton charges often react by either fighting back or dispersing into small groups to engage in property destruction. Those watching on TV may be motivated to come out and defend those being attacked in a similar manner.

People have the right to protest despite the presence of violence or property destruction nearby. Even when there is isolated criminal conduct within a demonstration, police have an obligation to target those engaged in the illegal behavior without criminalizing or brutalizing the entire demonstration, as long as its primary character remains peaceful. The First Amendment guarantees the right to protest and American criminal law requires the police to act on individualized suspicion. Collectively punishing protestors because they are protesting while others are setting fires is an abridgement of fundamental rights.

Alternatives

A more effective approach might try to do two things. First, political leaders, who bear ultimate responsibility for the outcomes in Ferguson, could have attempted a political solution to their problems. The governor could have initiated a real conversation about the economic, social, and political dynamics that have contributed to the profound alienation of African Americans in the Saint Louis area (if not more broadly). Openly rethinking the hodgepodge of poorly funded municipalities and schools, largely designed to facilitate white flight from Saint Louis, as well as the basic functions of the criminal justice system, could have gone a long way to restore public trust and divert attention from the specifics of Darren

Wilson's case. Local politicians knew that a criminal indictment was highly unlikely but took no steps to reduce the rage they knew would result.

Second, local officials could also have attempted to dial back the police's posture toward protest as threatening and illegitimate. Protests are by their nature disruptive and disorderly. The attitude of police in Saint Louis County has been to treat that as a fundamental threat to the social order. There really is almost no legitimate reason to deploy armored vehicles and snipers to manage protests—even those where some violence has occurred. Officer protection is an issue, but so are police legitimacy and constitutional rights.

In response to the events in Ferguson, Representative Hank Johnson from Georgia introduced a House bill ending the 1033 weapons program. It was unsuccessful but may have contributed to President Obama's decision to reduce the program slightly. In 2016, however, the Obama administration announced that it was reconsidering even these limited reforms in the face of opposition from military hardware producers and local police.[50] President Trump is likely to expand these programs, leaving it up to local jurisdictions to decide the extent of military equipment they want their police to have.

Groups like the Million Hoodies Movement for Justice and the ACLU continue to organize nationally against this militarized approach to policing. In 2016 a group of Los Angeles high school students forced the LA School District to return a variety of military equipment obtained under 1033, including MRAP grenade launchers and automatic weapons.[51] These weapons programs should be abandoned and military equipment returned and destroyed. Even when the weapons are not used, they contribute to police viewing the public as a constant threat and conceiving of the world as divided between evildoers and the good guys. Human nature is profoundly more complicated than that, and a police force that lacks a nuanced understanding of this will invariably slide into intolerance, aggression, and violence.

However, getting rid of the weapons and returning to a negotiated-management style of protest policing is not without potential problems. Negotiated management is only useful when protest actions are orderly and organized. Police need cooperative partners to communicate with. This approach also presumes the legitimacy of a system that severely restricts the time, place, and manner of protest activity, in line with Supreme Court rulings that prioritize order over the right to assembly. Instead, we need to reduce the political conflicts that generate disruptive protest movements. American democracy has been continually undermined by concentrations of wealth and political power in the hands of a smaller and smaller group of wealthy donors and corporate interests; contentious protest activity will increase as long as there is the freedom for it to do so. When normal political channels are closed off, street politics become more common. This can be seen in the rise of the Tea Party, Occupy Wall Street, and Black Lives Matter, all of which expressed profound alienation from existing political arrangements and took to the streets as an alternative.

Decisions about the granting of permits and the plans for deploying police should be largely removed from police control. Police may share their views about traffic management and serious security risks, but decisions should be in the hands of elected leaders operating within legal frameworks that protect the right to dissent. This shift will not be without problems; some leaders will undoubtedly politicize the decision-making process in ways that benefit some groups and not others. This will, however, make clearer the lines of accountability that today are often masked by a technocratic framework. Police make discretionary decisions about when, where, and how groups can protest based on their own threat assessments, which have always been clouded by political bias. That political influence is hidden behind the police bureaucracy.

Police have no legitimate role to play in monitoring, much less actively subverting social movements not actively engaged in violence and property destruction. Widespread surveillance, intelligence gathering, and the use of paid informants and undercover officers should be forbidden unless there is specific evidence of serious criminal activity; even then, investigations should be severely limited in scope and overseen by civilians. Without oversight, abuses always emerge. The temptation to cast a broad net and to interfere with movements that disrupt the social order is too great. If the threat of politically motivated violence is so large, why not involve outside monitors to ensure that police don't overstep their authority? Concerns about secrecy and professional expertise are specious at best; there is no reason to think that suitable guardians of the public interest can't be found. Judges confronted by the abuses of political policing should appoint such monitors on a permanent, not temporary, basis and give them full access to all records and personnel. Our basic democratic values demand nothing less.

The role of police in terrorism investigations must be similarly curtailed. As with the Palmer Raids, the threat has been at times severely overstated to encourage public support for broad-reaching police powers that are almost always used against nonviolent domestic political groups. The drive to get results has encouraged entrapment and guilt-by-association tactics that fly in the face of fair judicial process—something far too many judges have been willing to overlook.

We must also confront the role of US domestic and foreign policy in producing political violence. George W. Bush worked very hard to prevent any discussion of the US role in fomenting a terrorist backlash by labeling the terrorists as "evildoers." The reality is that US foreign policy in the Middle East has played a major role in inspiring such movements and making us a prime target for their anger. We need to rethink our relationship to Gulf oil countries that practice despotic rule and provide ideological and financial support to terrorists. We must also rethink our largely uncritical relationship with Israel, whose actions in the region have been incredibly destabilizing and whose behavior in Gaza and the West Bank have inspired widespread revulsion, some of which blows back on the United States in the form of both international and domestic terrorism.

The best way to avoid political violence is to enhance justice at home and abroad. Rather than embracing a neoconservative framework of retribution, control, and war, we should look to a human rights and social justice framework that seeks to ensure universal health care, education, housing, and food as well as equal access to the political process—goals we are far from achieving.

Conclusion

Policing needs to be reformed. We do indeed need new training regimes, enhanced accountability, and a greater public role in the direction and oversight of policing. We need to get rid of the warrior mindset and militarized tactics. It is essential that police learn more about the problems of people with psychiatric disabilities. Racist and brutal police officers who break the law, violate the public trust, and abuse the public must be held to account. The culture of the police must be changed so that it is no longer obsessed with the use of threats and violence to control the poor and socially marginal.

That said, there is a larger truth that must be confronted. As long as the basic mission of police remains unchanged, none of these reforms will be achievable. There is no technocratic fix. Even if we could somehow implement these changes, they would be ignored, resisted, and overturned—because the institutional imperatives of the politically motivated wars on drugs, disorder, crime, etc., would win out. Powerful political forces benefit from abusive, aggressive, and invasive policing, and they are not going to be won over or driven from power by technical arguments or heartfelt appeals to do the right thing. They may adopt a language of reform and fund a few pilot programs, but mostly they will continue to reproduce their political power by fanning fear of the poor, nonwhite, disabled, and dispossessed and empowering police to be the "thin blue line" between the haves and the have-nots.

This does not mean that no one should articulate or fight for reforms. However, those reforms must be part of a larger vision that questions the basic role of police in society and asks whether coercive government action will bring more justice or less. Too many of the reforms under discussion today fail to do that; many further empower the police and expand their role. Community policing, body cameras, and increased money for training reinforce a false sense of police legitimacy and expand the reach of the police into communities and private lives. More money, more technology, and more power and influence will not reduce the burden or increase the justness of policing. Ending the War on Drugs, abolishing school police, ending broken-windows policing, developing robust mental health care, and creating low-income housing systems will do much more to reduce abusive policing.

In the twentieth century, two major areas of policing were eliminated when alcohol and gambling were legalized. These two changes reduced the scope of policing without sacrificing public safety. Prohibition had led to a massive increase in organized crime, violence, and police corruption but had little effect on the availability of alcohol; ending it reduced crime, enhanced police professionalism, and incarcerated fewer people.

Similarly, fruitless attempts to stamp out underground lotteries, sports betting, and gambling proved totally counterproductive, empowering organized crime and driving police corruption. Government control and regulation of gambling has raised revenue and undermined the power of organized crime. By creating state lotteries, regulating casinos, and only minimally enforcing sports betting, the state has limited police power without sacrificing public safety. There is no reason the same couldn't be done for sex work and drugs today. The billions saved in policing and prisons could be much better used putting people to work and improving public health.

We don't have to put up with aggressive and invasive policing to keep us safe. There are alternatives. We can use the power of communities and government to make our cities safer without relying on police, courts, and prisons. We need to invest in individuals and communities and transform some of the basic economic and political arrangements in our society. Chemical dependency, trauma, and mental health issues play a huge role in undermining the safety and stability of neighborhoods. People who are suffering need help, not coercive treatment regimes or self-help pabulum; they need access to real services from trained professionals using evidence-based treatments. Even children and teens with some of the most serious personal problems can be helped with sustained and intensive engagement and treatment. They need mentors, counseling, and support services for themselves and their families. These "wraparound" approaches show promising results and cost a lot less than cycling young people through jails, courts, emergency rooms, probation, and parole.

People adapt their behaviors to a dysfunctional environment where unemployment, violence, and entrenched poverty are the norm. Even after twenty years of declining crime rates, there are neighborhoods where violence remains a major problem. These areas are almost all extremely poor, racially segregated, and geographically and socially isolated. The response of many cities has been further intensive policing. Recent crime increases and social unrest in places like Chicago, Milwaukee, and Charlotte attest to the failure to end abusive policing or produce safety. The most segregated and racially unequal cities in the country are its most violent.

Decades of deindustrialization, racial discrimination in housing and employment, and growing income inequality have created pockets of intense poverty where jobs are scarce, public services inadequate, and crime and violence widespread. Even with intensive overpolicing, people feel unsafe and young people continue to use violence for predation and protection. Any program for reducing crime and enhancing social wellbeing, much less achieving racial justice, must address these conditions. No one on the political stage is talking seriously about this reality. Racial segregation in the United States is as bad today as it has ever been. Poor communities need better housing, jobs, and access to social, health, recreational, and educational services, not more money for police and jails, yet that's what's on offer across the country. From Chicago to New York to California,[1] local politicians continue to hold out more police and new jails as the solution to community problems. This must stop.

These communities also need more political power and resources to develop their own strategies for reducing crime. Concepts like restorative justice and Justice Reinvestment offer alternatives. The money that would be saved by keeping people out of prison could be spent on drug and mental health services, youth programs and jobs in the community. At the same time, offenders could be asked to make restitution to their victims and the community through community service projects, agreements to stay clean and sober, and participation in appropriate programing. The Justice Reinvestment movement also looked to use savings achieved by reducing incarceration rates to invest in high-crime communities. Unfortunately, many of these programs ended up only moving money around within the criminal justice system and excluding communities from any role in the process.[2] The basic ideal remains sound, but new efforts at realizing it are needed and communities need to play a major role in deciding how the resources are used. But not all problems can be solved at this level. Access to decent housing and employment and the ongoing problems of polarized income structures and racial discrimination in housing must be dealt with systemically. Raising the minimum wage, restoring transit links, and cracking down on housing discrimination are big problems that operate largely outside these poor neighborhoods. If we want to make real headway in reducing the concentrated pockets of crime in this country, we need to create real avenues out of poverty and social isolation.

The Black Youth Project in Chicago envisions a program for economic development that would substantially improve the lives of people in high-crime communities as an alternative to relying on police and prisons. Their "Agenda to Build Black Futures" calls for reparations to address the long legacy of systematic exploitation of African Americans, from slavery through Jim Crow and into the current era.[3] Just as importantly, it focuses at length on decent jobs that can sustain a family above the poverty line. That means raising the minimum wage through direct government action, as well as giving workers the right to self-organize for better wages. Most of the advances that working Americans have made in the last century have come through the process of unionization and workplace activism, but in the last thirty-five years governments have moved systematically to reduce worker and union power. Private-sector protections have been largely erased, leading to massive union-busting drives and decimating union membership rates. The public sector retains more protections, but austerity economics have substantially eroded earnings and many Republican politicians and conservative courts are actively moving to break unions and further drive down wages. Unfortunately, many unions have resisted racial integration historically, and some remain incredibly white even today, so government protection of unions in the absence of a racial justice program will not be sufficient.

The Movement for Black Lives has also outlined a plan for economic and political justice that includes greater investment in schools and communities based on priorities developed by black communities.[4] At the heart of their program is a set of economic justice proposals, including reparations, which would reduce inequality, enhance individual, family, and community wellbeing and protect the environment. They call for major jobs programs, restrictions on free trade and Wall Street exploitation, and vigorous protections of worker rights. They specifically demand that funding for criminal justice institutions should be shifted to education, health, and social services. To make this possible, they demand political reforms and are developing plans for grassroots mobilizations. This is what police reform has to look like if it's going to bring meaningful changes.

Rural areas need help as well. The growth in opioid use is closely linked to the downward mobility of the rural poor and the expansion of the destructive War on Drugs. While simplistic protectionism and jingoistic anti-immigrant mania are unlikely to bring long-term stability, our rural areas must become more economically sustainable and livable, with green jobs, infrastructure development, and nontoxic food production. Reducing subsidies to multinational corporations that move jobs overseas to countries with little in the way of labor rights or environmental protections would also be a good place to start, replacing "free trade" with "fair trade."

None of these initiatives by themselves will eliminate all crime and disorder. They need to be combined and new ideas would need to be developed and tested, but those who would benefit from this process lack the political will and power to do so. US culture is organized around exploitation, greed, white privilege, and resentment. These are derived in large part from our economic system, but even profound economic changes do not automatically produce positive cultural changes, at least not overnight. Cultural norms also impede efforts to change these systems. What's needed is a process in which the very struggle for change produces cultural shifts. By working together for social, economic, and racial justice, we must also create new value systems that call into question the greed and indifference that allow the current system to flourish. We must take care of each other in a climate of mutual respect if we hope to build a better world. One of the more positive aspects of the Black Lives Matter movement has been its embrace of differences of identity and the diversity of people engaged in leading it. We can't fight racism while embracing homophobia, any more than we can fight mass incarceration by embracing a politics of punishment.

Both of our major political parties have accepted the politics of austerity that globalized capital has imposed on us. The neoliberal movement has been incredibly successful in normalizing the view that the only way to move forward is to unleash the creative power of a small number of economic elites by stripping away all regulations, worker protections, and financial obligations so that they can maximize their wealth at the expense of the rest of us. For thirty years we've been told that the result will be a rising tide for everyone; a trickling down of the spoils—but we're still waiting. Wages and living standards for all but the wealthiest continue to decline. The middle class is being eviscerated, poverty and mass homelessness are increasing, and our infrastructure is collapsing. When we organize our society around fake meritocracy, we erase the history of exploitation and the ways the game is rigged to prevent economic and social mobility.

When people complain about these realities, they are told it's their own fault, that they didn't try hard enough to be part of the glorious "1 percent," that they don't have what it takes and thus deserve to be degraded. This justifies defining all problems in terms of individual inadequacy, calling those left behind the architects of their own misery. Rather than using government resources to reduce inequality, this economic system both subsidizes inequality and criminalizes those it leaves behind—especially when they demand something better. The massive increases in policing and incarceration over the last forty years rest on an ideological argument that crime and disorder are the results of personal moral failing and can only be reduced by harsh punitive sanctions. This neoconservative approach protects and reinforces the political, social, and economic disenfranchisement of millions who are tightly controlled by aggressive and invasive policing or warehoused in jails and prisons.

We must break these intertwined systems of oppression. Every time we look to the police and prisons to solve our problems, we reinforce these processes. We cannot demand that the police get rid of those "annoying" homeless people in the park or the "threatening" young people on the corner and simultaneously call for affordable housing and youth jobs, because the state is only offering the former and will deny us the latter every time. Yes, communities deserve protection from crime and even disorder, but we must always demand those without reliance on the coercion, violence, and humiliation that undergird our criminal justice system. The state may try to solve those problems through police power, but we should not encourage or reward such short-sighted, counterproductive, and unjust approaches. We should demand safety and security—but not at the hands of the police. In the end, they rarely provide either.

Notes

1 The Limits of Police Reform

1 Parts of this chapter appeared previously in *Nation*, *Gotham Gazette* and Al Jazeera America.
2 Killed by Police.net, 2015; "Police Shootings Database 2015," *Washington Post*, 2015; "The Counted," *Guardian*, continually updated.
3 Nicole Flatow, "Report: Black Male Teens Are 21 Times More Likely to Be Killed by Cops than White Ones," *ThinkProgress,* October 10, 2014; Jeff Kelly Lowenstein, "Killed by the Cops," *ColorLines.com,* November 4, 2007.
4 Jaeah Lee, "Exactly How Often Do Police Shoot Unarmed Black Men?" *Mother Jones,* August 15, 2014.
5 Jennifer H. Peck, "Minority Perceptions of the Police: A State-of-the-art Review," *Policing: An International Journal of Police Strategies and Management* 38, no. 1 (2015): 173–203.
6 Victoria Bekiempis, "Why Do NYC's Minorities Still Face So Many Misdemeanor Arrests?" *Newsweek*, February 28, 2015, http://www.newsweek.com/nypd-race-arrest-numbers-309686.
7 Shane Dixon Kavanaugh, "NYPD officers stop-and-frisk Harlem teen, threaten to break his arm: audio recording," *nydailynews.com,* October 9, 2012.
8 Helene Cooper, "Obama Criticizes Arrest of Harvard Professor," *New York Times*, July 22, 2009.
9 Sue Rahr and Stephen Rice, "From Warriors to Guardians: Recommitting American Penal Culture to Democratic Ideals," *New Perspectives in Policing* (April 2015).
10 Simone Weichselbaum and Beth Schwartzapfel, "When veterans become cops, some bring war home." *USA Today,* March 30, 2017.
11 Radley Balko, *Rise of the Warrior Cop: The Militarization of America's Police Forces* (New York: PublicAffairs, 2013).
12 James Q. Wilson and George Kelling, "Broken Windows: The police and neighborhood safety," *Atlantic*, March 1982.
13 Edward Banfield, *The Unheavenly City: The Nature and the*

Future of Our Urban Crisis (Boston: Little Brown and Co, 1970).

14 Frederick Siegel, *The Future Once Happened Here: New York, D.C., L.A., and the Fate of America's Big Cities* (New York: Free Press, 1997).

15 James Q. Wilson and Richard Herrnstein, *Crime and Human Nature: The Definitive Study of the Causes of Crime* (New York: Simon & Schuster, 1985).

16 Ibid.

17 Richard Herrnstein and Charles Murray, *The Bell Curve: Intelligence and Class Structure in American Life* (New York: Simon & Schuster, 2010).

18 "Fair and Impartial Policing," www.fairimpartialpolicing.com.

19 Joaquin Sapien, "Racist Posts on NY Cop Blog Raise Ire at Time of Tension," *ProPublica*, April 16, 2015, http://www.propublica.org/article/racist-posts-on-ny-cop-blog-raise-ire-at-time-of-tension.

20 Melissa Crowe and Bianca Montes, "Victoria police officer investigated for tasing driver, 76," *Victoria Advocate*, December 13, 2014.

21 Peter Moskos, *Cop in the Hood: My Year Policing Baltimore's Eastern District* (Princeton, NJ: Princeton University Press, 2008). David Couper, *Arrested Development: A Veteran Police Chief Sounds Off about Protest, Racism, Corruption, and the Seven Necessary Steps to Improve our Nation's Police* (CreateSpace Independent Publishing Platform, 2012).

22 Seth Stoughton, "Law Enforcement's 'Warrior' Problem," *Harvard Law Review* 128, April 2015.

23 Jon Swaine, "Ohio Walmart video reveals moments before officer killed John Crawford," *Guardian,* September 25, 2014.

24 Jon Swaine, "Video shows John Crawford's girlfriend aggressively questioned after Ohio police shot him dead in Walmart," *Guardian*, December 14, 2014.

25 Jason Hanna, Martin Savidge and John Murgatroyd, "Video shows trooper shooting unarmed man, South Carolina police say," CNN, September 26, 2014.

26 "Close Quarters Battle: SRT Training, CQB Training, SWAT Training, High Risk Entry Training, Combat Training, Hand-to-Hand Combat," www.cqb.cc.

27 "Trojan Securities International," trojansecurities.com/military.html.

28 Balko, *Rise of the Warrior Cop.*

29 Brian A. Reaves, "Local Police Departments, 2007," US Department of Justice: Office of Justice Programs, Bureau of Justice Statistics (2010).

30 Robert Friedrich, *The Impact of Organizational, Individual, and Situational Factors on Police Behavior* (University of Michigan:

Ph.D. Dissertation, 1977); Joel Garner, Thomas Schade, John Hepburn, and John Buchanan, "Measuring the Continuum of Force Used by and Against the Police," *Criminal Justice Review* 20 (1994): 146–68; James McElvain and Augustine Kposowa, "Police Officer Characteristics and Internal Affairs Investigations for Use of Force Allegations," *Journal of Criminal* Justice 32, no. 3 (2004): 265–279; William Terrill and Stephen Mastrofski, "Situational and Officer-Based Determinants of Police Coercion," *Justice Quarterly* 19, no. 2 (2002): 215–248. John McCluskey, William Terrill, and Eugene Paoline, "Peer Group Aggressiveness and the Use of Coercion in Police-Suspect Encounters," *Police Practice and Research* 6, no. 1 (2005): 19–37; Brian Lawton, "Levels of Nonlethal Force: An Examination of Individual, Situational, and Contextual Factors," *Journal of Research in Crime and Delinquency* 44, no. 2 (2007): 163–184.

31 Bernard Cohen and Jan Chaiken, *Police Background Characteristics and Performance: Summary* (Santa Monica, CA: RAND Corporation, 1972). Ivan Sun and Brian Payne, "Racial Differences in Resolving Conflicts: A Comparison between Black and White Police Officers," *Crime and Delinquency* 50, no. 4 (2004): 516–541. Robert Brown and James Frank, "Race and Officer Decision Making: Examining Differences in Arrest Outcomes between Black and White Officers," *Justice Quarterly* 23, no. 1 (2006): 96–126.

32 Ryan Martin, "Having more black officers not a 'direct solution' for reducing black killings by police, IU research show," *Indy Star*, February 27, 2017.

33 Steven Brand and Meghan Stroshine, "The Role of Officer Attributes, Job Characteristics, and Arrest Activity in Explaining Police Use of Force," *Criminal Justice Policy Review* 24, no. 5 (2014): 551–572.

34 President's Task Force on 21st Century Policing, *Final Report of the President's Task Force on 21st Century Policing* (Washington, DC: Office of Community Oriented Policing Services, 2015).

35 President's Commission on Law Enforcement and Administration of Justice, *The Challenge of Crime in a Free Society: A Report by the President's Commission on Law Enforcement and Administration of Justice* (Washington, DC: United States Government Printing Office, 1967).

36 National Advisory Commission on Civil Disorders, *Report of the National Advisory Commission on Civil Disorders* (New York: Bantam Books, 1968).

37 *Omnibus Crime Control and Safe Streets Act of 1968*, Pub. L. 90–351, 90th Cong. (June 19, 2007).

38 Monica Bell, "Police Reform and the Dismantling of Legal Estrangement," *Yale Law Journal* 126:7 (2017).
39 Civil Rights Division of the United States Department of Justice, *Report on the Investigation of the Ferguson Police Department* (Washington, DC, March 4, 2015).
40 James Comey, "Speech at Georgetown University," (Washington, DC, February 12, 2015), FBI.gov; Christopher Mathias, "Bratton Says Police to Blame for 'Worst Parts' of Black History, but Reform Advocates are Unimpressed," *Huffington Post*, February 24, 2015, http://www.huffingtonpost.com/2015/02/24/william-bratton-nypd-slavery-history-broken-windows_n_6746906.html.
41 Steve Herbert, *Citizens, Cops, and Power: Recognizing the Limits of Community* (Chicago: University of Chicago Press, 2006).
42 Kimberly Kindy and Kimbriell Kelly, "Thousands Dead, Few Prosecuted," *Washington Post*, April 11, 2015.
43 *Graham v. Connor*, 490 U.S. 386 (1989).
44 Judith Browne Dianis, "Why Police Shootings are a Federal Problem," *Politico*, April 13, 2015.
45 *Cause of Action, U.S. Code* 42 (1994), § 14141.
46 Simone Weichselbaum, "Policing the Police," Marshall Project, May 26, 2015.
47 David Harris, *Driving While Black: Racial Profiling on our Nation's Highways* (New York: American Civil Liberties Union, 1999).
48 Mark Berman, "Six Cleveland Police Officers Fired for Fatal '137 Shots' Car Chase in 2012," *Washington Post*, January 26, 2016.
49 Robin Meyer, "Body Cameras are Betraying their Promise," *Atlantic*, September 30, 2016.
50 Min-Seok Pang and Paul A. Pavlou, "Armed with Technology: The Impact on Fatal Shootings by the Police," Fox School of Business Research Paper No 60-020. September 8, 2016.
51 Alex S. Vitale, "A New Approach to Body Cameras," *Gotham Gazette*, May 2, 2017.
52 Barry Friedman, *Unwarranted: Policing Without Permission* (New York: Farrar, Straus and Giroux, 2017).
53 "The Counted," *Guardian*. https://www.theguardian.com/us-news/series/counted-us-police-killings.
54 American Civil Liberties Union (ACLU), *War Comes Home: The Excessive Militarization of American Policing* (New York: ACLU Foundation, 2014).
55 Peter Kraska, *Militarizing the American Criminal Justice System: The Changing Roles of the Armed Forces and the Police* (Lebanon, NH: University Press of New England, 2001).

56 Tina Chen, "Baby in Coma after Police 'Grenade' Dropped in Crib During Drug Raid," *ABC News*, May 30, 2014.
57 Greg Smithsimon, "Disarm the Police," *MetroPolitics*, September 29, 2015.
58 Chris Hayes, *A Colony in a Nation* (New York: W.W. Norton and Co., 2017).
59 Brady Dennis, Mark Berman, and Elahe Izadi, "Dallas Police Chief Says 'We're Asking Cops to Do Too Much in This Country,'" *Washington Post*, July 11, 2016.
60 Saki Knafo, "A Black Police Officer's Fight Against the NYPD," *New York Times*, February 18, 2016.

2 The Police Are Not Here to Protect You

1 David Bayley, *Police for the Future* (Oxford, UK: Oxford University Press, 1996), 25–28.
2 Naomi Murakawa, *The First Civil Right: How Liberals Built Prison America* (Oxford, UK: Oxford University Press, 2014).
3 David Bayley, "The Development of Modern Policing" in *Policing Perspectives: An Anthology*, ed. Larry Gaines (Oxford, UK: Oxford University Press, 1998), 67.
4 Allan Silver, "The Demand for Order in Civil Society," in *The Police*, ed. David J. Bordua (New York: John Wiley and Sons, 1976), 21.
5 Kristian Williams, *Our Enemies in Blue: Police and Power in America* (Oakland, CA: AK Press), 119.
6 Mash Neocleous, The Fabrication of Social Order: A Critical Theory of Police Power, Pluto Press, 2000.
7 Galen Broeker, *Rural Disorder and Police Reform in Ireland, 1812–36* (Abingdon, UK: Routledge, 2015).
8 Donald Read, *Peterloo: The 'Massacre' and its Background* (Manchester, UK: Manchester University Press, 1958); Robert Walmsley, *Peterloo: The Case Re-opened* (Manchester, UK: Manchester University Press, 1969).
9 F.C. Mather, *Public Order in the Age of the Chartists* (Manchester, UK: Manchester University Press, 1984).
10 Roger Lane, *Policing the City: Boston, 1822–1885*, (New York: Atheneum, 1971).
11 Paul Gilje, *The Road to Mobocracy: Popular Disorder in New York City, 1763–1834* (Chapel Hill, NC: University of North Carolina Press, 1987).

12 Raymond Blaine Fosdick, *Crime in America and the Police* (New York: The Century Co., 1920).
13 Sam Mitrani, *The Rise of the Chicago Police: Class and Conflict, 1850–1894* (Chicago: University of Illinois Press, 2013).
14 Lane, *Policing the City.*
15 Eric Monkkonen, *Policing Urban America: 1860–1920* (Cambridge, UK: Cambridge University Press, 1981).
16 Roger G. Dunham and Geoffrey P. Alpert, *Critical Issues in Policing: Contemporary Readings, Seventh Edition* (Long Grove, IL: Waveland Press, Inc., 2015).
17 Daniel Czitrom, *New York Exposed: The Gilded Age Police Scandal that Launched the Progressive Era* (Oxford, UK: Oxford University Press, 2016).
18 Spencer J. Sadler, *Pennsylvania's Coal and Iron Police* (Chicago: Arcadia Publishing, 2009).
19 Alfred McCoy, *Policing America's Empire: The United States, The Philippines, and the Rise of the Surveillance State* (Madison, WI: University of Wisconsin Press, 2009).
20 Pennsylvania State Federation of Labor, *The American Cossack* (New York: Arno Press & The New York Times, 1971).
21 "Pennsylvania State Police [Politics] Historical Marker," *ExplorePAhistory.com*, http://explorepahistory.com/hmarker.php?markerId=1-A-3BB.
22 Jeremy Kuzmarov, *Modernizing Repression: Police Training and Nation-Building in the American Century* (Amherst, MA: University of Massachussetts Press, 2012), 39.
23 Ibid.
24 Mike Cox, *The Texas Rangers: Wearing the Cinco Peso, 1821–1900* (London, UK: Macmillan, 2008).
25 William Carrigan and Clive Webb, *Forgotten Dead: Mob Violence against Mexicans in the United States, 1848–1928* (Oxford, UK: Oxford University Press, 2013).
26 Aaron Cantu, "The Chaparral Insurgents of South Texas," *New Inquiry*, April 7, 2016; Rebecca Onion, "America's Lost History of Border Violence," *Slate*, May 5, 2016.
27 Benjamin Johnson, *Revolution in Texas: How a Forgotten Rebellion and Its Bloody Suppression Turned Mexicans into Americans* (New Haven, CT: Yale University Press, 2005).
28 Julian Samora, Joe Bernal, and Albert Peña, *Gunpowder Justice: A Reassessment of the Texas Rangers* (Notre Dame, IN: University of Notre Dame Press, 1979).
29 Walter Webb, *The Texas Rangers: A Century of Frontier Defense* (Boston: Houghton Mifflin, 1935).
30 Walter Webb, *The Texas Rangers: A Century of Frontier Defense,*

2nd ed. (Austin, TX: University of Texas Press, 1965).

31 Sally Hadden, *Slave Patrols: Law and Violence in Virginia and the Carolinas* (Cambridge, MA: Harvard University Press, 2001).

32 Richard Wade, *Slavery in the Cities: The South 1820–1860* (Oxford, UK: Oxford University Press, 1967), 80.

33 Ibid, 82.

34 Hadden, *Slave Patrols*, 4.

35 Douglas Blackmon, *Slavery by Another Name: The Re-Enslavement of Black Americans from the Civil War to World War II* (New York: Anchor Books, 2008).

36 Williams, *Our Enemies in Blue*, Ch. 4.

37 Micol Seigel, "Objects of Police History," *Journal of American History* 102, no. 1 (2015): 152–161.

38 Kuzmarov, *Modernizing Repression*, 235.

39 Christian Parenti, *Lockdown America: Police and Prisons in the Age of Crisis* (Brooklyn, NY: Verso Books, 2000).

40 Jonathon Simon, *Governing Through Crime: How the War on Crime Transformed American Democracy and Created a Culture of Fear* (Oxford, UK: Oxford University Press, 2007).

41 Michelle Alexander, *The New Jim Crow: Mass Incarceration in the Age of Colorblindness* (New York: The New Press, 2013).

42 Jeffrey Reiman, *The Rich Get Richer and the Poor Get Prison: Ideology, Class, and Criminal Justice* (Boston: Pearson, 2007).

43 Alexander, *The New Jim Crow*, 224–5.

44 Simon, *Governing Through Crime*.

3 The School-to-Prison Pipeline

1 "Justice League NYC," gatheringforjustice.org/justiceleaguenyc.

2 Lucinda Gray and Laurie Lewis, *Public School Safety and Discipline: 2013–2014* (Washington, D.C.: National Center for Education Statistics, U.S. Department of Education, 2015). Retrieved July 15, 2016 from http://nces.ed.gov/pubsearch.

3 "COPS in Schools (CIS)," *U.S. Department of Justice Community Oriented Policing Services*, http://www.cops.usdoj.gov/default.asp?Item=54.

4 John DiIulio, "The Coming of the Super-Predators," *Weekly Standard*, November 27, 1995, 23; James Q. Wilson, "Crime and Public Policy," in *Crime*, eds. James Q. Wilson and Joan Petersilia (San Francisco: Institute for Contemporary Studies Press, 1995).

5 DiIulio, "The Coming of the Super-Predators."

6 Melissa Sickmund and Charles Puzzanchera, eds., *Juvenile*

Offenders and Victims: 2014 National Report (Pittsburgh, PA: National Center for Juvenile Justice, 2014).

7 Advancement Project, *Test, Punish and Push Out: How Zero Tolerance and High-Stakes Testing Funnel Youth into the School-To-Prison Pipeline* (Washington, D.C.: Advancement Project, January 2010).

8 Ibid, 32.

9 Ibid, 31.

10 Augustina Reyes, *Discipline, Achievement, and Race: Is Zero Tolerance the Answer?* (New York: Rowman and Littlefield, 2006).

11 Annette Fuentes, *Lockdown High: When the Schoolhouse Becomes and Jailhouse* (Brooklyn, NY: Verso, 2013).

12 Abigail Thernstrom and Stephen Thernstrom, *No Excuses: Closing the Racial Gap in Learning* (New York: Simon and Schuster, 2004).

13 Kate Taylor, "At a Success Academy Charter School, Singling Out Pupils Who Have 'Got to Go,'" *New York Times*, October 29, 2015.

14 *PBS Newshour*, "Is kindergarten too young to suspend a student?" October 12, 2015.

15 Taylor, "At a Success Academy Charter School."

16 US Department of Education Office for Civil Rights, "Data Snapshot: School Discipline," Civil Rights Data Collection, no. 1 (March 2014).

17 Libby Nelson and Dara Lind, "The school to prison pipeline, explained," Justice Policy Institute, February 24, 2015.

18 Tamar Lewin, "Black Students Face More Discipline, Data Suggests," *New York Times*, March 6, 2012.

19 Ibid.

20 Project Nia, "Data on School 2013–2014," *Policing Chicago Public Schools* 3 (2015).

21 Daniel Losen and Russell Skiba, *Suspended Education: Urban Middle Schools in Crisis* (Montgomery AL: Southern Poverty Law Center, 2010).

22 Jonathan Brice, "Baltimore Leader Helps District Cut Suspensions," *Education Week*, February 6, 2013; Rachel Graham Cody, "Expel Check," *Williamette Week*, September 24, 2013; Jill Tucker, "Oakland schools to get suspension monitor," *SF Gate*, September 27, 2012; Lewin, "Black Students Face More Discipline"; Children's Defense Fund—Ohio, "Issue Brief: Zero Tolerance and Exclusionary School Discipline Policies Harm Students and Contribute to the Cradle to Prison Pipeline," *Kids Count*, November 2012.

23 US Department of Justice and US Department of Education, "Dear Colleague Letter: Nondiscriminatory Administration of School Discipline," January 8, 2014.
24 Susan Ferriss, "Update: How kicking a trash can became criminal for a 6th grader," *Center for Public Integrity,* September 3, 2015.
25 Ibid.
26 American Civil Liberties Union, "Kentucky Case Spotlights Problem of Untrained Law Enforcement Disciplining Students with Disabilities," August 3, 2015.
27 Niraj Chokshi, "School police across the country receive excess military weapons and gear," *Washington Post*, September 16, 2014.
28 American Civil Liberties Union, "South Carolina Students Were Terrorized by Police Raid with Guns and Drug Dogs, ACLU Lawsuit Charges," December 15, 2003.
29 Rebecca, Leung, "Ambush at Goose Creek: Drug Worries Lead to Raid at S. Carolina High School," *CBS News*, February 2, 2004.
30 Bethany Peak, "Militarization of School Police: One Route on the School-to-Prison Pipeline," *Arkansas Law Review* 68, no. 2 (2015): 195–229.
31 Fuentes, *Lockdown High*, 155.
32 Dana Goldstein, "In Your Face: Does Tear Gas Belong in Schools? Do Police?" Marshall Project, January 26, 2015.
33 Emma Brown, "Judge: Police can no longer pepper-spray students for minor misbehavior at school," *Washington Post*, October 1, 2015.
34 Elliot McLaughlin, "Texas student tased by police exits coma, enters rehabilitation, attorney says," CNN, February 3, 2014.
35 Thad Moore, Nicole Hensley, and Corky Siemaszko, "Deputy involved in body-slam arrest of Spring Valley High student is dating a black woman so he can't be racist, sheriff says," *New York Daily News*, October 27, 2015.
36 "Police Brutality—Officer Beats Special Ed Kid," YouTube video, 3:29, posted by "StopTheBrutality," October 27, 2010, https://www.youtube.com/watch?v=HU5fAGOVvEM.
37 Jaeah Lee, "Chokeholds, Brain Injuries, Beatings: When School Cops Go Bad," *Mother Jones*, July 14, 2015.
38 Eva Ruth Moravec, "Teen shot by Northside officer identified," *My San Antonio*, November 15, 2010.
39 James Pinkerton, "Local school police used force on students hundreds of times in recent years," *Houston Chronicle*, March 27, 2015.
40 "Additional counselors at Price Middle School after shooting," *WGCL-TV Atlanta,* February 28, 2013.

41 Chongmin Na and Denise Gottfredson, "Police Officers in Schools: Effects on School Crime and the Processing of Offending Behaviors," *Justice Quarterly* (2011): 1–32.
42 Barbara Raymond, "Response Guide No. 10: Assigning Police Officers to Schools," Center for Problem-Oriented Policing, 2010.
43 US Department of Education, *Guiding Principles: A Resource Guide for Improving School Climate and Discipline* (Washington, D.C.: US Department of Education, 2014).
44 Seth Stoughton and Josh Gupta-Kagan, "Why are Police Disciplining Students?" *Atlantic*, October 29, 2015.
45 R.E. Hamilton, "School, Police, and Probation: A Winning Team in Fresno," *School Safety* (Spring 1996): 20–23.
46 Kevin Quinn, "My View: More school resource officers, more safe school," CNN, January 17, 2013.
47 I. India Thusi, "Systemic Failure: The School-to-Prison Pipeline and Discrimination Against Poor Minority Students," *Journal of Law and Society* 13 (2011): 281–299; Peak, "Militarization of School Police."
48 Lisa Thurau, "Cops and Kids: We Need New Thinking," *Crime Report*, April 2, 2015.
49 US Department of Education, Office of Special Education Programs, "Positive Behavioral Interventions and Supports," pbis.org.
50 New York City School-Justice Partnership Task Force, *Keeping Kids in School and Out of Court: Report and Recommendations* (Albany, NY: New York State Permanent Judicial Commission on Justice for Children, 2013).
51 Urban Youth Collaborative, "The $746 Million a Year School-to-Prison Pipeline," Center for Popular Democracy, 2011.
52 American Federation of Teachers, "Community Schools," http://www.aft.org/position/community-schools.
53 Emma Brown, "Some Baltimore youth have fears of police reinforced in their schools," *Washington Post*, May 2, 2015.
54 Ibid.
55 Collaborative for Academic, Social, and Emotional Learning, "What is Social and Emotional Learning?" n.d.
56 John Payton, Roger Weissberg, Joseph Durlak, Allison Dymnicki, Rebecca Taylor, Kriston Schellinger, and Molly Pachen, *The Positive Impact of Social and Emotional Learning for Kindergarten to Eighth Grade Students: Findings from Three Scientific Reviews* (Chicago, IL: Collaborative for Academic, Social, and Emotional Learning, 2008).
57 J. Lawrence Aber, Sara Pederson, Joshua Brown, Stephanie Jones, Elizabeth Gershoff, *Changing Children's Trajectories of Development: Two-Year Evidence for the Effectiveness of a School-Based*

Approach to Violence Prevention (New York: National Center for Children in Poverty, 2003).

58 National Dropout Prevention Center/Network, "Model Program: Bry's Behavioral Monitoring and Reinforcement Program," n.d.

59 Matthew Mayer and Peter Leone, "A Structural Analysis of School Violence and Disruption: Implications for Creating Safer Schools," *Education and Treatment of Children* 22, no. 3 (1999): 333–356.

60 Ibid, 349.

61 Ibid, 352.

4 "We Called for Help, and They Killed My Son"

1 The chapter title is taken from a news report. See Michael Pearson, Christina Zdanowicz and David Mattingly, "'We called for help, and they killed my son,' North Carolina man says," CNN, January 7, 2014.

2 Egon Bittner, "The Police on Skid-Row: A Study of Peace Keeping," *American Sociological Review* 32, no. 5 (1967): 699–715.

3 *Guardian*, "The Counted."

4 Doris Fuller, H. Richard Lamb, Michael Biasotti, and John Snook, *Overlooked in the Undercounted: The Role of Mental Illness in Fatal Law Enforcement Encounters* (Arlington, VA: Treatment Advocacy Center, 2015).

5 Powell Shooting (Cell Phone Camera), YouTube video, posted by Sol Rayz, August 20, 2014, www.youtube.com/watch?v=j-P54MZVxMU&feature=youtu.be&bpctr=1470409330.

6 Naomi Martin, "Video: Dallas cops fatally shoot mentally ill man wielding screwdriver," *Dallas Morning News*, March 17, 2015.

7 Joseph Berger, "Officer Fatally Shoots Man After Stabbing in Brooklyn Synagogue," *New York Times*, December 9, 2014.

8 Alexandra Sims, "Nicholas Salvador became 'obsessed' with beheading videos weeks before killing grandmother Palmira Silva," *Independent*, June 24, 2015.

9 Ben Cohen, "This is How UK Police Stop Someone with a Knife," *Daily Banter*, August 21, 2014.

10 Daily Mail Reporter, "The moment thirty riot police tackled machete-wielding man with a wheelie bin," *Daily Mail*, May 20, 2011.

11 Rebecca Allison, "UK's first 'suicide by cop' ruling," *Guardian*, May 9, 2003.

12 Independent Commission on Mental Health and Policing, "Report," May 2013, http://news.bbc.co.uk/2/shared/bsp/hi/pdfs/10_05_13_report.pdf.

13 Fuller et al, *Overlooked in the Undercounted*; Martha Williams Deane, Henry Steadman, Randy Borum, Bonita Veysey, Joseph Morrissey, *Emerging Partnerships Between Mental Health and Law Enforcement* (Arlington, VA: American Psychiatric Association, 1999); Melissa Reuland, Matthew Schwarzfeld, and Laura Draper, *Law Enforcement Responses to People with Mental Illnesses: A Guide to Research-Informed Policy and Practice* (New York: Council of State Governments Justice Center, 2009).

14 National Association on Mental Illness (NAMI), "Jailing People with Mental Illness," n.d.

15 E. Fuller Torrey, Mary Zdanowicz, Aaron Kennard, H. Richard Lamb, Donald Eslinger, Michael Biasotti, and Doris Fuller, "The Treatment of Persons with Mental Illness in Prisons and Jails: A State Survey," (Arlington, VA: Treatment Advocacy Center, 2014).

16 Martin Kaste, "The 'Shock of Confinement': The Grim Reality of Suicide in Jail," NPR, July 27, 2015.

17 NAMI, "Jailing People."

18 Substance Abuse and Mental Health Services Administration, *Results from the 2011 National Survey on Drug Use and Health: Mental Health Findings* (Rockville, MD: U.S. Department of Health and Human Services Substance Abuse and Mental Health Administration, 2012).

19 Dennis Culhane, Stephen Metraux, and Trevor Hadley, "Public Service Reductions Associated with Placement of Homeless Persons with Severe Mental Illness in Supportive Housing," *Housing Policy Debates* 13, no. 1 (2002): 107–163; Robert Rosenheck, Wesley Kasprow, Linda Risman, and Wen Liu-Mares, "Cost-effectiveness of Supported Housing for Homeless Persons With Mental Illness," *Archives of General Psychiatry* 60, no. 9 (2003): 940–951; Thomas Chalmers McLaughlin, "Using Common Themes: Cost-Effectiveness of Permanent Supported Housing for People With Mental illness," *Research on Social Work Practice* 21, no. 4 (2011): 404–411; David Cloud and Chelsea Davis, *Treatment Alternatives to Incarceration for People with Mental Health Needs in the Criminal Justice System: The Cost-Savings Implications* (New York: Vera Institute of Justice, 2013).

20 Andy Newman, "Disturbed Man Wielding a Hammer Is Killed by Police in Brooklyn," *New York Times*, August 31, 1999.

21 Vivian Ho, Jenna Lyons, and Kale Williams, "Killing by S.F. police sets off public debate," SFGate, December 4, 2015.

22 CIT International, "Memphis Model," n.d., www.citinternational.org/training-overview/163-memphis-model.html.

23 Saki Knafo, "Change of Habit: How Seattle Cops Fought an

Addiction to Locking Up Drug Users," *Huffington Post*, August 28, 2014.

24 Lauren Almquist and Elizabeth Dodd, *Mental Health Courts: A Guide to Research-Informed Policy and Practice* (New York: Council of State Governments Justice Center, 2012).

25 Christian Henrichson, Joshua Rinaldi, and Ruth Delaney, *The Price of Jails: Measuring the Taxpayer Cost of Local Incarceration* (New York: Vera Institute of Justice, 2015).

26 Linda Teplin, "Keeping the Peace: Police Discretion and Mentally Ill Persons," *National Institute of Justice Journal* (July 2000): 8–15.

27 Michael Biasotti, "Policing the Mentally Ill," *Law Enforcement Today*, November 20, 2014, http://www.lawenforcementtoday.com/2014/11/20/policing-the-mentally-ill/.

28 Michael Koval, "Chief Koval's Blog: Madison Police Department Announces a new Mental Health Officer pilot program," *cityofmadison.com*, January 26, 2015, *http*://www.cityofmadison.com/police/chief/blog/?Id=6324.

29 David Ovale, "In Miami-Dade, hope, help for offenders with mental illness," *Miami Herald*, September 29, 2014.

30 Cloud and Davis, *Treatment Alternatives to Incarceration.*

31 Ovale, "In Miami-Dade, hope, help."

5 Criminalizing Homelessness

1 National Law Center on Homelessness and Poverty, *No Safe Place: The Criminalization of Homelessness in U.S. Cities* (Washington, D.C.: National Law Center on Homelessness and Poverty, 2014).

2 Katherine Beckett and Steve Herbert, *Banished: The New Social Control in Urban America* (Oxford, UK: Oxford University Press, 2009).

3 Alex Vitale, "The Safer Cities Initiative and the Removal of the homeless: Reducing crime or promoting gentrification on Los Angeles' Skid Row," *Criminology and Public Policy* 9, no. 4 (2010): 867–873; Forrest Stuart, *Down and Out and Under Arrest: Policing and Everyday Life in Skid Row* (Chicago: Chicago University Press, 2016).

4 Rick Rojas and Joseph Kolb, "Albuquerque Officers Are Charged with Murder in Death of Homeless Man," *New York Times*, January 12, 2015.

5 Kate Mather, Joel Rubin, and Gale Holland, "Video of LAPD

killing turns harsh light on skid row," *Los Angeles Times*, March 2, 2015; Kate Mather, James Queally, and Gale Holland, "L.A. Police Commission clears officers in skid row shooting but faults officer in Burbank killing," *Los Angeles Times,* February 2, 2016.

6 Kate Mather, "LAPD killing of unarmed homeless man in Venice was unjustified, Police Commission says," *Los Angeles Times*, April 12, 2016.

7 Vitale, *City of Disorder*. Alex Vitale, "Enforcing Civility: Homelessness, 'Quality of Life,' and the Crisis of Urban Liberalism" (City University Graduate School: Ph.D. dissertation, 2001).

8 David Firestone, "3 Tell Council They Beat Homeless to Clear Out Business District," *New York Times*, May 11, 1995.

9 Ross MacDonald, Fatos Kaba, Zachary Rosner, Allison Vise, David Weiss, Mindy Brittner, Molly Sherker, Nathaniel Dickey, and Homer Venters, "The Rikers Island Hot Spotters: Defining the Needs of the Most Frequently Incarcerated," *American Journal of Public Health* 105, no. 11 (2015): 2262–2268.

10 Ibid, 2262.

11 Jonathan Wrathall, Jayme Day, Mary Beth-Ferguson, Aldo Hernandez, Alyson Ainscough, Kerry Steadman, Rachelle Brown, Patrick Frost, and Ashley Tolman, *Comprehensive Report on Homelessness: State of Utah 2013* (Salt Lake City, UT: Utah Housing and Community Development Division, 2013).

12 Paul Guerin and Alexandra Tonigan, *City of Albuquerque Heading Home Initiative Cost Study Report Phase 1* (Albuquerque, NM: University of New Mexico Institute for Social Research, 2013).

13 Gregory Shinn, *The Cost of Long-Term Homelessness in Central Florida: The Current Crisis and the Economic Impact of Providing Sustainable Housing Solutions* (Orlando, FL: Central Florida Commission on Homelessness, 2014).

14 Michael Cousineau, Heather Lander, and Mollie Lowery, *Homeless Cost Study* (Los Angeles, CA: United Way of Greater Los Angeles, 2009).

15 Andrew Liese, "We Can Do Better: Anti-Homeless Ordinances as Violations of State Substantive Due Process Law," *Vanderbilt Law* Review 59, no. 4 (2006): 1413–1455; Robert C. Ellickson, "Controlling Chronic Misconduct in City Spaces: Of Panhandlers, Skid Rows, and Public Space Zoning," *Yale Law Journal* 105, no. 5 (1996): 1165–1248; Maria Foscarinis, "Downward Spiral: Homelessness and Its Criminalization," *Yale Law and Policy Review* 14, no. 1 (1996): 1–63.

16 Kirk Johnson, "Property of a Homeless Man is Private, Hartford Court Says: Justices break new ground on the rights of the homeless," *New York Times*, March 19, 1991; Bob Egelko, "Homeless

have right to reclaim property," *San Francisco Chronicle*, August 9, 2014; Gale Holland, "Seize a homeless person's property? Not so fast, a federal judge tells L.A.," *Los Angeles Times*, April 13, 2016.

17 US Department of Justice, "Justice Department Files Brief to Address the Criminalization of Homelessness," August 6, 2015.

18 United States Interagency Council on Homelessness, *Searching Out Solutions: Constructive Alternatives to the Criminalization of Homelessness* (Washington, D.C.: United States Interagency Council on Homelessness, 2012).

19 Bob Egelko, "U.N. panel denounces laws targeting homeless," *San Francisco Chronicle*, May 2, 2014.

20 Judicial Branch of Arizona Maricopa County, "Homeless Court," n.d.

21 National Low Income Housing Coalition, "Rental Inflation Drives Homelessness and Housing Instability for the Poor," May 1, 2015.

22 Virginia Housing Alliance, "Governor McAuliffe Announces 10.5 percent Decrease in Overall Homelessness in Virginia," July 21, 2016.

23 Maria La Ganga, "Utah says it won 'war on homelessness,' but shelters tell a different story," *Guardian*, April 27, 2016.

24 *Kitsap Sun*, "Opinion: Further questions about housing first," July 14, 2016.

25 Hasson Rashid, "Restoring Bread and Jams for the Homeless," Alliance of Cambridge Tenants, June 21, 2014.

26 *San Francisco Homeless Resource*, "Mission Neighborhood Research Center," n.dhttp://sfhomeless.wikia.com/

27 Alex Vitale, "Why are New York cops shaming homeless people?" *Al Jazeera America*, August 16, 2015.

6 The Failures of Policing Sex Work

1 Susan Dewey, "On the Boundaries of the Global Margins: Violence, labor, and Surveillance in a Rust Belt Topless Bar," in Susan Dewey and Patty Kelley, eds., *Policing Pleasure: Sex Work, Policy, and the State in Global Perspective* (New York: NYU Press, 2011).

2 Katherine Beckett and Steve Herbert, *Banished: The New Social Control in Urban America* (New York: Oxford, 2009).

3 Lisa Duggan, "What the Pathetic Case Against Rentboy.com Says About Sex Work," *Nation*, January 7, 2016.

4 Melissa Gira Grant, "The NYPD Arrests Women for Who They Are and Where They Go—Now They're Fighting Back," *Village Voice*, November 22, 2016.

5 Kamala Kempadoo, ed., *Trafficking and Prostitution Reconsidered: New Perspectives on Migration, Sex Work, and Human Rights* (Boulder, CO: Paradigm Publishers, 2012).

6 Damien Cave and Frances Robles, "A Smuggled Girl's Odyssey of False Promises and Fear," *New York Times*, October 5, 2014.

7 Donna M. Hughes and Tatyana A. Denisova, "The Transnational Political Criminal Nexus of Trafficking in Women from Ukraine," *Trends in Organized Crime* 6, no. 3/4 (2001): 43–68; Tim Rhodes, Milena Simić, Sladjana Baroš, Lucy Platt, and Bojan Žikić, "Police violence and sexual risk among female and transvestite sex workers in Serbia: qualitative study," *British Medical Journal* (2008): 307; Monica Rao Biradavolu, Scott Burris, Annie George, Asima Jena, and Kim M. Blankenship, "Can sex workers regulate police? Learning from an HIV prevention project for sex workers in southern India," *Social Science and Medicine* 68, no. 8 (2009): 1541–1547.

8 "St. James Infirmary," stjamesinfirmary.org.

9 Noah Berlatsky, "Child Sex Workers' Biggest Threat: The Police," *New Republic*, January 20, 2016.

10 Joana Busza, "Sex Work and Migration: The Dangers of Oversimplification: A Case Study of Vietnamese Women in Cambodia," *Health and Human Rights* 7, no. 2 (2004): 231–249; Rhodes et al., "Police violence and sexual risk"; Biradavolua et al., "Can sex workers regulate police?"

11 Rick Rojas and Al Baker, "New York Officer Ran Prostitution Ring at Motels, Authorities Say," *New York Times*, February 2, 2016; Henry Lee, "Sheriff's sergeant arrested for promoting prostitution at coffee stands," Q13 Fox, June 26, 2013.

12 Johnny Archer, "Veteran Officer Accused of Sexual Assault and Coercion," nbcdfw.com, December 21, 2014; Elissa Repko, "Updated: Veteran Dallas police officer arrested on charge of sexual assault," *Dallas Morning News Crime Blog*, December 21, 2014; "Lubbock Police Arrest Fellow Officer Tuesday Evening," *Everything Lubbock*, February 18, 2015.

13 Joshua Fechter, "Report: Central Texas officer arrested on child prostitution charge," *My San Antonio*, March 2, 2015; Associated Press, "Ocala officer fired after arrest for sex with underage girl," January 18, 2015.

14 "Seattle SWAT officer arrested for drugs, theft, prostitution," *Live Leak*, June 20, 2014.

15 "Ex-cop charged with stealing $450,000 from woman he'd arrested," SF Gate, April 22, 2015.

16 *Lowell Sun,* "Ex-Lowell police officer gets two years in jail for extorting prostitutes," April 25, 2013.

17 Juhu Thurkral, Melissa Ditmore, and Alexandra Murphy, *Behind Closed Doors: An Analysis of Indoor Sex Work in New York City* (New York: Sex Workers Project at the Urban Justice Center, 2005).
18 Jazeera Iman, Catlin Fullwood, Naima Paz, Daphne W, and Shira Hassan, *Girls Do What They Have To Do To Survive: Illuminating Methods Used by Girls in the Sex Trade and Street Economy to Fight Back and Heal* (Chicago: Young Women's Empowerment Project, 2009).
19 Ronald Weitzer, *Legalizing Prostitution: From Illicit Vice to Lawful Business* (New York: NYU Press, 2012), 67.
20 Molly Crabapple, "Special Prostitution Courts and the Myth of 'Rescuing' Sex Workers," *Vice*, January 2015.
21 Elizabeth Bernstein, "Militarized Humanitarianism Meets Carceral Feminism: The Politics of Sex, Rights, and Freedom in Contemporary Antitrafficking Campaigns," *Signs* 36, no. 1 (2010): 45–71; Elizabeth Bernstein, "Carceral politics as gender justice? The 'traffic in women' and neoliberal circuits of crime, sex, and rights," *Theory and Society* 41, no. 3 (2012): 233–259.
22 Empower Chiang Mai, *A Report by Empower Chiang Mai on the Human Rights Violations Women Are Subjected to When "Rescued" by Anti-Trafficking Groups Who Employ Methods Using Deception, Force, and Coercion*, June 2003.
23 Dewey, "On the Boundaries of the Global Margins."
24 Niels Lesniewski, "Brothel Responds to Reid's Prostitutes/2016 GOP Convention Remarks," *Roll Call*, February 21, 2014.
25 For a detailed description of these cities, see Weitzer, *Legalizing Prostitution*.
26 New Zealand Government, *Report of the Prostitution Law Review Committee on the Operation of the Prostitution Reform Act of 2003*, May 2008.

7 The War on Drugs

1 Sarra L. Hedden, Joel Kennet, Rachel Lipari, Grace Medley, Peter Tice, Elizabeth Copello, and Larry Kroutil, *Behavioral Health Trends in the United States: Results from the 2014 National Survey on Drug Use and Health* (Rockville, MD: Center for Behavioral Health Statistics and Quality, 2015).
2 William Campbell Garriott, *Policing Methamphetamine: Narcopolitics in Rural America* (New York: NYU Press, 2011).
3 Mike Mariani, "How the American opiate epidemic was started

by one pharmaceutical company," *Pacific Standard*, March 4, 2015.

4 Kevin Hill, "Medical Marijuana for Treatment of Chronic Pain and Other Medical and Psychiatric Problems: A Clinical Review," *Journal of the American Medical Association* 313, No. 24 (2015): 215–225.

5 Craig Reinarman and Harry Levine, *Crack in America: Demon Drugs and Social Justice* (Los Angeles, CA: University of California Press, 1997); Steven Belenko, *Drugs and Drug Policy in America: A Documentary History* (Westport, CT: Greenwood Press, 2000); David Musto, *The American Disease: Origins of Narcotic Control* (Oxford, UK: Oxford University Press, 1999).

6 Johann Hari, *Chasing the Scream: The First and Last Days of the War on Drugs* (New York: Bloomsbury, 2015).

7 Howard S. Becker, *Outsiders: Studies in the Sociology of Deviance* (New York: The Free Press, 1963).

8 Alexander, *New Jim Crow*.

9 Dan Baum, *Smoke and Mirrors: The War on Drugs and the Politics of Failure* (Boston: Little Brown, 1996).

10 Dan Baum, "Legalize It All: How to Win the War on Drugs," *Harper's Magazine*, August 18, 2016.

11 Thomas Rowe, *Federal Narcotics Law and the War on Drugs: Money Down a Rat Hole* (Portland, OR: Book News, Inc., 2006).

12 Tina Dorsey and Priscilla Middleton, *Drugs and Crime Facts* (Washington, D.C.: United States Department of Justice, 2010).

13 Daniel Mejia and Joanne Csete, *The Economics of the Drug War: Unaccounted Costs, Lost Lives, and Missed Opportunities* (New York: Open Society Foundations, 2016).

14 Balko, *Rise of the Warrior Cop*.

15 John Worrall, "Addicted to the drug war: The role of civil asset forfeiture as a budgetary necessity in contemporary law enforcement," *Journal of Criminal Justice* 29, no. 3 (2001): 171–187.

16 Wendy Ruderman and Barbara Laker, *Busted: A Tale of Corruption and Betrayal in the City of Brotherly Love* (New York: HarperCollins, 2014).

17 Robert Daley, *Prince of the City: The True Story of a Cop Who Knew Too Much* (Kingston, RI: Moyer Bell, 2004).

18 Milton Mollen, *Report of the Commission to Investigate Allegations of Police Corruption and the Anti-Corruption Procedures of the Police Department* (New York: City of New York, 1994).

19 Carmen George, "Fresno deputy police chief arrested in federal drug investigation," *Fresno Bee*, March 26, 2015.

20 "Former Scott County sheriff's deputy indicted," *Knoxville News Sentinel*, March 31, 2015.

21 Paula McMahon, "NYC cop served as insurance in drug deal, friend says," *Sun Sentinel*, March 8, 2015.
22 David Ovalle, "Miami-Dade police lieutenant pleads guilty to aiding cocaine smugglers," *Miami Herald*, March 31, 2015.
23 Kent Faulk, "Former Winston County deputy sentenced to federal prison in meth extortion," *Birmingham News*, March 27, 2015.
24 Peter Hermann, "Ex-FBI agent charged with 64 criminal counts in theft of heroin evidence," *Washington Post*, March 20, 2015.
25 Kevin Connolly, "Former Titusville police officer gets 10 years in prison in DEA coke sting," *Orlando Sentinel*, March 31, 2015.
26 Sari Horwitz and Carol Leonning, "Report: DEA agents had 'sex parties' with prostitutes hired by drug cartels," *Washington Post*, March 26, 2015.
27 Stopthedrugwar.org, "Police Corruption," n.d.
28 Alexander, *New Jim Crow;* Lisa Moore and Amy Elkavich, "Who's Using and Who's Doing Time: Incarceration, the War on Drugs, and Public Health," *American Journal of Public Health* 98, no. 5 (2008): 782–786; Lawrence Bobo and Victor Thompson, "Unfair by Design: The War on Drugs, Race, and the Legitimacy of the Criminal Justice System," *Social Research* 73, no. 2 (2006): 445–472.
29 Jeffrey Fagan and Amanda Geller, "Profiling and Consent: Stops, Searches and Seizures after Soto," *SSRN Working Paper Series* (2010).
30 Peter Moskos, *Cop in the Hood: My Year Policing Baltimore's Eastern District* (Princeton, NJ: Princeton University Press, 2009).
31 Natassia Walsh, *Baltimore Behind Bars: How to Reduce the Jail Population, Save Money and Improve Public Safety* (Washington, D.C.: Justice Policy Institute, 2010).
32 Maggie Taylor, "Former Baltimore Mayor Kurt Schmoke: Ahead of his Time," Drug Policy Institute, February 20, 2014, http://www.drugpolicy.org/blog/former-baltimore-mayor-kurt-schmoke-ahead-his-time.
33 "Law Enforcement Against Prohibition (LEAP)," leap.cc.
34 Hans Sherrer, "Travesty in Tulia, Texas: Frame-up of 38 Innocent People Orchestrated by a County Sheriff, Prosecutor and Judge," *Justice: Denied*, no. 23 (2004): 3–5.
35 John Sullivan, Derek Hawkins, and Pietro Lombardi, "Probable Cause: Pursuing drugs and guns on scant evidence, D.C. police sometimes raid wrong homes—terrifying the innocent," *Washington Post*, March 5, 2016.
36 Marc Santora and Benjamin Weiser, "Officer in Ramarley Graham Shooting Won't Face U.S. Charges," *New York Times*, March 8, 2016.
37 Alexander, *New Jim Crow.*

38 Rowe, *Federal Narcotics Law and the War on Drugs*.
39 National Center for Health Statistics, "National Overdose Deaths: Number of Deaths from Heroin," National Institute on Drug Abuse (NIDA), December 2015.
40 Amar Toor, "Russia has a serious HIV crisis, and the government is to blame," *Verge*, July 2, 2015; Karsten Lunze, Anita Raj, Debbie Cheng, Emily Quinn, Carly Bridden, Elena Blokhnia, Alexander Walley, Evgeny Krupitsky, and Jeffrey Samet, "Punitive policing and associated substance use risks among HIV-positive people in Russia who inject drugs," *Journal of the International AIDS Society* 17 (2014).
41 Harry Levine, "Global drug prohibition: its uses and crises," *International Journal of Drug Policy* 14 (2003): 145–153.
42 Human Rights Watch, *Neither Rights nor Security: Killings, Torture, and Disappearances in Mexico's "War on Drugs"* (New York: Human Rights Watch, 2011).
43 McCoy, *Politics of Heroin;* Peter Watt and Roberto Zepeda, *Drug War Mexico: Politics, Neoliberalism and Violence in the New Narcoeconomy* (New York: Zed Books, 2012).
44 Oscar Martinez, *A History of Violence: Living and Dying in Central America* (Brooklyn, NY: Verso Books, 2016).
45 Pew Charitable Trusts Public Safety Performance Project, "Federal Drug Sentencing Laws Bring High Cost, Low Return," August 27, 2015.
46 Shelli Rossman, John Roman, Janine Zweig, Michael Rempel, and Christine Lindquist, *The Multi-Site Adult Drug Court Evaluation: Executive Summary* (Washington, D.C.: Urban Institute Justice Policy Center, 2011).
47 Drug Policy Alliance, *Drug Courts Are Not the Answer: Toward a Health-Centered Approach to Drug Use* (New York: Drug Policy Alliance, 2011).
48 Center for Court Innovation, *A Statewide Evaluation of New York's Adult Drug Courts* (New York: Center for Court Innovation, 2012).
49 Marsha Weissman, "Aspiring to the Impracticable: Alternatives to Incarceration in the Era of Mass Incarceration," *New York University Review of Law and Social Change* 33: 235–269.
50 Rebecca Tiger, *Judging Addicts: Drug Courts and Coercion in the Justice System* (New York: NYU Press, 2012).
51 Maia Szalavitz, "How America Overdosed on Drug Courts," *Pacific Standard*, May 18, 2015.
52 Jeremy Galloway, "The Worst Place to Die: How Jail Practices Are Killing People Going Through Opioid Withdrawals," *The Influence*, March 23, 2016.

53 Teresa Gowan and Sarah Whitestone, "Making the criminal addict: Subjectivity and social control in a strong-arm rehab," *Punishment and Society* 14, no. 1 (2012): 69–93.
54 Ashley Peskoe and Stephen Stirling, "Want heroin treatment in N.J.? Get arrested," *NJ.com*, January 18, 2015.
55 Drug Policy Alliance, *Drug Courts Are Not the Answer*.
56 Justice Policy Institute, *Addicted to Courts: How a Growing Dependence on Drug Courts Impacts People and Communities* (Washington, D.C.: Justice Policy Institute, 2011).
57 Drug Policy Alliance, *Approaches to Decriminalizing Drug Use and Possession* (New York: Drug Policy Alliance, 2016).
58 Harry Levine and Deborah Peterson Small, *Marijuana Arrest Crusade: Racial Bias and Police Policy in New York City 1997–2007* (New York: New York Civil Liberties Union, 2008); Andrew Golub, Bruce Johnson, and Eloise Dunlap, "The race/ethnicity disparity in misdemeanor marijuana arrests in New York City," *Criminology and Public Policy* 6, no. 1 (2007): 131–164; Bruce Johnson, Andrew Golub, Eloise Dunlap, Stephen Sifaneck, and James McCabe, "Policing and Social Control of Public Marijuana Use and Selling in New York City," *Law Enforcement Executive Forum* 6, no. 5 (2006): 59–89.
59 Glenn Greenwald, *Drug Decriminalization in Portugal: Lessons for Creating Fair and Successful Drug Policies* (Washington, D.C.: Cato Institute, 2009).
60 Drug Policy Alliance, *Supervised Injection Facilities* (New York: Drug Policy Alliance, 2016).
61 Michael Reznicek, *Blowing Smoke: Rethinking the War on Drugs without Prohibition and Rehab* (Lanham, MD: Rowman & Littlefield, 2012).
62 Garriott, *Policing Methamphetamine*.
63 Ta-Nehisi Coates, "The Case for Reparations," *Atlantic*, June 2014.

8 Gang Suppression

1 Charles Katz and Vincent Webb, "Police Response to Gangs: A Multi-Site Study," (Washington, DC: National Institute of Justice, 2004).
2 Federal Bureau of Investigation, "Violent Gang Task Forces," n.d.
3 Malcolm Klein, *Gang Cop: The Words and Ways of Officer Paco Domingo* (Lanham, MD: AltaMira Press, 2003).

4 Megan Garvey and Patrick McGreevy, "LA mayor seeks federal aid to combat gangs," *LA Times*, January 4, 2007.
5 Joe Domanick, *Blue: The LAPD and the Battle to Redeem American Policing* (New York: Simon and Schuster, 2015), 65.
6 Ibid.
7 Jeffrey Reiman, *The Rich Get Richer and the Poor Get Prison: Ideology, Class, and Criminal Justice* (Boston: Pearson, 2007); William Chambliss, "The Saints and the Roughnecks," *Society* 11, no. 1 (1973): 24–31.
8 Klein, *Gang Cop*.
9 Ibid.
10 Ibid.
11 Ibid.
12 Victor Rios, *Punished: Policing the Lives of Black and Latino Boys* (New York: NYU Press, 2011).
13 Susan Pennell and Roni Melton, "Evaluation of a Task Force Approach to Gangs," *Responding to Gangs: Evaluation and Research* (Washington, DC: United States Department of Justice, National Institute of Justice, 2002).
14 Susan Phillips, *Operation Fly Trap: L.A. Gangs, Drugs, and the Law* (Chicago: University of Chicago Press, 2012).
15 Ana Muñiz and Kim McGilll. *Tracked and Trapped: Youth of Color, Gang Databases and Gang Injunctions* (Los Angeles: Youth Justice Coalition, 2012).
16 Ana Muñiz, Police, Power and the Production of Racial Boundaries (Brunswick, NJ: Rutgers University Press, 2015).
17 Beth Caldwell, "Criminalizing Day-to-Day Life: A Socio-Legal Critique of Gang Injunctions," *American Journal of Criminal Law* 37, no. 3 (2010): 241–290.
18 K. Babe Howell, "Gang Policing: The Stop-and-Frisk Justification for Profile-Based Policing," *University of Denver Criminal Law Review:* 5 (2015): 1–31.
19 US Department of Justice, Office of Juvenile Justice and Delinquency Prevention, *Best Practices to Address Community Gang Problems: OJJDP's Comprehensive Gang Model* (Washington, DC: U.S. Department of Justice, Office of Justice Programs, 2010).
20 David Kennedy, "Pulling levers: Chronic offenders, high-crime settings, and a theory of prevention." *Valparaiso University Law Review*: 31, no. 2 (1996): 449–484.
21 Jack Katz, *The Seductions of Crime: Moral and Sensual Attractions in Doing Evil* (New York: Basic Books, 1988).
22 Domanick, *Blue*.
23 Connie Rice, *A Call to Action: The Case for a Comprehensive*

Solution to L.A.'s Gang Violence Epidemic (Los Angeles: Advancement Project, 2007).

24 Youth for Justice, "LA For Youth—1 Percent Campaign," n.d., www.youth4justice.org.

25 Elliott Currie, *Crime and Punishment in America: Why the Solutions to America's Most Stubborn Social Crisis Have Not Worked—and What Will* (London: Macmillan, 1998).

26 Currie, *Crime and Punishment in America.*

27 Michael Fortner, *The Black Silent Majority: The Rockefeller Drug Laws and the Politics of Punishment* (Cambridge: Harvard University Press, 2015).

28 Todd Clear and David Karp, *The Community Justice Ideal: Preventing Crime and Achieving Justice* (Boulder, CO: Westview Press, 1999).

29 Emily Badger, "How Mass Incarceration Creates 'Million Dollar Blocks' in Poor Neighborhoods," *Washington Post,* July 30, 2015.

30 David Kennedy, *Don't Shoot: One Man, A Street Fellowship, and the End of Violence in Inner-City America.* (New York: Bloomsbury, 2012).

31 Elizabeth Palley and Corey S. Shdaimah, *In Our Hands: The Struggle for U.S. Childcare Policy* (New York: NYU Press, 2014).

32 "Cure Violence," cureviolence.org.

33 City of Minneapolis Health Department, *Minneapolis Blueprint for Action to Prevent Youth Violence* (Minneapolis: Department of Health, 2013).

9 Border Policing

1 *People v. Hall,* 4 Cal. 399 (1852).

2 Joseph Nevins, *Operation Gatekeeper and Beyond: The War on "Illegals" and the Remaking of the U.S.–Mexico Boundary* (Abingdon, UK: Taylor & Francis, 2010).

3 Kelly Lytle Hernandez, *Migra!: A History of the U.S. Border Patrol* (Berkeley: University of California Press, 2010).

4 Kitty Calavita, *Inside the State: The Bracero Program, Immigration and the INS* (New York: Quid Pro Books, 2010).

5 Hernandez, *Migra*, 172

6 US Customs and Border Protection, "Border Patrol Staffing by Fiscal Year," September 19, 2015.

7 Amanda Peterson Beadle, "Cost of a Broken System: US Spent More on Immigration than All Other Enforcement Agencies Combined," *ThinkProgress*, January 7, 2013.

8 Martha Menchaca, *Recovering History, Constructing Race: The Indian, Black, and White Roots of Mexican Americans*, (Austin: University of Texas Press, 2002).
9 United States v. Brignoni-Ponce, 422 U.S. 873 (1975).
10 American Civil Liberties Union, "The Constitution in the 100-Mile Border Zone," n.d.
11 David Horsey, "Border Patrol is becoming an occupying army in our borderlands," *Los Angeles Times*, August 20, 2013.
12 Nevins, *Operation Gatekeeper and Beyond.*
13 Judith Greene, Bethany Carson, and Andrea Black, *Indefensible: A Decade of Mass Incarceration of Migrants Prosecuted for Crossing the Border* (Charlotte, NC: Grassroots Leadership, and Brooklyn, NY: Justice Strategies, 2016).
14 Ibid.
15 Sasha Von Oldershausen, "The Cost of Justice," *Texas Monthly,* May 10, 2016.
16 Ibid.
17 Jon Greenberg, "Conservative host: Noncitizens are 25percent of federal inmates," *PunditFact,* July 10, 2015.
18 Alice Speri, "The Justice Department Is Done with Private Prisons. Will ICE Drop Them Too?" *Intercept*, August 18, 2016.
19 Nina Bernstein, "Officials Hid Truth of Immigrant Deaths in Jail," *New York Times*, January 9, 2010.
20 American Civil Liberties Union, Detention Watch Network, and National Immigrant Justice Center, *Fatal Neglect: How ICE Ignores Deaths in Detention* (New York: ACLU, 2016).
21 Monica Varsanyi, "Rescaling the 'Alien,' Rescaling Personhood: Neoliberalism, Immigration, and the State," *Annals of the Association of American Geographers* 98, no. 4 (2008): 877–896.
22 Jacinta Ma, "Department of Homeland Security—The President's Fiscal Year 2017 Budget," *National Immigration Forum*, February 11, 2016.
23 Inter-American Commission on Human Rights, *Report on Immigration in the United States: Detention and Due Process* (Washington, DC: Organization of American States, 2010), 55–57.
24 Margot Mendelson, Shayna Strom, and Michael Wishnie, *Collateral Damage: An Examination of ICE's Fugitive Operations Program* (Washington, DC: Migration Policy Institute, 2009).
25 "Fugitive Operations," U.S. Immigration and Customs Enforcement, n.d.
26 Marie Gottschalk, *Caught: The Prison State and the Lockdown of American Politics* (Princeton: Princeton University Press, 2015), 222.
27 Andrew Becker, G.W. Schulz, and Tia Ghose, "Four of five Border

Patrol drug busts involve US citizens, records show," Center for Investigative Reporting, March 26, 2013.

28 "Missing Migrants Project: Tracking deaths along migratory routes worldwide," Missing Migrants Project, http://missingmigrants.iom.int/.

29 Seth Freed Wessler, *Shattered Families: The Perilous Intersection of Immigration Enforcement and the Child Welfare System* (New York: Applied Research Center, 2011).

30 Maria Sacchetti, "Lawmakers call for US to be a refuge for Central Americans," *Boston Globe*, July 11, 2016.

31 Todd Miller, *Border Patrol Nation* (San Francisco: City Lights Books, 2014)

32 Cristina Costantini and Elise Foley, "Anastasio Hernandez-Rojas Death: Border Patrol Tasing Incident Complicated by New Footage," *Huffington Post*, April 24, 2012.

33 "Killed by Border Patrol," Southern Border Communities Coalition, July 2016.

34 Costantini and Foley, "Anastasio Hernandez-Rojas Death."

35 Guillermo Cantor, Walter Ewing, and Daniel Martinez, *No Action Taken: Lack of Accountability in Responding to Complaints of Abuse* (American Immigration Council, May 2014).

36 Esther Yu Hsi Lee, "The $5 Million Proposal to Hold Border Patrol Agents Accountable for Shootings, *Think Progress*, February 11, 2017.

37 Sam Howe Verhovek, "After Marine on Patrol Kills a Teen-Ager, a Texas Border Village Wonders Why," *New York Times*, June 29, 1997.

38 Rich Jervis, "National Guard at border gets mixed reviews in Texas," *USA Today*, July 31, 2014.

39 Ibid.

40 Brady McCombs and Stephen Ceasar, "Border program has vague goals, little oversight," *Arizona Daily Star*, November 15, 2009.

41 Jon Greenberg, "Ramos: 40 percent of undocumented immigrants come by air," *PunditFact*, September 8, 2015.

42 Miller, *Border Patrol Nation*; Sylvia Longmire, *Border Insecurity: Why Big Money, Fences, and Drones Aren't Making Us Safe* (New York: Palgrave Macmillian, 2014).

43 Longmire, 79.

44 Pradine Saint-Fort, Noëlle Yasso, and Susan Shah, *Engaging Police in Immigrant Communities: Promising Practices from the Field* (New York: Vera Institute of Justice, 2012).

45 Reece Jones, *Violent Borders: Refugees and the Right to Move* (Brooklyn, NY: Verso, 2016).

46 David Bacon, *Illegal People: How Globalization Creates Migration and Criminalizes Immigrants* (Boston: Beacon Press, 2008).
47 Bacon, *Illegal People.*
48 Watt and Zepeda, *Drug War Mexico.*
49 Greg Grandin, "The Clinton-Backed Honduran Regime Is Picking Off Indigenous Leaders," *Nation*, March 3, 2016.
50 Immigrant Movement International, "International Migrant Manifesto," November 5, 2011.

10 Political Policing

1 William Stanley, *The Protection Racket State: Elite Politics, Military Extortion, and Civil War in El Salvador* (Philadelphia: Temple University Press, 2010).
2 Jennifer Schirmer, *The Guatemalan Military Project: A Violence Called Democracy* (Philadelphia: University of Pennsylvania Press, 1998).
3 Naomi Klein, *The Shock Doctrine: The Rise of Disaster Capitalism* (London: Macmillan, 2010).
4 Daniel Egiegba Agbiboa, "Protectors or Predators? The Embedded Problem of Police Corruption and Deviance in Nigeria," *Administration and Society* 47, no. 3 (2015): 244–281.
5 K.S. Subramanian, *Political Violence and the Police in India* (Uttarakhand, India: SAGE Publications India, 2007).
6 Saurav Datta, "Freedom of assembly is our fundamental right, but Indian police just won't let us exercise it," *Scroll.in*, February 24, 2015.
7 Philip Stead, *The Police of France* (London, Macmillan, 1983).
8 Y. Guyot, *La Police* (Paris: 1884).
9 Robert Booth, "Anarchists should be reported, advises Westminster anti-terror police," *Guardian*, July 31, 2011.
10 Ibid.
11 Paul Lewis and Rob Evans, *Undercover: The True Story of Britain's Secret Police* (London: Faber & Faber, 2013).
12 Rob Evans, "Met police to pay more than £400,000 to victim of undercover officer," *Guardian*, October 23, 2014.
13 Lauren Collins, "The Spy Who Loved Me: An undercover surveillance operation that went too far," *New Yorker*, August 25, 2014.
14 Beverly Gage, *The Day Wall Street Exploded: A Story of America in Its First Age of Terror* (Oxford: Oxford University Press, 2009).
15 Edwin Palmer Hoyt, *The Palmer Raids, 1919–1920: An Attempt to Suppress Dissent* (New York: Seabury Press, 1969), 40.

16 Robert Dunn, *The Palmer Raids* (New York: International Publishers, 1948).
17 Ibid, 61.
18 Ibid.
19 Ibid, 65.
20 Brian Glick, *War at Home: Covert Action Against U.S. Activists and What We Can Do About It* (Boston: South End Press, 1989).
21 Frank Donner, *Protectors of Privilege: Red Squads and Police Repression in Urban America* (Berkeley, CA: University of California Press, 1990).
22 LEIU: Law Enforcement Intelligence Units, "About LEIU," n.d., leiu.org.
23 Ed Pilkington, "Burglars in 1971 FBI office break-in come forward after 43 years," *Guardian*, January 7, 2014.
24 Donner, *Protectors of Privilege*, 348.
25 Juan Gonzalez and Amy Goodman, "NYPD Surveillance Unveiled: City Claims to Lose Docs on 1960s Radicals, Then Finds 1 Million Records," *Democracy Now!*, June 17, 2016.
26 American Civil Liberties Union, "In Response to NYCLU Demand, Police Stop Interrogating Protestors About Political Activity," April 10, 2003.
27 Colin Moynihan, "Questioning of Garner Protestors in New York Renews Concerns About Police Practices," *New York Times*, April 28, 2015.
28 American Civil Liberties Union, "Policing Free Speech: Police Surveillance and Obstruction of First Amendment-Protected Activity," June 29, 2010.
29 American Civil Liberties Union of Colorado, "Spy Files Documents Reveal Political Spying by FBI's Joint Terrorism Task Force," 2012.
30 Ann Davis, "Use of Data Collection Systems Is Up Sharply Following 9/11," *Wall Street Journal*, May 22, 2003.
31 Nick Madigan, "Spying uncovered," *Baltimore Sun*, July 18, 2008.
32 Amy Forliti, "Documents mistakenly left behind by FBI in Minneapolis home shed light on probe of activists," *Twin Cities Pioneer Press*, May 18, 2011.
33 Dia Kayyali, "Congress Must Not Authorize More Chilling of the First Amendment with Material Support Laws," Electronic Frontier Foundation, May 29, 2015.
34 US Department of Homeland Security, "Fusion Centers and Emergency Operations Centers," n.d.
35 Michael German and Jay Stanley, *What's Wrong with Fusion Centers?* (New York: American Civil Liberties Union, 2007).
36 R. Jeffrey Smith, "Senate Report Says National Intelligence Fusion

Centers Have Been Useless," *Foreign Policy*, October 3, 2012.

37 Michael German and Jay Stanley, *Fusion Center Update* (New York: American Civil Liberties Union, 2008).

38 Missouri Information Analysis Center, "The Modern Militia Movement," *MIAC*, February 20, 2009; The Constitution Project, "Recommendations for Fusion Centers" (Washington, DC: The Constitution Project, 2012).

39 Beau Hodai, *Dissent or Terror: How the Nation's Counter Terrorism Apparatus, in Partnership with Corporate America, Turned on Occupy Wall Street* (Madison, WI: Center for Media and Democracy, 2013).

40 Gavin Aronsen, "What the FBI's Occupy Docs Do—and Don't—Reveal," *Mother Jones*, January 7, 2013.

41 Glenn Greenwald, *No Place to Hide: Edward Snowden, the NSA, and the U.S. Surveillance State* (New York: Metropolitan Books, 2014).

42 Human Rights Watch, *Illusions of Justice: Human Rights Abuses in US Terrorism Prosecutions* (New York: Human Rights Watch and Columbia Law School Human Rights Institute, 2014).

43 Matt Apuzzo and Adam Goldman, *Enemies Within: Inside the NYPD's Secret Spying Unit and bin Laden's Final Plot Against America* (New York: Simon & Schuster, 2013).

44 New York Civil Liberties Union, "Raza v. City of New York (Challenging the NYPD's Muslim Surveillance Program)," June 18, 2013.

45 Mazin Sidahmed, "NYPD's Muslim surveillance violated regulations as recently as 2015: report," *Guardian*, August 24, 2016.

46 Clark McPhail, David Schweingruber, and John McCarthy, "Policing Protest in the United States: 1960–1995," in *Policing Protest: The Control of Mass Demonstrations in Western Democracies*, eds. Donatella della Porta and Herbert Reiter (Minneapolis: University of Minnesota Press, 1998).

47 David Schweingruber, "Mob Sociology and Escalated Force: Sociology's Contribution to Repressive Police Tactics," *Sociology Quarterly* 41, no. 3 (2000): 371–89.

48 Alex Vitale, "The Rise of Command and Control Protest Policing in New York," in *The New York City Police Department: The Impact of Its Policies and Practices*, ed. John Eterno (Boca Raton, FL: CRC Press, 2015); Alex Vitale, "The Command and Control and Miami Models at the 2004 Republican National Convention: New Forms of Policing Protests," *Mobilization* 12, no. 4 (2007): 403–15; Alex Vitale, "From Negotiated Management to Command and Control: How the New York Police Department Polices Protests," *Policing and Society* 15, no. 3 (2005): 283–304.

49 Vitale, "The Command and Control and Miami Models."
50 Alex Thomas, "Obama May Backtrack on Military Equipment Ban For Police," *Reason*, July 26, 2016.
51 Jorge Rivas, "How high school teens got a police department to get rid of its military equipment," *Fusion*, June 3, 2016.

Conclusion

1 *Northern California Patch*, "Public Q&A Meeting Set This Evening to Discuss New Santa Clara Co. Jail," September 22, 2016.
2 Judith Greene et al., *Ending Mass Incarceration: Charting a New Justice Re-Investment*, Justice Strategies, 2013.
3 "Agenda to Build Black Futures," Black Youth Project 100, agendatobuildblackfutures.org.
4 "Platform," The Movement for Black Lives, policy.m461.org.

Further Reading

Alexander, Michelle. *The New Jim Crow: Mass Incarceration in the Age of Colorblindness*. New York: The New Press, 2013.

Apuzzo, Matt and Adam Goldman. *Enemies Within: Inside the NYPD's Secret Spying Unit and bin Laden's Final Plot Against America*. New York: Simon & Schuster, 2013.

Balko, Radley. *Rise of the Warrior Cop: The Militarization of America's Police Forces*. New York: Public Affairs, 2013.

Beckett, Katherine and Steve Herbert. *Banished: The New Social Control in Urban America*. Oxford, UK: Oxford University Press, 2009.

Currie, Elliott. *Crime and Punishment in America: Why the Solutions to America's Most Stubborn Social Crisis Have Not Worked—and What Will*. London: Macmillan, 2013.

Czitrom, Daniel. *New York Exposed: The Gilded Age Police Scandal that Launched the Progressive Era*. Oxford, UK: Oxford University Press, 2016.

Dewey, Susan and Tonia St. Germain. *Women of the Street: How the Criminal Justice-Social Services Alliance Fails Women in Prostitution*. New York: NYU Press, 2017.

Domanick, Joe. *Blue: The LAPD and the Battle to Redeem American Policing*. New York: Simon and Schuster, 2015.

Friedman, Barry. *Unwarranted: Policing Without Permission*. New York: Farrar, Straus and Giroux, 2017.

Fuentes, Annette. *Lockdown High: When the Schoolhouse Becomes and Jailhouse*. Brooklyn: Verso, 2013.

Garriott, William Campbell. *Policing Methamphetamine: Narcopolitics in Rural America*. New York: NYU Press, 2011.

Hari, Johann. *Chasing the Scream: The First and Last Days of the War on Drugs*. London: Bloomsbury Publishing, 2015.

Herbert, Steve. *Citizens, Cops, and Power: Recognizing the Limits of Community*. Chicago: University of Chicago Press, 2006.

Hernandez, Kelly Lytle. *Migra!: A History of the U.S. Border Patrol*. Berkeley, CA: University of California Press, 2010.

Jones, Reece. *Violent Borders: Refugees and the Right to Move*, Brooklyn: Verso, 2016.

Klein, Malcolm. *Gang Cop: The Words and Ways of Officer Paco Domingo*. Lanham, MD: AltaMira Press, 2003.

McCoy, Alfred. *Policing America's Empire: The United States, The Philippines, and the Rise of the Surveillance State*. Madison, WI: University of Wisconsin Press, 2009.

Miller, Todd. *Border Patrol Nation*. San Francisco: City Lights Books, 2014.

Mitrani, Sam. *The Rise of the Chicago Police: Class and Conflict, 1850–1894*. Chicago: University of Illinois Press, 2013.

Moskos, Peter. *Cop in the Hood: My Year Policing Baltimore's Eastern District*. Princeton, NJ: Princeton University Press, 2008.

Muñiz, Ana. *Police, Power, and the Production of Racial Boundaries*. New Brunswick, NJ: Rutgers University Press, 2015

Murakawa, Naomi. *The First Civil Right: How Liberals Built Prison America*. Oxford, UK: Oxford University Press, 2014.

Nevins, Joseph. *Operation Gatekeeper and Beyond: The War on "Illegals" and the Remaking of the U.S. Mexico Boundary*. Abingdon, UK: Taylor & Francis, 2010.

Phillips, Susan. *Operation Fly Trap: L.A. Gangs, Drugs, and the Law*. Chicago: University of Chicago Press, 2012.

Rios, Victor. *Punished: Policing the Lives of Black and Latino Boys*. New York: NYU Press, 2011.

Ruderman, Wendy and Barbara Laker. *Busted: A Tale of Corruption and Betrayal in the City of Brotherly Love*. New York: HarperCollins, 2014.

Stuart, Forrest. *Down and Out and Under Arrest: Policing and Everyday Life in Skid Row*. Chicago: University of Chicago Press, 2016.

Tiger, Rebecca. *Judging Addicts: Drug Courts and Coercion in the Justice System*. New York: NYU Press, 2012.

Way, Lori Beth and Ryan Patten. *Hunting for Dirtbags: Why Cops Over-Police the Poor and Racial Minorities*. Boston: Northeastern Press, 2013.

Williams, Kristian. *Our Enemies in Blue: Police and Power in America*. Oakland, CA: AK Press, 2015.

Index